THE WINDS OF MALIBU
AN UNEXPLAINABLE MEMOIR

JEFF LUCAS

The Winds of Malibu
An Unexplainable Memoir
All Rights Reserved.
Copyright © 2019 Jeff Lucas
v11.0

The opinions expressed in this manuscript are solely the opinions of the author and do not represent the opinions or thoughts of the publisher. The author has represented and warranted full ownership and/or legal right to publish all the materials in this book.

This book may not be reproduced, transmitted, or stored in whole or in part by any means, including graphic, electronic, or mechanical without the express written consent of the publisher except in the case of brief quotations embodied in critical articles and reviews.

Lucas Bly LTD.

Paperback ISBN: 978-0-578-20814-5
Hardback ISBN: 978-0-578-20815-2

Cover © 2019 Jeff Lucas. All rights reserved - used with permission.
Photos © 2019 Jennifer Jacobson. All rights reserved - used with permission.

PRINTED IN THE UNITED STATES OF AMERICA

Dedicated to the Acting Bug

ACKNOWLEDGMENTS

My gratitude is expressed to Emilio Estevez and Martin Sheen for including me in their father/son autobiography, Along The Way. Thank you to Roderick Clark, publisher & Managing Editor for Rosebud magazine, who published my stories. Thank you to Brenda Boyd Moorehouse, who first typed up my diary in 1988 and then helped me with the first draft of this book. Thank you to the great Bill Noctor and to Roger Lott. Thank you to my wife Jennifer. Last but not least, thank you to everyone that I was able to contact for allowing me to use their real names.

*Jeff and Andrea Allgreen in Malibu. October, 1968.
Photo by Helen Allgreen.*

Jeff at the Deerhead Road Lucas house. Malibu, 1969.
Photo by Reba Dick.

Steve and Jeff Lucas in Playa Del Rey, 1972. Jeff is wearing his Viet Nam war POW bracelet on his left wrist. Photo by Reba Dick.

Paul Lucas on his Malibu property in 2003. Photo by Betty Lucas.

Table of Contents

1. The Carpenters 1
2. Trisexual 6
3. Friends Are Better Than Parents 17
4. Another Fine Mess 23
5. That's What She Said 50
6. What Hump? 71
7. The Sugar Blues Kid 86
8. The Most Refined Asshole 119
9. Prodigy 145
10. Centerpiece 160
11. Bicentennial 180
12. WANT 210
13. D 240
14. "What the hell," said Bix. 272
15. What the Peeper Saw 296
16. General Robert E. Lee High 321
17. August, 1978 328
18. July, 1979 336
19. February, 1980 345
20. March, 1982 351
21. August, 1983 356
22. February, 1984 360
23. May 12th, 1984 364
24. Epilogue 367
25. Index 369

PREFACE

When I was eleven, I walked on a path through dense trees in Malibu. Underneath a branch, I stopped in front of a caterpillar's cocoon, a tidy bag, translucent, with a skin membrane-thin. Almost a butterfly, black and yellow and red and blue. So vulnerable. The sun shone through it. I quietly stared.

"Let's see how tough you are." I rubbed across the top of the branch lightly with my index finger, like brushing away dust.

The cocoon tore off and dropped like an egg without a shell. I heard it land and watched it spread out in a puddle. The weakest form of life I had ever seen was motionless and began to dry up.

One

January, 1973, eleven years old

THE CARPENTERS

On the Pacific Coast Highway, three burned-out hippies drove a pickup truck stacked high with baggage. We followed them with a second load in our car. My father was behind the wheel, and behind us was his new woman in her green British sports car. I sat in back with my brother, squeezed between boxes, and stared at the faded paint of the tailgate.

We had lived in Playa Del Rey for two years, and it was back to Malibu for us. The hippies had rented out the house and were three months behind in the rent.

We turned right on Morning View Drive and drove upward amid the stunning scenery. Halfway up the mountain, we pulled into the long straight driveway of 5838 Deerhead Road.

The house was in disrepair and out of place in the panoramic view of the Pacific Ocean and the outline of the distant islands along the horizon, and in back of us a breathtaking sweep of the sharp mountain with green shrubs moving in waves with the breeze.

My father told me it was in 1948 that he creeped along the coast of Malibu in lustrous sunshine, in a sailboat, at the age of twenty, and made it the goal of his life to buy a house and property there.

I walked around my father's property. A four-foot pile of garbage rotted in a heap outside. Inside it smelled like sour milk and ashes. My father got on the hippies for smoking in the house. I didn't hear my father's words, but the hippies looked angry at him. My stepfather Jack told me that my father was one of those people who thought the world was out to screw him all the time, and when you think the world is out to screw you, you will get screwed.

Different parts of the house brought back memories. That first year in Malibu went well, before my father's anger caught up with him. I remembered the brightly lit, hellish living room at age six in the middle of the night.

"Are you fighting?" My mother hid her face behind the pale curtain and stared out at the black night. She was a beautiful brunette, with an impulsive, insensitive streak. She was Oklahoma, white-bread, a little better off than sharecropper poor, for generations. She was more my friend than my mother, though she was a best friend of mine. I realized by eleven that my mother was just another woman and it was best not to get too attached to her.

"No. Go to bed," she said. I glanced at my father with his massive, hairy fists and biceps as he stood in demanding control of the house.

My brother and I often hid from him under our beds and backed up against the wall as he reached for us and got us. If I have one memory of my pretty grandmother Lucas, when she visited, it is her urgent Czechoslovakian overtures to *"Leave them alone,"* which sounded like, "La zee min roo."

⟫⟪

Jenny was my new stepmother. Her face was not quite pretty, except for her wonderful blue eyes. She had a nose that shot downward, thin lips, and cropped blonde hair. She was an intelligent thirty-two-year-old British woman with a pale complexion. My dad said she looked like Puck. Her mind was black and white. You were in or you were out, and she was good at grudges. She had travelled to Africa and had brought back long, black masks and dark tribal statues that glittered. She placed several all around the Malibu house. They cast a Shamanistic glow across the walls and fireplace.

Two and a half years older than me was my brother Steve, and he helped plenty as we unpacked and cleaned up. Even as a baby, Steve looked like a man. I had always looked like a delicate imp. I felt depressed, mostly just confused. Malibu didn't look or smell like it did when we had moved away in 1970. The wind, the waves, the sun and haze were the same, but there was a rock-hard loneliness to what I looked at or breathed in. It couldn't just be the absence of my mother, or one Carpenters song after another on the radio.

"That is one woman's voice I cannot stand!" my father announced to us.

I stood and watched Jenny place a small glass tube on a shelf in the garage, which looked like it could hold a small flower. The hole at the top was as narrow as a coffee straw.

"What have you got there?"

"It is an opium pipe," she said. I stepped back.

"You're joshing, right?" She closed her mouth and unpacked

the rest of her interesting possessions.

"Jeff! Help us unpack!" yelled my father as he stomped around carrying heavy boxes. I helped out slowly, with no focus. When we had finished unpacking, he stood in the yard and we joined him. He had held on to this prized location after the divorce from Hell. He put his arms around us and we looked out onto the bright sea to Catalina Island and Whale Island and the horizon.

"We made it back," I said.

"Thanks for getting us back to Malibu, Dad," said Steve.

"Yep. You're welcome. The place reminds me of Tara in *Gone With the Wind* after it has been through the war." Jenny laughed.

"Well, at least we're here," I said.

"Just remember, when you return to a place you used to live, it's usually not quite the same," he told us.

"I'll keep that in mind," I said. Jenny held him with both arms on his right. Steve hugged him on his left, and I hugged him in front.

As we all sat around the embers in the fireplace that night and watched the wood crack and split, he told us a story.

"About a year ago, I dated a woman who was into voodoo. I am not superstitious, but we conducted a ceremony where I stuck pins into a Voodoo doll and I named the doll Reba, after your mother."

"Do you think she felt the pain?" I asked.

"I hope so," he said.

Jeff believing he is Godzilla. Deerhead Road Lucas property. Malibu 1973. Photo by Steve Lucas.

Two

February, March, 1973, eleven years old

TRISEXUAL

Over the next weeks, months, I played alone, and talked to myself. Malibu was still beautiful, and I knew that I was extremely privileged to live here again, friends or no friends. I missed Scott, from Playa Del Rey. I reminisced how Scott and I used to sing out the first two syllables of the song "America" and not sing the rest of it. Scott had also moved, and I rarely returned the letters he wrote to me from Boston. Since the age of ten, panic attacks seized me as I lay down to bed at night. My imaginary world helped calm me down.

Unlike my father, I enjoyed my own company. He was an engineer. He had a head shaped like a circus clown, minus the make-up, and a body like Max Baer Sr., the heavyweight boxer of the 1930s, his appearance was mismatched. His poppa was Jewish or mostly Jewish. His mom was a Gentile, or mostly a Gentile. He stood solid at six foot three, had an ass like a

Clydesdale horse, and a scarred, bulbous, doorknob nose, with wide, hairy nostrils. His nose turned red with acne every time he ate chocolate, and he loved chocolate. He was bald except for the sides, which stuck out like tufts of pubic hair, and he kept the sides of his head trimmed to lessen the clown effect.

When I saw black hairs of his around the house, I couldn't tell where on his body they had come from. At his best, when all cleaned up, he resembled the actor, Gene Hackman, except for the ball at the end of his nose. Once on an airplane, he was mistaken for Gene Hackman by someone who approached him and asked for an autograph. His mouth remained closed-lipped unless he talked, screamed, or yawned, or vigorously brushed his teeth. His toothbrushes were frayed sideways and crushed down.

"You are far handsomer than I ever was," he told me, and I was handsome, in a small-boned sort of way.

I squinted into the morning sun. It felt great to be on the way to school, down the rolling straw hills again back to good, old Juan Cabrillo Elementary School. As I stepped into the familiar one-story design, my heart sank a bit: my school of the 1960s had lost its luster.

I sat at my desk and glanced around at the other unwashed students in Mr. Shultz's fifth-grade classroom. Most of us bathed barely enough. Water in Malibu was expensive for the middle class, and we were all middle class. One student, Ladd, seemed like he was allowed to bathe less than the rest of us. Ladd's eyelids were crusty, and his long hair was stiff and wracked with dandruff. He was taller than the rest of us, wore a rumpled corduroy jacket, and smelled of old sweat. He sure was a good-natured boy, though. Ladd never hated anyone who bullied him, and I watched him as he was tormented on most school days. I can still see his face as he tolerated it. He just looked quietly sad until they were through with him.

Every home in Malibu had to have a septic tank that was costly to empty and had to be emptied regularly. In our house, we were limited to ten-minute showers every other day. I learned to grab the dry bar of soap first and turn on the limp water as it slowly warmed up. I partly rinsed and toweled off the remaining soap.

What would the bullies do if I entered my dream world during school? I stood with my back against the chain-link fence and slowly rocked on my heels back and forth, with my fingers wrapped in the wire. There were a few other students who were misfits also, and I watched them drift around the playground, with their hands in their pockets. Day after day, it was the same spot on the chain-link fence. I had one suit of clothes that my father had picked out especially for me; a bright, reddish-orange bell-bottom pants and jacket. It was an ugly suit, even by 1970s standards.

"Oh, it's a red dog!" a group of girls taunted and rubbed their faces at me, my old playmate Andrea was among them.

I imagined I was The *Planet of the Apes* movie characters, I believed I was Clyde Barrow, I believed I was the Universal Studios monsters of the 1930s, I believed I was Godzilla and the Japanese movie monsters in the rubber suits. I believed I was Manfred Von Richtofen, The Red Baron, I believed I was Peter O'Toole in *Lawrence of Arabia*, and I believed I was Mark Lester in *Oliver! The Musical*.

When I had the house all to myself, I embellished the story of Bonnie and Clyde. I imagined the lives of these criminals were more glamorous than movie stars. They were singers, songwriters, and by gunpoint they made their own records. Bonnie and Clyde never hid from danger, and they sometimes used no weapons when they robbed banks. The mere sight of their faces made tellers of the most secure banks turn over every cent.

The Arthur Penn masterpiece film was what kicked off my

fantasy. I finally got to see it on television. In my imagination, Clyde's car purred on and off the roads at one hundred and forty miles per hour. Clyde built the car like a tank with bullet-proof windows and a cannon-proof body. The tires were designed to withstand most any abuse.

All the battle scenes became ten times more exaggerated. The authorities hunted them. Ambushes and walls of bullets were what Bonnie and Clyde ate for breakfast. I turned on the sprinklers in the yard and dodged around jets of water, with two plastic machine guns in my hands.

I listened to the Bluegrass music of the soundtrack album loudly as I worked all this into my fantasy.

Bonnie and Clyde were tricked by a friend. Clyde walked into a room where he saw his friend welcome him over with a shit-eating grin. The door slammed behind Clyde, and a series of the most complex security mechanisms ever invented locked. The "friend" was safely out of harm's way, and bullets tore through Clyde furiously from gun spouts placed in every inch of the wall that faced him.

I filled up and turned on the bathroom Water Pik, set it on full blast, and let the cord dangle, as I writhed from one end of the wall to the other in a death dance. I staggered out of the bathroom as Clyde. My hands grasped for a gun that wasn't there, and I collapsed forward, dead.

I fell over the back of the couch on my stomach in the living room and lay there wet from head to toe for twenty minutes, to let it sink in that I wouldn't act this fantasy ever again. Bonnie's death scene followed the same format. I acted her part out too; I held my arms out in tragic feminine beauty, made it over to Clyde, and collapsed on top of him, dead also, with my eyes open. The bathroom walls were soaked, and so was the couch.

Jenny and I were trapped together in the house during a rain storm. When I was in my fantasy world she kept her distance. I set my Bachman Fokker D VII down on the TV and walked up to her in the dining room.

"Did you like the movie *Oliver!* with Mark Lester in it, from the '60s?" I asked in a British accent.

"Oh, it was all right."

"He is from England like you are. Did you ever meet Mark Lester?"

"No, but I saw him a few months ago in a new movie he made."

"Oh? I *have* to see that! I've always been a fan of his! What is the name of that movie?"

"*What The Peeper Saw-r*," her words ran together.

"Sorry. Say that title again. I didn't understand you." Jenny rolled her eyes and looked up from her magazine and yelled.

"*What… The… Peeper… Saw*! It was a film about a *creepy* little boy!" She glared at me. I dropped the British accent.

"I heard you that time. Where did you see it? What theater? I'd love to see anything with him in it." She went back to her magazine.

"They showed it at UCLA." I picked up my Bachman Fokker DR1 Tri-plane, placed it at eye level, and flew.

A list of chores was taped to the refrigerator door by Jenny, on yellow paper in small handwriting. Thunder rolled across the sky and outside the sliding glass door, lightening streaked down onto the ocean. Steve and I had to vacuum, clean the counters, set the table, and do the laundry and the dishes as well as pull up the hundreds of thorny weeds all around the house and pack them down in the trash cans.

My eyes narrowed. I didn't like the crisp attitude that she had as she taped it up there, and this first night was my turn to do all of it. The kitchen light blared down as I stayed up and wiped a rag across the dining room table and cleaned every dish before placing it neatly into the dishwasher, as my father demanded. In the other room, Walter Cronkite with the news was on television and Jenny put her feet up in front of the fireplace where four logs burned high, and she meditated into it.

I squeezed the big plates in the bottom rack and the cereal bowls into the top. A steak knife fell halfway through the bottom and jammed the dishwasher. I couldn't slide it open or closed. My anger burst out of my mouth and surprised even me.

"It is your job to clean the kitchen and vacuum the house! It is your job, if that is how clean you want this house to be, lady! I don't need this house to be that clean! It never was when my mom was here! Why should it be now?"

Jenny took her feet down off the fireplace and walked to the bedroom that she shared with my father. I went into my room and stood high on my single bed.

"You are not my mom. You are nothing like her!"

Five minutes later, my father entered my room with uncharacteristic calmness. He spoke quietly, with tension in his voice. He sat on my bed.

"I understand you are upset. Jenny is not your mother and she never will be, but we all have to learn to get along."

"Dad, are we going to have to do all those chores? Why should this house have to be spotless? It's like Cinderella."

"Yes, you will have to do those chores," he said.

Jenny made us all get tetanus shots a week later under the wet reflecting trees in our yard. If we all got five tetanus shots within two weeks we wouldn't need another for ten years, is how she put it. She had brought home the serum and syringes from UCLA and after dinner she shot us all up. She knew damn well that I was the only one of us who was terrified of needles.

She and I were by ourselves in the house again. She was at the kitchen counter slicing lemons. Their bedroom door was open. I glanced in and noticed a black, round sock on her dresser. I entered their room and poked it with my finger. It was filled with coins, loose change, and was tied off in a hard knot. Her petty cash stash.

I picked it up and carried it into the kitchen.

"What are you doing?" I asked.

"I am making lemon curd."

"You are?" I smiled mischievously and held up the black sock.

"Look what I found." Jenny glanced at it sideways and paused.

"Oh…and where did you find that?" she said quietly.

"I just found it lying around, that's all." I had my smug look on. We stood there and didn't say anything else. I looked up at her and she didn't look back. I went into my room and set the black sock on my dresser. I forgot all about it and went outside and believed I was Godzilla for an hour. When I came back in, the sock was not on my dresser. It was back on hers.

It was a hike up to our house after school. Sometimes I had to shit, which was easy, because you had privacy everywhere outdoors. I learned which leaves were best to wipe with. I hoped that I had time to shit and that I was not being stalked by a dog.

I had nightmares about fangs. Vicious large brutes of canines ran loose throughout Malibu. I never knew what surprises awaited me around each curve along the rural hillside roads. Fangs of terror leapt out of bushes at every other property line. It was usually a long standoff of the dog and I staring at each other as it growled on and on. I felt lonely. I wanted to change my route home from school.

My best friend of the 1960s, Andrea Allgreen, still lived at the bottom of the mountain. She had an abundance of friends now. She had never had to move away. She abandoned our imaginary world as if she wanted to bury that part of her.

We were the same age. Andrea was huskier than I was. She was the ultimate tomboy. When we acted out scenes, she was not only always a male character; she was also the more dominant of the two of us. For instance, when we acted out the movie, *Oliver, The Musical!* I was always Oliver Twist and she was always The Artful Dodger.

When we were six-, seven-, and eight-year-olds, Andrea and I had done *everything* together. Our imaginations were the best part of life on planet Earth. It was just the two of us with no one else around. We made it a point to get away from everybody on most days during those years. We acted out movies and TV shows, until we got the scenes correct, the way we wanted. We were very lucky to have that freedom. It wasn't just an average children's dream world. It really felt like we were *acting*.

Her new friend, Louise Engelhardt, was tall, blonde, and popular and lived on a property near the end of Deerhead Road. Louise was nice; I liked her, but I was locked out from everybody, Louise included. The house could not be seen from the road, but maybe Andrea was up there. I began up the steep driveway. I hesitated and rested my right hand on the wall of the dirt slope that lined the driveway. I heard a deep jingle of a heavy collar, of two heavy collars. Here came one healthy, enormous, and fully grown Briard dog, followed by a second enormous Briard dog. Both dogs were on the loose with no owner about. They both moved toward me, their basketball-sized, white, furry heads held high and steady.

The male stopped in front of me and leaned in slowly and smoothly and sniffed me with a black nose larger than my fist. He pressed his nose against my chest, as I noticed that both dogs were on higher ground, which gave them even more advantage. I stood still except that I trembled. An ominous bass growl began which had the unlimited feel of an earthquake, and grew louder. The female beside him joined in. I turned my head all around me. I was in trouble again. Their eyes looked like a sheet of hair.

"Nice doggie. Good doggie."

I slowly moved my hand forward. I felt their heavy breath as my thumb brushed across an upper fang as sharp as an ice pick. They growled again, and I turned to face the stone bricks that held in the ice plant-covered slope. I grabbed onto the finger-like ice plant leaves and put my right leg on the wall edge and hoisted myself up. The ledge was too high, but I tried again and made it over when the male Briard dog moved toward me, and with the loudest growl yet, lunged forward and sank its fangs into my left buttock and locked its jaws together.

Thankfully, I was able to scream loudly.

"AH! HELP! AH!" I saw the Engelhardt parents make their way around the top of the driveway and stand there looking down. Mr. Engelhardt clapped his hands rapidly and sharply and yelled something. **They** began down the steep driveway.

.

"Let him be! That boy didn't do anything to you," said Mr. Engelhardt. The fangs reluctantly unclamped. My butt hurt, and I shook and wept and held to the ice plant with wide eyes.

"Is Andrea here?!"

"No. She was here yesterday," said Mr. Engelhardt. They led the Briard dogs placidly up the driveway by their collars, turned right and were gone.

I limped home and up our driveway. No matter where you walked in Malibu, you had to have a long-legged stride, but not today. My father was out somewhere with Jenny. There was his car at the top. I opened my father's car door and crouched backwards in the front seat with my knees on the seat. I adjusted the rear view mirror, pulled my pants and shorts down and looked around to my left in the mirror. Two big, sad, fang punctures on my butt showed trickles of dried blood.

I wanted to shoot those dogs with my father's rifle, but it was too big for me to use, and his BB gun would make those Briard dogs laugh in my face. I didn't know what to do. I thought about using the kitchen knives on them. There was no way for me to kill the Engelhardts' dogs. I wanted them carved up bloody and I wanted it now. Saw off both of their heads and hang them down by our mailbox.

I told my father and Jenny about it. Jenny kept a smirk on her face and didn't say anything. I showed my father the fang marks.

"Huh. The Engelhardts' dogs did that to you? Huh," he said in a tired voice. "Well, that should heal up okay."

"I don't care! I want those dogs to die!"

"You should thank Jenny for the tetanus shots," he said. I gave her a calculating, contemptuous glare.

The Engelhardts' male Briard dog sat and waited for me with his balls hanging out every school day in the center of Deerhead road on the walk home, and chased me to my driveway until I discovered an alternate route.

We sat in Mr. Shultz's class.

"Give this your undivided attention. Who wants to divide seven into four hundred and sixty-three for me?"

"Not I, said the Little Red Hen," shot back the coolest, most popular student, Arthur Lake, from his desk. Arthur's mom was J. P. Morgan. He had a show business family.

My seat was in the center of the room. I occasionally glanced around for a quirky student who was as disinterested as I. I found one toward the front and on my right, named Shane. We looked at each other. I raised an eyebrow and smirked, and so did he.

I glanced down at my math paper. I couldn't get into it. It was impossible to get into it. I peered out to my left through the windows at the empty playground. Then I looked over at a girl named Nora. I was starting to like her a lot. She just tolerated me. She was the skinniest girl in the classroom and had a beautiful, freckled face.

I looked at the chalkboard and zoned out at all the numbers. I got an intense hard-on out of nowhere. Not for Nora, for I put her on a pedestal. My groin needed my *undivided attention*.

All the students were apparently busy with their math equations as I put my hands underneath my desk, unzipped, and pulled it out of my shorts. I pushed it to the right on my leg and up against the cold metal of the desk and rubbed away. I knew my face must look either strained or relaxed, I didn't know which, though nobody seemed to notice. My hands pressed down against the top of my desk. I breathed unevenly and laughed at how crazy this was.

Nine minutes went by on the clock on the wall and I couldn't stop. My first orgasm trembled through me from my black-haired scalp down to my toenails.

I was surprised that it hurt when it was over, like someone had kicked me in the crotch. I looked around the room. Everyone seemed normal except me. If anyone had noticed, they were polite about it, even the teacher. I reached beneath the desk and zipped up, amazed that I had gotten away with it. Somehow that seemed like an accomplishment.

Three

April, May, June, 1973, eleven years old
Friends Are Better Than Parents

I was on the edge of my father's bed in front of his TV on a Friday night as he snored behind me. I kept the volume low as I watched an old black-and-white Jerry Lewis and Dean Martin movie titled *That's My Boy*. Jerry Lewis ran up and down a football field. He scored for the wrong team and I laughed so hard I fell off the bed. I laughed as quietly as I could, so as not to awaken the beast in back of me.

At every commercial break, Jerry Lewis's facial expressions came easily for me in my father's bedroom mirror. I wanted to get the expressions down accurately. After the movie, I got up off the bed and went into the other room to practice. I had always liked him and remembered his television show from the '60s. Over the weekend, all I did was act like Jerry Lewis.

For the Nutty Professor, I wore my father's reading glasses on the end of my nose and bucked out my teeth. My father and Jenny glanced over at me as I got into character. Jenny frowned.

"Jerry Lewis is revolting. He's all *greasy*."

"I used to kind of like his TV show."

"I find him appalling."

"You're a shmageggy, you know that?" said my sleepy father.

"Do you have glasses you could give me?"

"I have got my father's glasses, if that would help you."

"Can I have these really?"

"Sure, go ahead," he shrugged. They had a thick black rim. I couldn't see when I put them on, so I broke out the lenses with my thumb and bled on the kitchen counter.

I carried the glasses on Monday morning. I walked with big steps ahead of my brother. The cut on my bandaged thumb would heal nicely and I strode confidently down the mountain. I touched the school gate in a new way and the dew that had collected there broke under my hands like tears of joy. A strange anticipating look came over my face until the recess bell rang.

I felt like I was at the start of a championship race of some sort, and the recess bell was my signal to rush out of the gate. I walked past my usual spot on the fence and went to the center of the playground, with the most popular long-haired tough boys, not a misfit in sight. I stood proudly pigeon-toed in the middle of the playground like a wacky Jerry Lewis. The students stopped to watch the weirdo in the reddish orange bell-bottoms. Some looked like they were in shock, which only made me laugh inside and behave weirder.

I cut to the front of the handball line, in full character, the glasses at the end of my nose and I bucked out my teeth. No one bothered me. They couldn't beat me up. They were afraid to.

"Listen! You fellers particularly mind if I play ball? ...that's ah…what I really want to do…so…I mean, ball is naturally what I'm gonna transpire to accomplish presently—so…" I cleared my throat. "Hmm it's my …hmm! I think it's my…Hmm…turn." I tucked the ball under my left armpit. "Let's get a start." I held a pose to hit the ball but didn't. Six boys stood still and looked at me with scoffing incomprehension.

"It's not your turn. You'll have to go to the end of the line," said the stud behind me. He smiled a bit.

"Get the fuck out of here," snarled another.

"Very well," I said. As soon as I had walked smoothly to the end of the line, I turned around and went back up to the front as a different character, with a British accent. I repeated this until the recess bell rang.

I smiled pallidly on the walk home. I felt a lot of air in my mind. I stopped, alone, on the property of the Ball family.

"I am going to be a famous actor." I stared forward. The winds blew the straw in slow waves shaped like an arrow. I nodded my head once and continued home. I concentrated on the dogs instead. When I didn't have to face those monsters alone, it was easier. It was time to choose a friend.

Tommy Pringle chose me for a friend. He was skinny, with cords in his neck, and he had a natural tan that was probably just dirt. He had jagged sharp teeth and could barely see without his glasses. Grime in his ears could be seen from thirty yards away. He was dressed well enough, in short-sleeved shirts and long pants that were clean and too big for him, the flap of his belt stuck out. He was about my height, maybe a bit taller, and smelled dusty, sort of mummy-like. Tommy seemed slow in his mind, but he was loyal. Jenny liked him. My father bristled at the sight of him.

I chose Shane Smith. He was the one ahead of me on the right in class. I had flunked first grade, so my hormones were slightly advanced than some of the rest of the class. I got Shane's attention. I pantomimed I crawled inside a vagina bigger than I was and got lost in there as I sat at my desk. He topped that by doing a pantomime of climbing into an even larger vagina and doing cartwheels inside the vagina.

I could never make Shane laugh unless it was seriously at somebody else's expense. I think it was the mean streak in him. Shane always wore clean, expensive clothes. He was the best-dressed student. He was a good athlete and could do fancy tricks on the handlebars and run faster than anyone in the school. My brother Steve said that Shane looked like Johnny Crawford from the TV show, The Rifleman. I visited him often at his house, a long walk up to the very top of the mountain in Malibu Park.

"Do you like any girls in school?" he asked as we hiked the zig-zag road.

"I like Nora. I'm crazy about her. How about you?"

"No. Nora is okay, except she is so skinny! Her butt looks like a peanut!"

We were almost to his house when we saw Mr. Poole in front of his mailbox. He was a teacher down at the junior high school adjacent to our elementary school. Mr. Poole looked like the classic farmer. He stood at the end of his driveway, deep in thought.

"You boys don't know it yet, but these are the best years of your lives."

We couldn't disagree. Shane and I nodded and said, "Hmm." We glanced back: the view of Malibu sprawled below almost brought on a fear of heights.

I liked Shane, except for his current kleptomaniac stage. He wanted to steal all the time, and since he was my new friend, I stole too. I stole half as much as he did, and I didn't even want it. I threw most of it away. We nearly half depleted the candy aisle at Trancas market. Shane stole cigarettes too and I watched him smoke them at the bottom of a canyon in back of his house. He just stuffed everything inside of a Corduroy jacket and walked out with it. When he got bold enough, he walked out with a six-pack of Elephant Malt Liquor, and we split that and got drunk.

Shane looked around inside the fancy student store of Malibu Park Junior High School. We had no student store at our elementary school. The locked door, located on the side of the office, had an upper bolt as well as a big locked lower door knob. Shane went to work with a screwdriver and an ice pick while Tommy Pringle and I sat on a nearby green lunch bench, feeling lost.

"Tommy, we are what is known as an accomplice."

"What's that?" he asked.

"An accomplice is somebody who feels as lost about everything as we do," I told him.

Tommy took off his glasses and pressed together the tape in the middle that connected his busted glasses. Shane walked out with an expensive pencil sharpener that he had unscrewed from the wall, and two notebooks.

"I'm in!" he sneered. I went to see. Tommy stayed seated. Shane switched on a light and we looked around.

"Oh shit, they took the money with them!" he said.

He spied a pair of well-used industrial pliers on a shelf.

"Hey, look at these!" He walked out with the pliers and I reached in the office and shut the door. It closed with a thick click.

We walked over to Tommy.

"What's the matter, Pringle?" he taunted.

"Yeah, what's the matter, Tommy? Don't like being an accomplice, or what?"

"We could get into trouble," said Tommy in his simple voice.

"Oh yeah?" teased Shane, "The only trouble you're going to get into is this!" He reached out and clasped the pliers onto

Tommy's crotch and then let go.

"Ow. That makes me mad at both of you," said Tommy. Pringle looked deranged when he was angry.

"Let me see those pliers," I said.

Shane handed me the pliers.

"Say there, Pringle," I said, "What's the name of that guy on *The Beverly Hillbillies*? You know…the star of the show. Jed… what?"

"*Clampett!*" yelled Tommy. Tommy got clamped in the crotch again with the pliers after that answer. I laughed but not as hard as Shane laughed.

I got no thrill out of any of this.

"I don't even want any of this stuff," I told him as he stuffed a pillow case.

"Really? What kind of juvenile delinquent are you?"

"A different kind, I suppose."

My father sometimes took Steve and me horseback riding in the Malibu hills. We rented horses from the famous Egon Merz, who rode with us. He was always in a good mood when we did that. My brother had joined the Boy Scouts. On a ten-mile hike, my father recognized someone he went to high school with that he hadn't seen since then. He was one of the dads there on the trail, but they barely spoke to each other. My dad never had a true, trusted friend in his life. I hiked along and swigged water out of a shared thermos and thought about that.

Four

July, 1973, through February, 1974 eleven years old

ANOTHER FINE MESS

"Do you want to see my balls?" asked Shane.

"No, that's okay," I said. We were standing in the middle of the street near his house in the bright sunlight.

"You sure? I'll show you my balls right now."

"No uh...no, that's okay." I waved my hand, and we walked up his steep, short driveway and into his house, and stood in the kitchen.

"I think I'm finished with stealing," I said. There was a pause.

"*One* more," said Shane, "and if anything goes wrong, we can call it quits and never steal again."

"No. I should say no. Why aren't I saying no? We have already made the Malibu Park school newspaper, Shane, and they are in hot pursuit looking for who stole all that from the student store. What is it?" I glared at him. I never got headaches, but I had one.

"Okay. I've thought it all out. Can you picture how great it would be to have our own mini-bike? We could go anywhere in Malibu we wanted!"

"And where is this mini-bike?" I blinked.

"At the Pringles' house! It's Pringle's brother's mini-bike."

"*The Pringles?* You want to fuck with the Pringle family? Hey, Shane, they are *scary* people, in case you haven't noticed!"

"They may be scary, but you can't tell me they are smart. Now, tomorrow Tommy is going to work with his dad at Fox studios. So on the way home from school, you sidetrack Mrs. Pringle while she's in her garden, and I'll sneak the mini-bike out and we'll go for a ride."

"Since you are the only friend I have except for Pringle, I guess I'll say…yes."

"Good! Meet me after school," he said with exuberance. The only way I could get into this is if I thought of John Dillinger, Baby Face Nelson, Machine Gun Kelly, Pretty Boy Floyd, Bonnie and Clyde and the Smith and Lucas gang.

I talked to Mrs. Pringle in her garden as Shane snuck the mini-bike fifteen feet behind her and around the house. I could see where Tommy got his looks. Mrs. Pringle resembled one of the puppets from the *Mr. Rogers Neighborhood* TV show named Lady Elaine Fairchild.

"Take care, Mrs. Pringle. Tell Tommy I said hi."

"Okay, I will. Goodbye now," she squeaked. I caught up with Shane on Fillary Heights road. He got on and kicked the starter. I noticed he looked really cool when he did that. He tried to kick start it again and again.

"It's out of gas," he said.

"Your plans just keep getting better."

"You want to help push this thing?" said Shane. I rolled my eyes and took the mini-bike by the horns and pushed it up a small incline. It was a smooth road, but it felt like thick sand. I leaned it back over to Shane, who didn't take it.

"Here! You're the athlete! I'm the actor! Remember?

"This is just not me, Shane. I want you to know that we probably will not get away with this."

He shrugged his shoulders and took the handlebars back as we trudged down Phillip Avenue, even downhill the mini-bike was hard to push. It took a lot to make Shane huff and puff but now he was; his face turned red.

"Aren't you gonna help push? It's your mini-bike too, y' know. We're sharing it," he said.

"Oh no, you explained to me exactly how this was going to work. Now things have changed a little."

We made it to the Pacific Coast Highway. Cars and big rigs blew our hair all over the place. We trudged into the Mobil gas station beside Trancas Market.

"Okay, I've got enough money to fill us up," he said. He grabbed a dollar out of his gold corduroy pants. I looked to my right and saw Shane's mother turn in off the highway and into the gas station in her red 1970 Toyota mini-station wagon. It could be a coincidence, I thought. She wasn't filling up on gas, though. She pulled up alongside me and rolled the passenger's window down.

"Where is Shane?" she demanded, looking attractive and pissed. I took a deep breath of ocean air and leaned on my back heel.

"He is paying for some gas right at the moment."

"Well, let me go get him then." She got out and jabbered at him on his right ear. Shane's mouth was uncharacteristically shut as they went past me.

"Are you gonna put gas in or not?" I said. I gave him a look that said we were both assholes.

"We are putting that bike in the back!" she ordered. They got the mini-bike up and fit it in there without my help.

"There is a dollar of gas in the pump, Mom. Do you want it for your car?"

"*No!*" Shane and I got in the back seat together.

"Mr. Poole spotted you two with his binoculars and phoned me." Shane and I looked at each other.

"Tell me what happened!" I rolled my eyes.

"Well, ya see," said Shane, "Tommy's brother had this mini-bike and I didn't think he had any use for it, so we thought we would take it off his hands."

"Oh, is Jeff involved in this too?" She tilted her head up through the rear view mirror and watched us more than she watched the curves ahead.

"Well, *sort of*," whined Shane. I was on his left, trapped. We glanced at each other. I was sick of him.

"Is your father home?" she asked nasally.

"Unfortunately, yeah, he is." There was my father's blue car at the top of the driveway. She got out and walked around the house and came back.

"How do you get to the front door of this house?"

"The house is built crazy, like its inhabitants. The front door is around the side to your left." I pointed the way and she went.

"I don't have the kind of father that puts up with this," I said.

"I don't either," said Shane.

"Then why do you do it?"

"Because there is nothing else to do!"

She returned, and I got out of the car. They drove off and I went inside. There were my father's giant arms, folded. Jenny wasn't home yet.

"Go to your room," he said. I did and quietly shut the door. Ten minutes went by.

"*Jeff!* Are you sorry about what you did?" He was calm, as he frowned. He shook his big head slowly as he often did, with bulging eyes.

"Yes, believe me, it was him. I am really not a stealer. I have weird friends like Tommy Pringle, but you have to believe me."

"Go to your room for the rest of the night."

I stayed in my room. Jenny came home in a good mood and after a couple of hours he called me out, and my day of crime wasn't mentioned. We sat down and ate Welsh rarebit leftovers.

My father and Jenny had given me the bedroom next to theirs. I never asked for this to be my room and would have preferred Steve's room down the hall. Except for my large bedroom window, there was no way for me to leave my room without my dad and Jenny's bedroom door in front of my face.

Three decades later, three weeks before my father died, I finally got the truth out of him. Jenny thought that I constantly listened with bated breath at their bedroom door to listen to them have sex and tried to find a way to watch them have sex. This made her resist my father's sexual advances. My dad liked to get laid, and Jenny remained frigid because of me. When I went outside, Jenny thought I had my ear pressed to the wall, even though I would be a mile away at the time, or else I was in my room with the window open to hear the raspy ocean waves.

They were quiet in their bedroom, which was a little curious to me because when he had been married to my mother, the sound of near murder was in the air and the nights were loud consistently. Now, it was almost too quiet. Sometimes I left my room and listened just to make sure they were in the house at all, and all I heard was the wind outside and then maybe a slight rustle of a comforter, then I walked away. I didn't want that at all. They were gross people to me in that way.

The fact was, Jenny saw me as Mark Lester's character, Marcus, in the obscure movie, *What the Peeper Saw*. To Jenny, the destructive, perverted liar that manipulates his parents and commits matricide, and me, were similar children. Of course, she told my father what her feelings were toward me. I gave her the creeps, and this was the connection she made and she stuck to it for as long as we knew one other. If I had known that this was his false basis for banishing me from Malibu, I would have made more of a stand, but he was too much of a prude to flat-out tell me.

I tried to be nicer to my stepmother, but the damage had already been done. When *OLIVER!* came on TV as The Movie of the Week, we all watched it in the living room and talked during commercial breaks.

"I think he is a fag," said Jenny.

"Who?" asked my father, "Oliver? Oh, bullshit! He's too young to be a fag!" Jenny crossed her arms.

"Well, that's what *I* think!" she said. My father put his bare feet up on the coffee table and snapped his toes. He was double jointed. His big toe could lunge out and snap loudly against the rest of his foot. It was louder than a finger snap. He did this with both of his feet. He looked like a crab.

"Dad, I can't hear the movie," said Steve. He kept doing it.

"I *find* your toes am*u*sing," smiled Jenny. She leaned over, made an eager sound and gave my father a peck on the lips.

He caught me as I got the Nutty Professor voice down correctly in the bathroom mirror at night, with those glasses slid down my nose.

"Jennifer. Jennifer, you crazy bird!" I bucked my teeth out. He looked depressed when I glanced at him, his hands in his blue pockets. I learned to rehearse with the bathroom door shut.

I spent my summer vacation at my mother and stepfather

Jack's house in Mar Vista, an hour's drive from Malibu. My stepfather, Jack Dick, looked like the dad on *The Brady Bunch*. I said hello to my stepfather's girls from a previous marriage: Terri, who had dark wavy hair; Kelly, who had straight light-brown hair; and Michelle, who had curly blonde hair. They were from Texas. We all knew Terri Lynn Dick would make a wonderful mother someday. She thought all matters through more than her sisters did, more than I did. She had a protective quality about her. Not quite as pretty as her younger sisters, she was still attractive, and intelligent boys with good hearts were interested in her.

The peer pressure was on us all to see *The Exorcist* together. The volume in the theater was exceptionally loud. I sat through the matinee of *The Exorcist* with my thumbs in my ears and my fingers tightly over my eyes.

A desire gripped me to keep a journal. No one else I knew needed to keep a diary. I only wanted Terri, who I saw once a year, to give it to me for my birthday. She forgot and apologized. I smiled and hugged her.

"I'll just wait until next year. I will not have a diary until you give me one."

"Why me?"

"I don't know…but it's got to be you, and only you."

Sixth grade began with a week-long school field trip high in the mountains somewhere. It was there I chose my best friend, Frank Kratochvil, who slept in the bunk across from me. Frank dressed neatly and cleanly. He didn't overdo it and he didn't underdo it. He wore a white V-neck sweater with a red stripe on the V, and white t polo shirts. His hair was always short, with bangs down his forehead. He had tan horn-rimmed glasses, and he was as pale as I was. We were never tan. Frank lived in Malibu's Sycamore Park. Sycamore Park's distinctive features are its rolling hills and the canyon formed by Escondido Creek. Here, in this idyllic setting, Frank lived part time with his mother and part time with his father.

We ate bowls of Life cereal at his mom's rented house. Then we passed a mellow couple of hours together and made each other laugh. He sat in the main chair like he owned the place. I was on the couch.

"Is your mom still here?"

"She is in her room," said a relaxed Frank.

"It's really quiet. Is she asleep?"

"No, she is having a drink," he said, and smiled slightly.

"Oh."

I felt tremendous freedom there. Frank raised his left eyebrow behind his glasses and jutted out his lower lip in a comical sneer. He rotated his head counter-clockwise, with his right eye shut. He looked like the Kaiser of Germany. I laughed easily. I went into the Nutty Professor routine, with my gapped front teeth out.

"Well, that's marvelous, actually, as the night spins forth," I glided my tongue over my front teeth. Frank raised his right hand beneath his nose and laughed.

"Do you feel like driving around?" I sat up.

"Driving? You mean in a *car?*"

"Yes," he said calmly.

"An automobile? A jalopy?"

"Yes." He slowly blinked his eyes once.

"I can't drive. Can you drive?" Frank sat still.

"You *can?*"

"Yes," he said, with a wise smile.

"Let's go, I guess…do you mean your mom's car?"

"Yes." Frank leaped out of the chair with built-up energy and picked up his mother's keys off the counter.

"I'm twelve, Frank. How old are you?" We went into the garage.

"Eleven," he said. I laughed. He picked up a remote control and pointed it at the garage door. Frank's comic timing was excellent.

"Push the button, Max," said Frank. The movie *The Great Race* was never far from our minds. The garage door chugged open and we climbed into the light-blue 1969 Volkswagen mini station wagon. We put on our seatbelts. He started the engine, and we backed out of the garage, down the driveway, and into the street. He put it in drive and shot up the side of the mountain. I stayed quiet so I wouldn't distract him, but I watched him as he held his head up, his steady eyes through his glasses on the road just over the top of the steering wheel. We pulled into a driveway.

"This is where my friend Frank Weatherwax lives. His dad breeds the Lassie dogs for the TV show," he said. Though the ride was far from smooth, Frank drove with lots of confidence as we moved at quite a clip. He slammed on the brakes at the bottom of Sycamore Park, and we both flew forward.

"My dad lives there in a condominium," he showed me, and we glanced at a small two-story complex. Frank turned the car around, and we were on our way back up the mountain. Frank's headlights seemed like the only lights in Sycamore Park. He turned into his mom's driveway, opened the garage door with the click of a button, and headed in. He switched off the motor, and we got out.

"Do you just like comedians?" he asked.

"Yes. I like a lot of comedians, though. Do you know who you remind me of? The guy from the *Get Smart!* show."

"Don Adams?"

"Yes. I mean you look like him. You also look like Arty

Johnson from the show *Laugh- In*." Frank smiled wide and whipped a hand in the air and stomped his foot.

"I *love* when people tell me *that!*"

"Who do you like?"

"Evil Kneivel."

"You mean, daredevils?"

"Yeah, I want to be a daredevil like Evil Knievel."

"You are definitely heading in that direction," I told him.

I got up off of my bed and went down the hallway to Steve's room. He was propped up on his double bed and didn't look up. He continued to sketch an interesting design with a pen on a pad.

"Hi."

"You're the only guy I know who smiles vertically," he said.

"Tell me more about the acting class at your school."

"I hate the acting department. Mr. Thacker threw a kid off the stage one time."

"He did?"

"That's what I heard, and I believe it. He kind of intimidates me. He makes me never want to act in anything."

"I *would love* to get on any stage," I said.

"Not me." He rolled something between his right index finger and thumb.

"So, Ffej, if ya *had* to have a million dollars, would you take it?"

"No. I want to earn it from acting."

"Here, I peeled off the back of a bumper sticker today and I saved it for you. Do you want some gobbeldy goop? It's a present," he said.

"Honest?"

"Honest."

"Honest, or hhh-onest?"

"Honest," he said.

"Sure," I said, and took the gobbeldy goop from his fingers. I could feel the consistency wasn't smooth enough, and I knew what it was.

"This is a fucking booger! You're an asshole!" I laughed. I flicked the booger back into his room and went into the bathroom and looked into the mirror and studied my face. There was no way I was going to let Mr. Thacker intimidate *me*.

"You just do it, that's all. You make it happen."

I spoke to my excellent black hair in the mirror.

The best place to start was on the side of my school, in front of a tan wall, where everyone passed on their way to and from the cafeteria or playground. After the lunch bell rang, I stood in front of the wall.

"*This* is Doctor Jekyll and Mister Hyde," I announced, and went into it. I walked with an imaginary cane and exaggerated dignity. I pulled off the tip of the cane and poured mysterious liquid inside the cap, drank it and waited. I shrugged my shoulders and headed east. I convulsed violently, fell to the warm blacktop, got spastic, and lurched up.

I was a monster now. I ran around, roared, grabbed my throat, and slammed my cane to the ground. I drank from the cane crudely and became Jekyll again, smoothed down my hair, and walked away with dignity.

Seven students sat where they had never sat before and watched, as I improvised a Frankenstein comedy. I played both doctor and monster. As the doctor, I twiddled my fingers upward to pantomime the smoke of test tubes all around. Two dumpsters clanged across the school yard.

"I can see my neighbor is also making a *monster*." My new

audience loved it.

At the end of recess, I saw eighteen students laughing with me. They clapped their hands and I smiled back at them. This was a miracle to me.

These wall shows were freaky popular. Students and faculty from the elementary school and also the junior high, who could see what was going on from their campus, came over. The fifty students brought their lunches with them and ate on the ground instead of at the cafeteria tables.

I imitated our teacher, Ms. Bolton, with her Texas accent, and her glasses on a chain around her neck, until she heard about it and called me over during class with a wagging index finger,

"Stop doing *me*," she said loudly in her John Wayne voice. The classroom shouted with laughter.

I did two performances a day at recess and lunch. My imitation of Laurel and Hardy got the best reaction. The way Oliver Hardy stares into the camera when things go wrong is how I stared at the audience, and Stan Laurel's fluid comic timing that never lets up. The students sat on the pavement, but the faculty always stood, and my space to perform got smaller.

(Short essay for school)

> *November 16th, 1973*
> I don't know whether the gasoline shortage will affect us or not but I think it will. We have small cars but my mom drives a pretty long way and my dad drives miles and miles. Just yesterday he drove two hundred miles! His ~~gas~~ company pays for his gas but still it's a waste of gas. The cars we have are a Maverick for my dad and a TR6 for my mom, an they both give pretty good ~~milage~~ mileage.

I waited to tell my dad about my wall shows until he was alone and in a fair mood in his easy chair.

"Dad, you might not believe this, but a big crowd gathers every day at school to watch me perform in front of a wall. Teachers watch me too. You should see them applaud!"

"Is that a fact?"

"Yes, it is."

"It sounds like wild exaggerations to me, Jeff." He smacked his tongue lightly on the roof of his mouth and folded his hands onto his cashmere sweater. "You know, my father, your grandfather, who came over from Hungary after World War One, tried like heck to make it in show business, and all he ever became was an unsuccessful composer of movies. He told me if I ever became an artist he would *break my arm*, and he meant it. We had no money and we suffered. When I was nine, I needed to have ten deep cavities filled and they took me to the dentist there in Chicago. My father couldn't afford to pay for Novocain or pain killer of any kind, or so he said. So, they drilled all ten cavities in my mouth and all they gave me for the pain was a quarter to jam my thumb through ...while the smoke whirled upward, *zhoom!*" His hands illustrated the smoke. "...and in those days, the drills were *so* slow, not like now, now they have high speed drills...and afterwards, they took the quarter away from me and my mother, your grandma, promised she would buy me a hamburger when the ordeal was over but...I never got one. That event changed me," he said while tightening his jaw. "So...show business is... not the business to get into. Stay out of it. Take it from me. That's the *one business* to avoid."

"Why?"

"Because it is virtually impossible to become successful in, that's why. Pick any business you want to get into, but I'd *very* much prefer you didn't go into that one."

He swiveled slowly and blew into a mug of coffee. I looked down at his large white socks on his heavy feet.

"So, you don't think I or anyone I know will ever make it in Hollywood?"

"No, I don't. There is really no possible *way*, unless by *a* total fluke, which won't happen. A lot of what is big in Hollywood is all just a bunch of hype anyway."

He waved his hand in the air and swiveled to his left and peered out the sliding glass door at the Pacific Ocean's horizon. I looked at the gleaming dome of his bald head.

"Your grandfather worked with some famous musicians."

"Didn't he have trouble getting along with people, though?"

"*Oh* yes, the man could be very hard to get along with. He would try attending Hollywood parties and such, but it usually didn't go so well." A sad smile was frozen to his face as he talked.

"Do you remember any stories about those parties?" He set his coffee mug down and sleepily folded his hands on top of his head.

"Well, there was one party. The famous Milton Berle was there, and my father was off by himself playing the piano and wasn't joining in. So, suddenly, my father looks up, and Milton Berle is standing there next to him with his pants unzipped and he had his… glory…all hanging out there to behold." He demonstrated a large penis dangling. I laughed.

"So, he has his…wand out, and all this sort of thing…and he plunks it down on the piano there, and my father was just aghast. He was in shock, really. And so, Milton Berle gestures toward it and he says, 'Take a good look at that. Have you ever seen anything quite as beautiful in all your life? Isn't that the most magnificent thing you've ever seen? So, Milton Berle got the reaction out of my father that he wanted."

He swiveled to his right and looked at me on the floor. He

slowly blinked his eyes and grinned and let out a laugh when he saw me immobile with laughter.

I wished he could stay sleepy like that forever. It was when he was well-rested that he became dangerous. Come to think of it, his anger hadn't erupted since we had moved back to Malibu. It was just a matter of time though. I looked into his sleepy eyes while the calmness lasted.

"Anyway, the entertainment field is a really hopeless business. Don't go into it, if you want my advice, and even if you *don't*," he concluded with a single nod of his head.

He paced in strides throughout the house and he saw me run a little old-fashioned blue car along the dining room floor.

"…mmmmm…." hummed the engine out of my throat. The jarring return to reality was his size-13 shoe. My old-fashioned car was the size of his middle toe buried inside his enormous Hush Puppy.

"*Jeff*, the whole world to you is just a *dream*, isn't it? You live in a *dream world*, and I am beginning to get a little *tired* of it, if you really want to know. I *want* you to stop playing with these cars. I do not *want* to see you doing that anymore," he said. "You just… live in a *total* dream world…and I *intend* to pull you out of it, if I at all *can*." He walked away with his large hands clenched into fists as usual. I put the blue car in my pocket and rested my elbow on the counter.

I hid in my room, with the flimsy bedroom door closed. I sat at my new fancy homework desk my father had bought for me and stared into the white Formica.

Who was the most originally funny person I knew? That was easy: Frank Kratochvil was funny in the bones, just the way he moved. I copied Frank's way of nodding yes, with a slow, back-and-forth, pigeon-head. Also the way he stuck his lower lip out and to the side to look regal. He never tapped his foot to music. Instead, he kept the beat of a song he liked by moving his arm up and down with a floppy wrist. I started my next performance with a Frank Kratochvil impression.

"Next is…the Wolfman." I gave them Lon Chaney Jr.'s Wolfman—stricken by the full moon, he transforms slowly into the wolf, with that look on his face like he is about to cry. On my tiptoes, spastically, with knees bent, I stalked the audience, ran through them, and roared up at the sky while crouched down. That went over well. That was one of the last acts I did for them.

I relaxed with Frank at recess. We strolled slowly toward the jungle gym. We walked a wide circle around an obscenely giant potato bug that we could hear scuttle along the blacktop.

"Frank, I would like you to be my manager and agent. What do you say?"

"Yes." We climbed to the tip of the jungle gym and sat on the bars overlooking the sea.

Vance, who was also an outcast, joined us. On the surface, Vance was just another Malibu white boy, handsome in a negative sort of way, with dark curly hair and brown eyes, but his personality was just as quirky as ours. We sat across from each other at the rickety perch, as seagulls glided a few feet over our heads. Our hair was always short, never long. Just that alone separated us from the others. Tommy Pringle started up.

"We don't want Pringle up here," said Frank. He began shaking the jungle gym. Then Vance and I chimed in. We all shook the old jungle gym in unison. The faded jungle gym had bolts missing and swayed violently. Tommy could not climb up. He finally stopped trying.

"I'll see you on the way home, Tommy," I said.

"We are at the summit. It is time for a summit meeting," said

Frank. Vance curled his thin lips into a downward slant, his upper lip to the left and his lower lip to the right.

"I like having the day off from my shows," I told them.

"Are you going to do the lunch show?" asked Vance.

"I just don't feel like doing a show today."

"Maybe you should," said Frank.

"If my manager says I should, then I will," I said to Frank.

"Well?"

"Why? I already proved it *can* be done. I'd rather relax here with you two. I am going to tell them I need a break from it. My mind is made up." Vance smiled mischievously. Frank remembered his responsibilities as my manager.

"Are you *sure?*"

"*Yes,*" I said primly. I stood, balanced on a narrow rung, and barked into the sea breeze.

"Shit, piss, and corruption!" I had learned that one from my father. A seagull below us in the sandbox answered me with ugly multiple squawks. I sat back down and leaned out and leaned in and rested my chin on the cool, gray, curved steel rung.

"I don't know if you are doing the right thing. When you do something that is good in show business, you have to stick with it until you get famous, but it's up to you," said Frank. I gave a sideways glance to both of them.

"When the lunch bell rings, you both just follow me around to the wall that I made famous."

"Okay!" grinned Vance.

Frank and Vance trailed behind me to the famous south wall at lunch.

"Okay, wait here." They stopped, and I turned the corner to the biggest audience I had yet seen. There was almost no room to perform. I guessed about seventy people sat on the hard ground. I walked to the front of them.

"I am not going to perform today. Thank you." I looked for and received a uniform frown on all the faces. They were quiet as I returned to Frank and Vance. We went down the hallway together. We casually glanced behind us to find that most of the audience had followed and were fifteen feet behind us and grinning.

"C'mon, they're after us!" yelled Vance. We ran behind Vance, and the crowd was in pursuit.

Frank led the way and cut us through a random classroom and back toward another building. Sixteen students chased after us when I looked. Frank led us through a front door and out the back door of another classroom, and then zig-zagged through the back door and out the front door of another classroom.

They hid me inside the boys' bathroom at the front of the school. Frank held the door shut while Vance stood up on a toilet and peeked out the high window that he cranked opened two inches.

"He's not in here! Okay, yes, he is in here!" yelled Vance out the window. I stepped up on the toilet seat next to Vance, placed my finger tips on the window ledge and peered over. I waved at them and the seven girls squealed.

"Come on, give us a show, please?" We wanna see Doctor Jekyll and Mister Hyde," said a tall blonde girl named Michelle Peters.

I looked at Vance, who was preoccupied with them. As we stood on the same toilet seat on our tiptoes, the sunshine showed the peach fuzz across the right side of his face.

"How come you are such a silly whore, Vance?" I asked. His eyes darted over at me.

"I know! Oh well!" he sneered.

They dispersed outside. Vance and I stepped down and I felt kind of emotional. Frank looked at me and understood, while

Vance just wanted someone to chase the crap out of us all day long.

Christmas vacation began with my father's nostrils ablaze as he glared at my report card.

"Go to your room. You are grounded for a full week. That's half of your vacation. Then you can go off with your mother, and I don't care what you do!" During my incarceration, I tried my hand at a screenplay about my favorite comedians all thrown in together. It was so bad that I got up in the middle of the night, balled up the pages and threw them in the garbage pail. I went back to bed and had one of my typical anxiety attacks.

I got up and switched on the light beside the door. Just below the light, a thick, hairy wolf spider gripped the wall and cast a shadow. I could swear I saw it breathing. Or maybe it was the wall that was breathing. I picked up my hardcover math textbook from my desk and balanced it on my hand like a waiter does a food tray. I aimed and heaved the book forward and ran as the book smacked into the wall and came down, spider and all.

"*TO BED, JEFF!*" screamed my father from the adjacent room. I heard an irritated sigh from Jenny.

"Okay," I said. I looked down. It was a direct hit. The wolf spider's legs were curled in and it was on its back, which was a damn good sign.

In the vibrant morning sun, I walked onto the enclosed patio, where my father and Jenny sat over pink grapefruit halves sprinkled with sugar. My father was worked up over Jane Fonda, and Jenny sat there in her quiet intelligence.

"That goddamn bitch! She should be shot as a traitor!" he growled, his voice echoed off the patio windows.

"What did Jane Fonda do?" I asked.

"She's a traitor! She went over to the other side in Vietnam and cheered them on, goddamn bitch!"

"Oh? I don't remember that."

"Well, you were too small."

"The only bad thing I thought she did was make the movie *Barbarella*. You took me to see that movie when I was five, and I haven't been the same since." I said. My father laughed.

"Oh, yeah, God, you were really upset. You were screaming," he reminisced.

"Can I take a little walk around?"

"Well, you're grounded, but okay." I left them there and re-immersed myself in my study of comedians. I decided I wasn't too fond of Abbot and Costello. I rarely laughed when I watched them on television. They looked like they did comedy just to make money out of it. I found them mean-spirited and rather dull. It felt good to narrow down my interests as I walked alone slowly.

My mother and Jack pulled up beside the mailbox to take me to their home in Mar Vista. My father waved me over just before I went down the driveway.

"Don't forget to give your mother a big kiss for me. Not on the left cheek, and not on the right cheek but right, square in the middle of her *you-know-what!*" He laughed bitterly.

"Yeah...I know what," I said, and got away from him quickly.

My mom dropped me off at Cinema-on-the-Mall in Santa Monica to see a new movie, *American Graffiti*. I saved the full-page ad in the calendar section of the *Los Angeles Times*. By the time I got up to piss halfway through, my life was changed. This movie vamped up my mind. I sculpted my hair with my fingernails with water from the lobby water fountain. I had never known about 1950s Americana, but I did now. I was instantly in love with a music called doo-wop that I had never heard before.

For the first time, I asked my father to give me a haircut. To save money, he cut our hair with his electric hair clipper kit that had dull blades. I combed my hair back with Vaseline into an uneven ducktail.

I tried another screenplay titled *Eggs*, inspired by *American Graffiti*, about Halloween night two months ago when I rode with my brother and his friends in a station wagon in Malibu West and we threw eggs at people on the sidewalks and they threw eggs at us. I gave it up and drew flying eggs.

My father barged in and stood over me with his hands in his pockets.

"What are you working on for school?" he leaned over my desk with a sour expression, his eyes fixed on my flying eggs. "Huh….Got any homework?"

"No," I lied.

In the morning I got out of bed. It was cold. Steve and I each ate a bowl of corn flakes mixed with granola, wheat germ, and milk before our walk to school together. I put on my shoes.

"Are you ready, Fej?" he asked from the kitchen door.

"Yep." We headed down the mountain.

Halfway through the meadow, I stopped to tie my shoe. Steve looked over his shoulder at me, rubber-necked, and stopped. I stood back up.

"Are you wearing your pajamas?" I was afraid to look down. I slowly did. Sure enough, I had my light-green, red-striped pajamas, bottoms and top. My shoes and socks were on neatly.

We were more than halfway to school.

"It feels comfortable," I grinned. Steve laughed.

"I can't believe you, man. Gawd! You're somethin' else!"

"To hell with it. I guess I'm going to school this way."

I just acted natural. Two hours of class went by. Then Ms. Bolton asked loudly across the classroom, "Jeff, are you wearing your pajamas today?" The class roared out. I stood up.

"This is a suit my dad bought for me; it's the latest!" I put my hands on my hips. I didn't have to do any impressions that day; my pajamas got the laughs.

I didn't worry about sports on the playground. They never picked me for their softball team and I didn't want to be picked, pajamas or no pajamas. I stayed close to Frank.

"After you stop laughing, I have to tell you about a new movie called *American Graffiti*. We have to go see it and you have to buy the soundtrack. Agreed?" Frank picked up a snail, dropped it, and kicked it over the fence.

"Okay." His face was red, and he shut his eyes so he wouldn't have to see me, as I struck tough-guy poses in my pajamas. I left him in a corner of the playground so he could catch his breath.

Two days later, Steve and I were on our way down through the meadow again as usual and right about at the same spot as before.

"*Again?*" I heard him shout. I stopped, clamped my eyes shut and slowly peered down. This time I only wore the top of my pajamas, and I had my normal bell-bottom jeans on.

"Yeah, I know," I said sadly.

I always sat next to Frank, and when Ms. Bolton stepped out to smoke a cigarette, the comedy began. Frank's latest was to hyperventilate as he sat at his desk. When the dizziness hit him, he stopped and sat still with his eyes closed and one eyebrow up.

"That's what it feels like to be drunk," he said. Then I tried it, but I couldn't hyperventilate as well as Frank.

I felt a tap on the back of my head, turned and saw the new guy in class. He grinned wide. Tiny wads of paper landed in my hair, and Frank's hair. I thought he was just another bully. His smile was a silent laugh. He had big teeth, high cheekbones, and was covered with dirt from his shoes to his straggly dark-blond hair. His dark, puffy jacket had dried snot on the sleeves.

I didn't know what to say to him. I watched him throw a couple of tiny paper wads at the back of Frank's head. We picked the wads out of our hair.

"Was that a spit wad or was it dry?" asked Frank. All we got is that laugh that had no sound.

"Stop that," Frank told him. "I will knock you out. I don't care if your dad is a famous director or what."

"Whose dad? His dad?" I whipped around to face him.

"His dad is a movie director. You don't know who his dad is? He is Sam Peckinpah." Frank put a stick of Juicy Fruit Gum in his mouth.

"Yeah? Who is that?"

"You don't know who Sam Peckinpah is? He directed the movie *The Wild Bunch*, and also *Straw Dogs* and *The Getaway* with Steve McQueen, and he also directed *Pat Garrett* and *Billy The Kid*." Frank turned and faced him.

"Sam Peckinpah is your dad, huh?"

"Yeah, Krap-a-shit, yeah, Frank Krap-a-shit," he said.

"Peckin*poo*!" said Frank back.

"So what's your name?" I asked.

"Matt," he said.

"How do you spell your last name?" I wrote it down in a margin of my math textbook. Matt spelled it out slowly,

"P-e-c-k-i-n-p-a...." Then he did the silent, laugh-grin before giving me the last letter. "h."

"Hey Dad, do you know who Sam Peckinpah is?"

"Sam Peckinpah...yeah...he is really famous. He is one of Hollywood's top movie directors."

"His son is in my class."

"No kidding. Yeah, he's big time," said my father. "Although his movies are really full of a lot of killing. He is known for putting way too much violence into his films. A theater probably wouldn't let you in to see his movies. You're too young."

Matt and I slowly drifted around the playground, avoiding all the sports.

"Does your dad live in Malibu?"

"Yeah, he lives in Paradise Cove."

"Oh? What's it like living in Paradise Cove?"

"I don't know. I live with my mom," he said vaguely.

"Oh."

I wasn't sure what to say to Matt. I was drawn to his dark sense of humor, though. I wanted to learn from him.

"Have you seen the movie *American Graffiti*?" I asked.

Matt lowered his head and said in a respectful tone, "Yeah, I saw it with my dad. He said it is an important movie."

"Oh good! It's too bad you missed the wall shows I was doing. I think you would have liked them."

"Why did you stop?"

"I ran out of ideas pretty much. If I was to start those shows over now, you'd be the only one in school who hasn't seen my comedy."

I walked with Matt to his mom's house, which looked even more run down than my house. A scruffy white dog leaped against the front gate.

"I'll see you later, Matt."

"Do you want to meet my dad?"

I turned and faced him. "Sure, if it is all right but only if it is all right."

"Okay," said Matt with a half grin. "We can go see him tomorrow."

The sky had a dense fog over it the next morning. Everybody else in my father's house had gone out to breakfast. I told them

I wanted to stay home. I put the *Bonnie and Clyde* soundtrack album on the living room turntable, paced the needle on the first track, and turned the volume all the way up. Three deer on our front lawn scuttered at the opening of "Foggy Mountain Breakdown". I watched the thick fog swirl down on the other side of the canyon, on cue to the Bluegrass music and it felt great. After the desired chill bumps, I phoned Matt.

"Meet me at the entrance to Paradise Cove at noon," he said.

Matt was there as I stepped off the bus. We hiked up the long grade to the trailer homes each as white and flimsy as the next.

Matt took a key from his pocket and opened the door of one unremarkable-looking trailer. We stepped into an air-conditioned, furnished living room with brown panel walls. The room was deserted.

"Come in here, Mathew," said a crackly booming, articulated voice in a room to the left of us. Matt stepped toward the partially opened door and quietly entered a darkened room.

"Hi, Dad. I brought a friend with me. Is it okay if he comes in?"

"Why, sure," said the voice slowly. Matt motioned for me to step into the room. To the left, Mr. Peckinpah was on a bed propped up on some pillows. He was shirtless and covered from the waist down by a blanket. He was in the company of two fully clothed, beautiful, brunette women who stood on either side of the bed. One of the women held an open screenplay in her hands.

"Joey and Natasha were reading to me from a screenplay that has some potential," Mr. Peckinpah told us with drawn-out words in his gruff voice. He looked older than I had expected though not as old as Tom Pringle's dad. The blinds were shut, and I wondered how a script could be read in such a dark room. Mr. Peckinpah lay there and held a bottle of whisky at his side.

"This is Jeff."

I stepped forward and spoke with a respectful little smile. "I just wanted to tell you that it is an honor to meet such a famous director."

Mr. Peckinpah smiled. "Well, that's quite all right. Thank you, I appreciate that," he said.

"We'll go outside now," said Mathew courteously.

"Okay, good. Let us *work*," said Mr. Peckinpah as he raised himself up on the pillows. The woman with the screenplay squinted at the page and got ready to read aloud. I walked out with Matt, who quietly shut the bedroom door. We went outside. He looked at me with his silent laugh.

"Well, I guess I'll go home now," I said.

"You have to go?" His smile dropped.

"Yeah, I should get going."

"Why? I'm not as fun to hang around as Kratochvil?"

"No, you're a barrel of monkeys, just like me. And meeting your dad was really something!" I studied his face.

"You don't want to go back in the trailer for a while?"

He shook his head no. "I'll see you tomorrow, Matt."

"Okay, bye," he said, and I walked to the bus stop. I looked over my shoulder and saw Mathew with his hands in his back pockets, his eyes to the ground, his long hair over his face as he stepped with uncertainty around the world's wealthiest trailer park.

Tommy Pringle's house was my first stop on my walk home.

"My dad invited you to go to his work with him at Twentieth Century Fox tomorrow. We can walk around the studio while he is working. You have to be ready at seven a.m., he said."

"Oh, I'll be here."

The lot was vacant. I yawned as we strolled through streets of sun-warped building fronts and square beige-colored stages. It looked like no movies were being filmed. A wind picked up and blew dust in our eyes. Then we noticed some action going on in one small stage. There was a white trailer in front of it with black curtains. The trailer door said Peter Boyle on it and we entered the dark studio uninvited. The director's chair said Gene Wilder across the back.

We stayed there the rest of the day and watched Gene Wilder direct a scene with Peter Boyle as a bald Frankenstein monster.

"I have never seen a bald Frankenstein monster before, and I have seen all of the Universal Studios Frankenstein movies. This must be some sort of joke!" I told Tommy between takes. Gene Wilder spoke to us nicely when they took a break.

We payed close attention when Peter Boyle slowly went down the outside steps in those big shoes, then up the tiny trailer steps and squeezed into the trailer door frame. He sat abruptly in a chair and the trailer swayed. The make-up man patiently applied touch-ups to his blue head. Tommy and I leaned in and stared from the trailer door. Peter Boyle turned in back of him and looked at us and lost his patience. "Boys, would you excuse us, PLEASE!" he yelled.

Tommy and I gasped and ran off the set and didn't look behind us.

Five

March through June, 1974, twelve years old
That's What She Said

My father understood what it was like to be a worried child. He had a bad childhood and he expected everyone else to have a bad childhood too. When I was ten, he showed me two exercises for nervous stomachs.

"Plug one side of your nose with your finger and breathe as slowly as you can, so that you can barely feel the air in your nose. Exhale just as slowly. Now try it on the other side of your nose. Keep doing that until you feel normal."

The other exercise was to tense up each part of your body separately and then relax it from your feet up. It helped.

"Thank you," I told him. My panic attacks were too severe now for those 1930s remedies. I asked Jenny for help.

"Try drawing a hot bath for yourself. That might help you calm down," she said.

"Did any of you find a better solution to nervous stomachs?"

I asked at the dinner table as we ate trifle, a sort of bread pudding with plenty of sherry in it that Jenny had made for us.

"Maybe all those hot baths you are taking are causing your panic," she said from across the table.

"But that's what you told me to do. Never mind," I managed to get down another bite.

"This doesn't feel right in my mouth," I said.

"Well, you don't have to eat it then," she said, with an *"I'll-get-you-for-this"* look on her face, or so I thought.

ACTING CLASS TAUGHT AT MALIBU CINEMA SATURDAY MORNINGS, $5.00 per class was pinned on the bulletin board at Mayfair market on Point Dume. I rode the bus to class. Two kids under the age of six and me were the only students. It was fun to be in an acting class at a movie theater. I could pretend that I was the movie. The teacher really liked my imitation of Jerry Lewis's Nutty Professor. I involved the two children in all the scenes like Jerry Lewis would. I picked them up and placed them in different seats of the theater. The teacher was ecstatic. She was thin and jittery and had no criticism for me even though I asked her for some. My father picked me up afterwards and paid her. Every time, the teacher raved about me with a huge smile.

"He does this great old man! Oh God! You have an extremely talented son! Don't let *go* of him! He is truly, *truly*, going places!" she told him in the lobby on our way out.

"Oh, no kidding…" said my father with a fake smile as we exited.

I looked over at him as he sat behind the wheel and did his yoga breathing exercises through his big nostrils. His belly rose and fell spasmodically.

"Did you hear all those good things she said?"

"She's probably a very dingy lady, Jeff. She sounds really

just…half out of her head, to be perfectly honest."

"All right, she seems kind of dingy, but a little of her praise might be on target." I faced him.

"I am not going to believe anything she says, Jeff, so drop it!"

I could never be as silly with Matt as I could with Frank. I had to adjust my mind to spend time with Mathew Peckinpah.

At the Paradise Cove entrance, I waited in the morning sun. For twenty minutes I dreamed about how much I wanted to be a Hollywood movie star, like my heroes from the '50s, Jerry Lewis and Dean Martin and Bob Hope. I wanted it so badly I could taste it, and it tasted great as I glanced across the mountain tops. A white van pulled up. I smiled and got into the van with Mr Peckinpah, his wife, Joey Goldenstein, and Mathew and three other people. We took the highway into Hollywood. I recognized the Hollywood sign and Grauman's Chinese theater, but otherwise I was lost, which made the city more magical.

We went into a building with a beautiful dark lobby, with various tall plants and a fancy waterfall that cascaded from twelve feet up across fake rocks. Matt and I tried to make ourselves invisible. He understood how to have good manners around his father, and he stood quietly. An overhanging mass of fern leaves was over our heads.

"What kind of plant is that?" I said.

"Shh…I don't know… something big," he whispered. He glanced up with his arms folded.

"It's a monster," I whispered. Matt stared at the ground with a small, closed smile.

I could hear Mr. Peckinpah's voice from somewhere on the first floor of the building. I couldn't hear anyone else, but I could hear every word Mr. Peckinpah penetrated. He was explaining what he would need.

"I bet your dad doesn't need a megaphone when he's directing," I said. Matt shushed me, index finger to his lips. It struck me that Sam Peckinpah sort of looked and sounded like an overly intense Burgess Meredith, the actor. He was also about that height. He wasn't very tall.

We got back in the van and headed home. I was seated between Matt and Mr. Peckinpah in the back seat while Joey rode up front. An ambulance rushed by us on Pacific Coast Highway with sirens and lights.

"I wonder where they're going," I quietly said.

"BOW YOUR HEADS! SAY A PRAYER!" shouted Sam Peckinpah. It was a fierce command, and all of us—even the driver—lowered our heads in unison. Mr. Peckinpah was taken to his trailer home and I was dropped off at the top of my father's driveway. I thanked Matt and the driver. I told my father about it.

"Huh…no kidding," he said.

Until my dad bought me a black leather jacket, I had to be on good terms with him. I wanted to look like the perfect 1950s teenager. My mother and Jack said they couldn't afford one, so I worked on my dad. It was kind of like working on a grizzly bear to wrestle a little control away from him.

"I'll buy you a brown one where your grandma works, Wilson's Suede and Leather. A black leather jacket looks too much like a hoodlum."

"But that's why I want one, to look like Marlon Brando in the '50s!"

"One more word, Jeff, and you're not getting either jacket!"

"Thanks, Dad." I shut my mouth and we visited my pretty Grandma Lucas. She didn't look anything like my father except maybe the cheekbones. I behaved sweetly and I got the brown jacket that we all knew I would grow out of in two years or so when I became gangly. I raised the collar in the back and kept the front points angled down and combed my hair into a messy ducktail. I checked myself in the bathroom mirror. *I had it going on!* Jenny stopped in the hallway.

"The jacket doesn't make you any less peculiar," she said and moved into the kitchen.

My acting class broke up after a month because the teacher couldn't find any more students. Frank and I were in my room. The night's festivities were devised on a half sheet of paper. Above all else, Frank refused boredom. I played "Annie Had A Baby" by Hank Ballard and The Midnighters on my record player.

"We could throw dirt clods at the horses next door." Frank jotted that down.

"So when do we have a drinky-poo?" he asked, in his German accent, rolling the 'r' in the back of his throat. I took a deep breath.

"You mean my dad's alcohol? Not 'til late, and absolutely no sneezing. He catches us and we are dead—or *I* am dead."

"Okay." Frank scribbled NO SNEEZING.

My father had a rolling liquor cart in the dining room. The hard alcohol in all those fancy bottles was strictly for a potential guest that never arrived. The bourbons and liquors would age much longer on that cart than they had in any barrel.

"What else? There is still room left on the paper. What neighbors do you have?"

"Well…do you know Andrea Allgreen?"

"No."

"I grew up with her. The Allgreens' home is way down below…but we don't have to go there." I grabbed Frank's pencil away and handed it back to him to get his attention.

"Listen, Frank, we can only sneak out when we know for sure that Jenny and my dad are asleep." He scribbled that down.

Jeff and Frank's plan to cause mischief on Deerhead road, in Frank Kratochvil's handwriting. 1974. From Jeff Lucas' souvenirs.

"After we're through with everything, maybe we can quietly listen to 1950s records," I said.

"Okay."

Frank folded the note into a neat, small square, and we went in to eat dinner. We shared a look with each other that said Jenny and my father were not our kind of people. Frank felt the controlling presence of my father. He sat at one end of the dinner table, and my father took his place at the head of the table. He glanced at each of us quietly without the usual adjusting of his glasses.

We dined on Jenny's Welsh rarebit with the thick, cheesy beer sauce over toasted English muffins, with brussels sprouts on the side that were loaded on the insides with boiled bugs that apparently only I could see. I liked Welsh rarebit, though I doubted if it was healthy. Frank was not used to any foreign cuisine and left his plate alone. He didn't even cut open a brussels sprout to see the bugs.

"*So*, how are your grades in school, Frank?" asked my father.

"Okay."

"Got any homework this weekend, Jeff?" my father needled.

"No," I said.

"Well, your report card should be here soon, so we'll soon find out if you're telling the truth or not." My father leaned back, grabbed his gut, and shook his belly, *"Uh-buh-buh-bup!"* he belched. Then he laughed and Frank laughed a little.

"Aren't you hungry, Frank?" asked my father. Frank raised an eyebrow and shifted uncomfortably.

"I am not that hungry."

"You should have let me know you weren't hungry. It's a shame to waste it," my father told him.

"In France, a belch is considered a compliment to the chef,"

Jenny told us all.

"See? I've just complimented you highly," joked my father.

Jenny looked at Frank directly for the first time that evening.

"Seeing as you didn't eat anything on your plate, then you can clean all the dishes." Frank did the dishes as my father supervised.

"*No*, you should rinse them off better than that before putting them in the dishwasher!" Frank re-rinsed a green ceramic plate and placed it back into the dishwasher.

"*No*, you should rinse that off some more!" Frank took the plate out of the dishwasher and rinsed it off some more.

"Now reach in and *stick it* all the way inside there as *far* as it can go," said my father. He grinned and looked at me and said his all-time favorite joke.

"That's what she said!" Frank placed the bowl in the back of the dishwasher with a hidden sneer.

"Can Frank and I go for a walk?" I asked.

"Unless you were lying to me about your homework, then yeah, I guess so." He turned and went into the living room. Frank dried his hands on a dishtowel and we stepped out the kitchen door and into the visual moonlight.

We approached the wooden fence along the Bergmans' property line. The nearest horse was twenty feet away—a dark-red, full-grown stud with its left profile to us. I reached down, gripped a dirt clod, and threw it in the direction of the horse. It fell apart in midair. Frank picked up a harder dirt clod the size of a ping-pong ball. Frank's aim was not just better than mine, it was accurate, and he nailed the horse on the ass. The horse lifted its right, rear leg a bit and rested on its hoof. We laughed, and I shushed him, my index finger to my lips. Frank nailed the horse again in the same spot.

"Okay, let's go inside before my dad catches us."

I turned to him halfway across the driveway,

"I didn't mean to ignore you when I was hanging out with Matt Peckinpah."

"Maybe his dad can help you with your career."

"Thanks for thinking of that."

Everyone had settled into their bedrooms. Frank and I read our list over.

"Next we dress weirdly and go down to the Allgreens'," said Frank. Frank drew a Charlie Chaplin mustache on me with a felt pen and I put a black bowler hat on my head. I drew a Groucho Marx mustache on Frank.

"Magic Markers stink. Eyeliner is what to use for a mustache. My mom gives me her eyeliner pencils, but I'm out," I said.

I turned out the light. We waited in silence until we could only hear the sound of my father's television.

"Are you ready?" he whispered.

"Yes. Let's go." I slid my bedroom window open and crawled out. My foot sank down into the weeds.

"Drop your leg slowly," I whispered. Frank hopped out and down onto dry loud leaves. "Shh." I carefully closed my bedroom window one inch at a time.

"The Allgreens and I were real close when I was a little kid."

"Yeah?"

"Yeah, Frank. Goddamn it. I am your best friend, but I want us to go easy on them," I said clearly. We went into the dark valley, and then further down the steep driveway to the small Allgreen house. We looked around us. There wasn't even a dog barking.

We stopped underneath a row of fruit trees along the left side of the driveway, which were just out of range of the flood light. Frank leaned on the trunk of a tree loaded with green, hard apricots. I picked an apricot and acted like Stan Laurel. I raised and lowered my eyebrows and examined it. I almost took a bite, and then I didn't. Frank laughed loudly as he reached up, picked two apricots, and threw them hard against the Allgreens' red-painted wood garage door. The thud echoed throughout the canyon.

I scrambled behind another tree. I considered throwing an apricot also, laughed quietly, and shook my head. When Frank did anything outrageous, I had to do it too.

I plucked an apricot and threw it badly. I missed the garage door and hit the roof; it rolled down and fell on the lawn. Frank threw five apricots at once, which sounded like machine-gun fire. He yelled out a laugh. I threw a round, but the apricots thudded on the picket fence.

The front door banged wide open, the porch light came on, and Mr. Allgreen, who had never stopped being paranoid about the Manson Family murders, stepped out with a shotgun. He was a large, fit man with a handsome, fleshy face. I took off my bowler hat. Frank and I looked down the barrel of the shotgun pointed at us.

We ran all the way up the moonlit mountain, the wind in our ears. We didn't look back until the top of my father's driveway. Mr. Allgreen was still on his porch. He squinted into the darkness with his shotgun ready. I saw my brother's head stick out of his window as we climbed inside. I turned my bedroom light on as Frank unfolded the instructions.

"*Drinky*-poo is next," he whispered in a German accent. I switched out the light and we tiptoed down the creaky hallway to my father's liquor cart. The house was treacherous, and our eyes were wide as Frank, daring and indignant, lifted an unlabeled decanter of whiskey, took out the fancy glass stopper, and had a good swig. He turned his head and his smile had a happy grimace to it as he handed me the bottle. I swallowed my first taste of whiskey and was surprised how much it burned. I handed it back to Frank, who took another big swig.

I leaned in to Frank's left ear and whispered, "No more, because he will notice. He never touches these bottles, but he does look at them, for no good reason at all." Frank put the bottle down and picked up another. It was peppermint schnapps.

"My dad will know there is booze missing," I grabbed his arm to make sure he understood. Frank went to the kitchen sink, turned on the faucet, and carefully added water to the bottles.

"*There*," said Frank, as he put the bottles back on the cart in the same place. He stepped back and studied them to make sure.

"What's left?" I asked. Frank started to take out the note and then remembered.

"Crankie," he whispered in a German accent. We sat at the dining room table. The loudest part of it was the buzz of the rotary phone as we dialed the numbers and it went around the circle.

"Try not to dial nines or zeroes," I whispered as Frank dialed a 457 Malibu number randomly.

A woman picked up.

"Hello? Is Sue there?" I asked.

"No, sir."

"Well, I'm looking for Sue."

"Sue who?"

"Sue your *ass*." Frank cracked up.

"No sir, you have the wrong number!"

"Have you ever licked a cunt? Have you ever seen *The Great Race* with Tony Curtis?" I asked.

"The cops are gonna get you."

I hung up. We covered our mouths and laughed.

Frank read from the list.

"Listen to records."

"Let's wash off our mustaches first," I said. We stood at the bathroom sink and got some of the black smudge off our upper lips. We went to my bedroom.

"Wait. Let's play a song called 'Oh Boy' by Buddy Holly."

"Okay."

"It's the last song on side one. There. Now just let the goose pimples happen."

After that, I put on the *American Graffiti* soundtrack, side three. The first song was "Ain't That a Shame" by Fats Domino, with background singers on the staccato beat. We danced in our beds. It was good exercise, fluid with the rhythm.

We slowly fell asleep, and when we awoke he smiled first and I smiled second. Our satisfaction with our activities had not diminished. Frank left early to catch the bus home. I watched him from my bedroom window as he walked down; his auburn hair disappeared behind some ice plant.

"That guy gets away with anything he wants," I said to myself.

"*Jeff*, come in here!" shouted my father from the kitchen. I looked at him, an expression of submissive tolerance in my eyes, a charcoal smudge on my upper lip.

"What happened last night? Were you out causing trouble?"

"No," I lied.

"Stevie said he saw you two outside." Mr. Allgreen knocked on the door. My father stepped outside and spoke with him. When he returned, his arms were folded, and his face was a scowl.

"You lied to me. You said you weren't causing trouble last night. You could have been shot…and I see you were in my liquor bottles also, or Frank was…I can tell. The liquor has an oily look. I am terribly disappointed in you. You think it's funny, Jeff? Now I want you to go down there and apologize to Helen, Mrs. Allgreen."

I left for the Allgreens'. Mrs. Allgreen was born and raised in Scotland. She had dark, wavy hair and constantly had a thoughtful expression. My sad face was an act, but when I saw her waiting for me in her driveway, I cried real tears. It poured out of me, and she hugged me. It felt good to be held.

"There, there, now Jeff," she said in her thick Scottish accent. "It's okay."

"I'm sorry."

"My husband never knows if the rest of the Manson Family might be on the loose is all. It's okay."

My dad didn't ground me, which almost made me suspicious, and I went with Matt to the beach at Paradise Cove. We trod along the sand together and climbed over the biggest boulder in front of us and slid down amid the tide pools. I stood. Matt sat down on a dry patch of sand.

"So what is your favorite song from *American Graffiti*?" I asked over the seagulls and crashing waves.

"You're obsessed with that music. I don't know. 'Runaway,' I guess."

"Del Shannon! Good choice!"

"You know what song I hate on the *American Graffiti* album? 'To the Ass…to the Asshole'!"

"You mean 'To the Aisle'?" We laughed. "Yeah, maybe that one's kinda shitty, I guess, but 'Runaway' is my favorite song ever recorded!"

Matt sighed and leaned toward a tide pool with a purple flower thing swaying in it. I dipped my foot down into the purple flower and it closed up around my shoe. I pulled my soaked foot out and entered the ocean with my blue jeans on.

"What are you doing?"

"Running away" I said.

Matt followed me in and a wave fell over us both and knocked us over. We floated and staggered to dry sand.

"I want to find out about the Juan Cabrillo School talent show," I said.

"I haven't heard anything. I think I'm getting crotch rot, though."

"Crotch rot? What's that?" I laughed.

"From salt water."

"Me too!" We walked on with straightened legs as our jeans constricted.

"Ow."

"Ow!"

"Damn, that hurts!"

"Ow!"

"Mrs. Bolton? I have some ideas about the big sixth-grade show." I approached her at her desk.

"What big sixth-grade show?" She looked me square in the eyes. I studied her face, amazed at how much she looked like John Wayne with a wig on.

"There *is* going to be a show, isn't there?"

"Maybe, maybe not; it depends who's interested."

"Well, I am extremely interested, and so are my friends. I am going to write a skit," I said.

"Let me know what you come up with."

Matt and I were the only reason there was an elementary school showcase that year. We performed two skits. One was about divorced parents. I lifted the jokes from the Bob Hope movie *Boy, Did I Get A Wrong Number*. Matt dressed in drag and played my wife and Frank and Vance were our kids. The next skit was about 1950s American teenagers. Matt played the tough guy ready to fight, and I was the good kid.

We both combed Vaseline in our hair. Matt's hair was too long for a ducktail so I tucked it under his collar and shaped his hair.

"What are you doing here, punk?" said Matt.

"Who, me?"

"No. I'm talking to the other fifty punks around here!" We took out our combs and struck an attitude. Principal Merriman got the classroom's attention.

"Let's see a show of hands. Which play did you like better? Raise your hands if you liked *The Divorce*." Half the hands went up.

"Who preferred the second routine about combing your hair?" Every hand went up.

Frank and I reminisced through our old school after hours and wandered into the kindergarten section.

"These trees look small now!" I reached and picked up a bird's nest and held it out. Four baby chicks were inside, eyes closed.

"I am a tree with a nest on my branch. I should put it back."

Frank grabbed up one of the birds and let out a laugh I had never heard from him. It was a madman's laugh. He didn't even smile, his blue eyes swimming in recklessness.

At the end of the laugh, he tore the baby bird's head off and threw both parts on the ground hard. I was afraid of him.

"Frank, why did you do that?" He grabbed up the other three baby birds out of the nest in my hand and tore all three heads off at once. I dropped the nest, held my own neck, and looked at Frank's hands. There was blood on them.

"Jesus, Frank. Was that necessary?" I followed the chirps of more birds over to another tree and stood by a nest with three baby chicks. Frank nudged in beside me.

"Their mother can't be far away," I said. Frank reached in, got a bird and plucked its head off and tossed head and body high in the air. I reached in the nest and picked up a bird. I could feel its soft featherless skin. I winced and plucked its head off and tossed both parts away.

Frank let out the same madman laugh. I turned my back to Frank, picked up the last bird and removed its head and almost gagged. I jumped away from the trees and laughed a what-the-hell laugh. I leaped on top of the red cement tube in the sandbox and danced on it, and so did he.

The school bell slammed out its last tone. I stood outside after everyone had gone and listened to the wind and the ocean. I felt foolish as if I was really going places in the world. I looked over at the massive junior high school gym, its red brick staring back defiantly. What would it be like there? I perched my right foot on a gas meter.

"I am going to tackle the Malibu Park junior high acting department," I said to no one. I balanced on top of the gas meter. I leaped as high as I could and stung my feet on the blacktop.

Along with my rotten report card, I carried my sixth-grade "yearbook," which was just a note pad with a blue jean cover and Mad Lib patches on it. My classmates and I signed each other's notepads in the library.

(Juan Cabrillo elementary school Yearbook)

"Have a nice summer, my best friend. Vance"

"Have a hot summer get it!' Craig Conklin"

"Have a nice bummer Jeff. From Dan S."

"roses are red, violets are blue, I only…roses are red, violets are pink, this is a waste of…Have a good summer, you old bat. Frank Kratochvil"

"Have a good summer and I hope you get to be an actor because you're good. Eric"

"To Stan, Charlie, Ollie, or whoever you'll be good luck. Michael Kim"

"I hope you get on TV. Christen"

"Roses are red, violets are blue, I only sign autographs to clods like you. Richard"

"Have a corny summer. I'm sure you will! Lisa Teel"

"Hope you have a good summer, brat, over-grown toe-nail, stale! Jenny"

"Have a bad summer. Steve"

"To Jeff, and a BLAH!!!! To you too. Anonamous"

"Have a summer. Steven"

"Jeff, you are a great actor, have a nice summer. Deanna"

"To the greates, Jeff. Tom Hanley"

"To Jeff, An outstanding young man with a talent for acting, a real nice sense of humor, and a pleasure to know. Best wishes for your future! Sincerely, Principal R. Merriman"

"Hope you make it to Hollywood. Your friend, Ray Gonzales"

"Have a nice summer, you old snake of a friend. Vance"

"Jeff, Roses are red, violets are pink, this is a waste of dam good ink. P.S. Just kidding hope ya have a fun summer. John Kelly"

"Good luck Jeff, in Junior High. Curtis"

"I hereby give my smallest to you. Shawn Wiley"

"Jeffie, Love you forever, Genie, _ Fake, Jack _ 5th grade"

"Jeff, I'm glad you're not taller than me! I enjoyed knowing you these last two years. If I can assist you, come see me. Mr. R. Shultz"

"Jeff, Have fun in summer. Michaela P.S. (I think you are a great actor and a nice person)"

"Have a career acting, see you next year, Craig K."

"Dear Jeff, I shall never forget you – keep your goals high & work high. Tons of fun this summer! Love, Miz B."

"Jeff, Have a neat summer and a hot one to. Brian"

"Have a nice summer, 5 foot 4 in. Greg Berry"

"Roses are red, violets are pink, this is a waste of God damn ink. Matt Guerrero"

"To Charlie Chaplin, Have a nice time with Ruth Buzzy! Bruce Bates P.S. Have a hot summer!"

"Jeff, Have a good summer and hope to see ya in 7th grade. April"

"Jeff, it has been really fun being in your class, see you around, Love, Charlie (Liz)"

"To Jeff, from a pal. Pickle 457-3103"

I handed my father the yearbook notepad making sure it was open to the page with principal Merriman's handwritten entry.

"This is from the school principal."

"Hmm…I am sure that you are quite the class clown, Jeff."

"And here is my report card." I held it up with my other hand. He grabbed it. When he saw the D+, he tossed the report card across the counter and slammed the notepad down as if it burned him.

He took long, slow strides over to his new tan colored upright piano, sat down, and pounded Beethoven's piano sonata number 8, the "Pathétique" in C minor. I stood to the right of him. He made a mistake and paused.

"Is this Brahms?"

"No, it's Beethoven."

"You prefer Beethoven to Brahms, don't you?"

"I prefer Beethoven, yes, but I don't believe he was the most talented composer who ever lived."

"And who was?"

"Mozart was a genius... Mozart was the most talented composer of all time," he continued playing. He made another mistake.

"What is a genius?" I asked. He lifted his hands from the keyboard.

"Genius has been defined as having the ability to be able to concentrate on one area, to the exclusion of all else, without wavering away from that single-minded concentration, over a long period of time."

"Does it matter what that area is?"

"Well, if we are talking about music, then music."

I nodded my head once and went quietly down the hall and lie on my bed. I heard him practice for ten more minutes, faltering. Then I heard him drop the lid over the keys, and step away from the piano.

Jenny poured sherry over the English trifle and placed it in the oven. I was in my room with the door closed, smelling it. I quietly felt good about my life. I had taped a picture of Jerry Lewis on my wall, along with a picture of Charlie Chaplin, the first advertisement of *American Graffiti*, photos of Laurel and Hardy, an interview with Jack Lemmon and his advice to out-of-work young actors, and an illustration of how Hollywood movies are made. I could hear my father and Jenny argue on the other side of the house.

"*JEFF!*" my father screamed contemptuously. I came out of my room quietly.

"Yeah?"

"*DINNER!*" he screamed gutturally like a good impersonation of Adolf Hitler's speech voice. We sat and ate that same sherry-soaked, sweet mushy bread. I watched my father hunched over his plate at the head of the table, looking dangerous.

"Can I be excused?" I asked.

"No, I want you to sit here." He finished his food angrily, and Jenny didn't say anything but sat up very straight.

"I decided I don't want you decorating your walls with all of that nonsense. It's just distracting you from doing your homework. It only leads to more daydreaming, so take it down. It's just pure crap."

I went crimson and wanted to turn the table over. Jenny sat across from me, calmly delighted. She leaned over in her flowered frilly blouse, crossed her competent pale hands firmly and looked directly at me.

"*Your* problem is *ingratitude*." I stood up. Steve didn't say anything—he was their angel.

I moved fast into my room and shut the door.

"You motherfuckers! I won't do it! I would rather go into your room and take everything off the walls! Then I will tape my beautiful things, on your walls! Best idea ever!" Had there been a lock, he would have broken down the door. My father moved like a wall of death toward me. He eclipsed the room.

With a closed fist, held me with one hand and pounded me with the other into my lower back. He had huge boxer's hands. I screamed like a panther, out of hatred. I did not sit still, though. I kind of walked as he struck me around the room, and since he held me with one hand we went in a counter-clockwise circle. I screamed so loudly I pictured the gym walls exploding at Malibu Park Junior High. He hit me in the back of the head and lifted me and threw me on my bed. I bounced and focused my eyes and looked for him. He had stomped out of the room. I waited for my bedsprings to calm down.

The bruises took six days to heal. I was glad I didn't have a show to do. I took the mementos off the walls as he had requested and lay down on my stomach to avoid my bruises.

Six

June through November, 1974, twelve years old

WHAT HUMP?

I stood in line by the front corner of the auditorium to register for summer school. I knew exactly what I wanted to take, but it seemed like no one else did, as the line inched slowly forward.

A stocky, athletic, tan seventh-grader was next to me. He wore short pants and a loose, mild-colored, short-sleeved shirt.

"What are you gonna take?" he asked me.

"Theater Arts. What are you gonna take?"

"Theater Arts."

I paused a few seconds.

"You like to act?"

"Well, my dad's an actor."

"He *is*? Mine sure isn't."

Five minutes went by, and we had moved forward two feet.

"Has your dad been in movies?" I asked in a polite tone. He nodded.

"Did you ever see *The Execution of Private Slovik*?"
"Yeah, I did! I sure *did*!"
"He was in that."
"What's your name?"
"Emilio."
"My name is Jeff. What's your Dad's name?"
"Martin Sheen."
"Oh," I said. "Emilio Sheen."
"No, it's *Estevez*. Emilio Estevez. Sheen is my dad's stage name."
We got to the table.
"TV production," he said.
"TV production," I said, and we walked out.
"I will be watching for *The Execution of Private Slovik* again," I waved.

He smiled. "See you in TV production."

The last half hour of the made-for-television *The Execution of Private Slovik*, was scary to watch, because I had to weep at Martin Sheen's incredible performance. My father even got misty-eyed. Every time I saw it, I sobbed for two hours after it was over, my face deep in my pillow so no one could hear me. I had seen the movie twice already, once with my father in his room. I studied the face of the lead actor and made the connection.

I finally got to meet the notorious Mr. Thacker.

"You have a brother, right?"

"Yes, Steve Lucas. He is not what you would call an actor." Mr. Thacker didn't argue. Emilio sat upright at a desk in the second row and drummed his fingers on one hand. By the end of the hour, Emilio and I were the only enthusiastic students. The other ten students talked about where they wanted to surf in that thick surfer drawl.

"Have you been to the Pipeline in Oahu?"

"No. Totally awesome, I bet."

What Hump?

"The waves are colossal. So gnarly. Dude, I fucking went there with my family. I just lived in the water the whole time. Rad."

"Oh, fer sure."

Mr. Thacker's assistant invited the class to come out to the parking lot adjacent the classroom on Monday and make a short film. Emilio and I were equally interested, but he was nowhere to be seen on the day.

"Has anyone seen Emilio? I know he wanted to be here," I said.

"It's a hot summer morning…Emilio decided to go surfing," a guy with hair over his eyes like a window shade said with a stoned grin.

"Are you sure?"

"No." He wavered a little. We headed over to the main parking lot to begin our black-and-white silent film. I wanted to play Professor Fate. I wore a black top hat and drew on a mustache with a black eyeliner pen.

"We don't have any sound. Any ideas?" the assistant teacher asked us.

"Yes, how about a comic villain who steals stuff from the student supply store and disrupts the whole school, and then he makes the school newspaper with his accomplice."

"How did you happen to come up with all that?"

"It just came to me…that's all." They all looked at me suspiciously.

"Does anybody else have any ideas? …Then I guess that is what we will go with. We are allowed only two takes for each scene."

I loved silent movies, so I put that into my performance. I moved in fast motion. The next day, I asked Emilio where he had been.

"I had something to deal with at home," he said quietly.

We turned out the lights and watched it, and I liked it more than I thought I would. We all did. My timing was good. I added little nuances not knowing if they would come across. In one scene, I went to sleep with my top hat on and a rock for a pillow. My head banged on the rock and I sat up, took off my hat, rubbed my head, and put the top hat back on and put my head back on the rock and slept. By the end, Emilio had a laughing smile on his face.

"I should have been here."

"I wish you had."

Matt invited me to spend the night at his dad's trailer. His father would not be home until later, so we had the place to ourselves. We took a walk down to the Sand Castle restaurant and ate two orders of French fries, 88 cents each. Then we listened to records that I had brought with me; a Laurel and Hardy album, a 1950s rock & roll double album, Jenny's Lawrence of Arabia soundtrack, and two singles; Joe Turner's "Shake, Rattle, and Roll" and Elvis Presley's "Don't Be Cruel." Matt listened intently to all of it.

"Why would you ever listen to the *Yellow Brick Road* album when you can listen to this?"

"I like the *Yellow Brick Road* album."

"And you should cut your hair, too. You should cut your hair and *only* listen to this great stuff." I held up my hand and twirled my fingers into a fist.

"You better listen to me."

"I'm listening."

It was dark after the second playing of the Laurel and Hardy album.

"What do we do now?" I asked.

What Hump?

"I don't know. Let's look around the trailer." We went through the bathroom cabinets and pulled out a can of his dad's shaving cream. He shook the can, sprayed a ball of foam into his left hand, and spread it around his face, and I did the same.

"Are we going to scrape this with a razor?"

"No, we are going to walk around the trailer park like this," he said. So, out we went into the Paradise Cove evening. People laughed at us from inside their trailer windows.

"I would love to be a movie actor with good roles. I can't even describe how much I want that."

"Yeah, that would be good. I was in some of my dad's stuff."

"Oh yeah? Which ones?"

"One called *Junior Bonner* with Steve McQueen. Some other stuff too."

"Tom Pringle and I saw Gene Wilder making a movie a few months ago. Pringle's dad took us to Twentieth Century Fox studios and we walked around on our own. Gene Wilder was on one of the sets. He was directing some kind of movie with a bald Frankenstein monster in it. It looked like a really cheap set. Remember Gene Wilder from the Willy Wonka movie?"

"Of course!"

"Gene Wilder talked to us a little bit and we pissed off the Frankenstein monster."

"That must've been cool!"

I could feel my face burn. I looked at Matt, who tapped his fingers through the shaving cream.

"Do you feel a burn?" I asked.

"Hell yes!"

"Let's get this shit off our faces!" I yelled. We ran back to his father's trailer and washed off our faces in the bathroom sink.

We waited for Mr. Peckinpah to come home as we sat in the living room with red stinging faces. In an hour, we heard the key in the door, and Matt's father walked in with his wife. She disappeared into the bedroom, and Mr. Peckinpah got a bottle of whiskey from a cabinet and a glass and sat in the center of the couch. He was not one for small talk.

"Here is what I want both of you to do for me." His index finger pointed to the middle of the room and he aimed the cone of a stand-up lamp where he had pointed. "Now, I will give you both a scene to do, and you two take it from there. Agreed?"

"Yes."

Jeff's stepfather, Jack, Jeff, and Mathew Peckinpah at Magic Mountain in June, 1974. Photo by Reba Dick.

What Hump?

He finished his drink and slowly poured another. Mr. Peckinpah liked silences after he spoke. We listened to the whiskey splash in his glass on the coffee table.

"You are both inside an elevator and the doors won't open."

Matt and I began. We pretended we didn't know each other. When I pressed the button for the elevator, I got an electric shock, which got a laugh from Mr. Peckinpah. We entered the imaginary elevator.

"That's just my luck… stuck here," I said.

"I guess now we have to wait and try not to go crazy," said Matt. I climbed on Matt's shoulders to escape out of the top of the elevator. Mr. Peckinpah ended it there.

"Okay," he said, and laughed and applauded a bit. "Now, I want you two to be at an amusement park together."

"We might as well go on the spinout ride," I said. Matt grinned. We were only - acting what had really happened recently on a trip to Magic Mountain amusement park together with my mom and Jack. The floor dropped, and the attendant would not stop the ride. Everyone threw up on everyone else.

"He is sadistic!" I yelled.

"Hey, that fat lady is spreading out!" yelled Matt.

"We are being smothered by fat!" I yelled. Mr. Peckinpah laughed, and clapped his hands.

"All right, boys, take a break!" he said with a great smile. He poured himself another glassful.

"That was good, boys. No bullshit. That was good."

Mr. Peckinpah took off his shoes, placed them beside the coffee table, and had some more drinks. I sat on the floor and Matt sat in a chair.

"That was good, boys, no bullshit. No bullshit," he said again. He stayed up, with his feet on the coffee table and the light on and the whiskey re-poured in his glass. Matt and I fell asleep on the floor. Just as I would doze off, I would hear "No bullshit, I liked that" again. The last thing I heard Sam Peckinpah say before I fell asleep was: "Something is trying to break through!"

Emilio and I sat together and yawned and yawned some more. We had to play second fiddle to the ninth-graders and didn't have much say. We carried out a slow conversation between our yawns.

"I hope when Thacker's drama class starts, we get to do more than we get to do in here," I told him. Emilio yawned and nodded his head.

"Hey, I did kind of a skit for Sam Peckinpah a few nights ago." Emilio's eyes opened up.

"You did?"

"Yeah, it went good! Me and his son, Matt, acted for him a little bit. I wish Matt were here in this class. If he was, he would be yawning too, I guess." Emilio laughed and folded his arms. It was a cold summer morning and the classroom door stayed propped open. He wore his usual short pants and short-sleeved polo shirt. I always wore long sleeves and long pants, because of my puny arms and white scrawny legs. Mr. Thacker announced a test about camera angles, and class ended.

Out into the south parking lot, Emilio and I waved as he slowly walked away toward Point Dume with another yawn. Everyone was walking away toward the Pacific Coast Highway. Only one person walked toward the classroom. It was Matt Peckinpah.

"Do you wanna go to my dad's again?"

"Of course I do."

When we stepped inside the trailer, Sam Peckinpah was on his feet as he paced through the front room like a Tyrannosaurus Rex. He had a most concerned look on his face. His eyes were peeled wide.

WHAT HUMP?

"The most basic of all emotions is fear. It wreaks havoc upon the world," he said slowly. Matt and I sat down quietly, both us afraid to move. Mr. Peckinpah turned to us and said, "If I had a penny for every time I said that, I'd be a rich man." He went into the kitchen and paused.

"Mathew, I want you to sweep the porch out here. It's got all kinds of dirt on it. Take this housewife's broom and sweep all this up." He handed Matt the broom and led him out to the porch. I followed them outside and noticed that the porch was clean, and I couldn't see any dirt on it. Matt swept the doormat and the little aluminum steps.

"That's not the right way to do it! There is a right way and a wrong way!" Mr. Peckinpah screamed. He grabbed Matt by his left shoulder and shook him violently, his long hair tossed around. Mr. Peckinpah then gently, stoically, handed the broom to me.

"Here. Now you try," he commanded.

I nervously took the broom from him and swept where I stood in front of my feet in the same careful strokes as Matt had done.

"There, that's the way it is done, now! You see? That's the way! See, Mathew, how he is doing that? He knows how to do it! There!" he yelled out across the trailer park. Mr. Peckinpah turned and went inside the trailer. He gently closed the door behind him.

Matt and I stood there.

"I guess I'd better go."

"Yeah, okay." His hair was a mess and he looked as though he had just fallen out of a tall tree. I tiptoed off the porch and walked away and wondered how long Matt would wait before he entered the trailer.

I stood at the top of the Malibu driveway and watched for Jack's Grand Prix down by the mailbox. My father watered some

Student Handbook

MALIBU PARK JUNIOR HIGH SCHOOL
MALIBU, CALIFONIA

Welcome

It is our hope that the years you spend at Malibu Park Junior High School will be filled with new discoveries, physical and mental growth, and creative accomplishment that will always be a part of you. What you do with your time in school will largely determine your effectiveness in meeting challenges and responsibilities. We, your teachers, can help but education is to a great extent a do-it-yourself task.

We know you will soon come to be as proud of Malibu Park as are the students and staff members who have been here for some time. We base our pride on the school spirit which the students and faculty have developed together.

A junior high school gives you some new opportunities; for example, a different teacher for each subject; an opportunity to explore new fields of study; a chance to feel more adult and to be treated as such by your teachers; a chance to reinforce self discipline; and a chance to experience the freedom to make choices, to face one's own faults, and to consider others.

This handbook is designed to be a source of information for you and your parents. Read it through to become familiar with its contents, then use it whenever you have a question concerning school rules and procedures. Put it in your notebook for safekeeping.

We have observed that successful students are involved in school programs, they participate in student activities, and they demonstrate a strong, positive attitude toward our school. We want you to be successful at Malibu Park.

William Delkener,
Principal

A Brief History Of Malibu Park Junior High School

Before Malibu Park was built, the land on which it now rests was a large open field of short grasses and tumbleweeds. Its most visible resident was a very fast and very busy roadrunner.

Our school opened in September 1963 with 268 6th and 7th grade students. Our first principal was Dr. Edward Wells. In September 1964 we added an 8th grade and the following year dropped the 6th grade and added a 9th grade.

Since the school opened, the two-story classroom building, library and main office building and the gymnasium and pool have been added. Our first library was in the back half of the auditorium with temporary partitions separating it from other parts of the building.

From 1964 to 1970 Dr. Donald G. Richardson was principal, and during this time all the present buildings were planned and built. In 1969 student body President Sandee Lambert and the Student Council placed a "time capsule" with information about the school, students and teachers of that time in the foundation of what is now our library building.

In September 1970 all our new buildings were completed and Mr. William Delkener became principal. As the 1973-1974 school year began Malibu Park was ten years old, had 660 students and 33 teachers.

What Is Malibu Park Junior High School?

Malibu Park is many things. Most important, it is a time in your life to explore a wide variety of topics, skills, interests, and experiences before you decide what to specialize in. It is an opportunity to practice self discipline and making choices and a chance to voice your opinions and share ideas with other people.

At Malibu Park, you will probably have a different teacher for each subject and you will attend seven different classes each day. You will meet in small groups and large groups, in classrooms, outside, in a library and even in a swimming pool.

Malibu Park is an exciting, sometime frustrating, but rewarding time in your life. The rewards are knowing and developing yourself and understanding your own world.

Public domain. From Jeff Lucas souvineers.

plants with his big, hairy fist around the green garden hose and his other hand in his blue pocket.

"Bye. They're here, Dad."

"Okay," he grinned, "Don't forget to give your mother a real big one for me right between her cheeks, tongue and all!"

"Right." I stepped away from his bitter laugh.

I had a great time away from my father. My stepsister Terri again forgot to give me a diary for my birthday. We laughed about it.

"Okay, next year, I will make sure. I promise," she told me.

My mother dropped me off at the bottom of the Malibu driveway in September. I entered quickly, smiling, then stopped like a fly on a windowsill. My father spun in his chair and eyed me, head on one side. Jenny sat uptight in the nook of the couch. They both had the identical stern frown. They didn't speak to each other.

"Hello," I said quietly. They didn't answer. Jenny shot out of the room. I tried to conceal my new Big Band double album under my arm. He stared at me and spoke in a low disgusted tone.

"So, how is your puke-y mother? Did you give her a big kiss for me like I asked you to?"

"Sort of." I drifted quietly into my room.

Junior high school looked imposing on the first day of the seventh grade. We all thought that, as we went up those long steps in front of the school. Steve told me what to expect and which teachers to dread. Most of his information was useless. I knew Physical Education would be my worst class. In the rest, the worst that could happen was that I would fail but in PE, I would not only fail but also get beaten up.

One glance at my list of classes and I became a bully myself. I stormed into the principal's office, furious. Mrs. Edgington called me to her desk before I could get to the principal.

"Yes? You must talk to me whenever you have anything to say to Mr. Delkner," she said with a big fake smile. "Now, what grade are you in?"

"Seventh." My face looked angry, and I was a little out of breath.

"Do you have all your classes lined up?"

"Yes."

"Well then, *everything* should be fine."

"*Why* isn't an acting workshop offered to seventh-graders?"

"Because not enough seventh-graders are interested in it."

"Well, I am interested in it, *very interested!*" She leaned forward and looked at me from behind her cat's-eye glasses.

"When eighth grade comes, you will get your chance to perform."

"You can't let *one* exceptional kid *in*, even if I prove myself?"

"Like it or lump it, those are the *rules*," she smiled, her hands folded in front of her.

I went out into the chilly ocean breeze. I paused feebly as the curtain drew open in my brain. I squinted up at the flagpole and figured out Plan A: Malibu was a movie colony, and Malibu Park junior high was the main school in Malibu. I would get an inside view of all school productions and spend as much time as I could around Mr. Thacker.

My clothes and hair styles alternated between the 1950s and 1940s. For the '40s, I combed more Vaseline into my hair and wore a long-sleeved white shirt with one of my father's ties. I had Glenn Miller in mind. I asked him for a tie in his room and he tossed me one. It was the only time we ever played catch together.

What Hump?

"I don't know why you would want it but...here you go."

"Thank you."

Autumn was soccer time, and we played on a large grass field encircled by the quarter-mile track located at the summit of the school. After we changed into our green shorts and short-sleeved yellow tops, Coach Bennett blew his whistle loudly and we ran laps.

I ran with Frank, who was a slow runner like me. We talked as we huffed and puffed. Frank leaned forward as he ran. He leaned into the steps, and his hands flopped around in front of him. I copied him, and it made running easier. We didn't have any other classes together.

"I am already getting D's in all of my classes. How are your grades?"

"I am getting B's in everything."

"I swear to God, all I want to be in the world is an actor and a comedian. It is that or nothing."

"Yeah, that is what you are good at."

Coach Bennett stood in the center of the field with a soccer ball. He blasted his whistle and we all walked over to him. I was the last one to arrive. The largest student in our PE class was Flaherty, and the smallest student was Graham. They were close buddies, Flaherty and Graham—their names flowed together like a vaudeville team. The coach blasted his whistle, and the game started.

I had stuck my lens-less, horn-rimmed glasses inside the elastic of my trunks. I put them on, scratched my eye through the glasses, and acted like the comedian Joe Flynn with his level head and hands at his sides, and monotone voice. I went up to a tough guy on the other team and stuck my face in his.

"Why, if I were you, I would pop him right in the weasel for pulling a stunt like that!" He shot me a confused look.

The other team scored a goal.

"Why, you try that again, and I'll let you have one!" I yelled at the other team. I held up my fist in character. Some of them laughed. Flaherty bent down and whispered in Graham's left ear and glanced at me in his unstable way. When Coach Bennett blew his whistle for the game to resume, I could see Flaherty and Graham were no longer interested in the ball. They ran toward me in a bee-line and both of them kicked me in the shins as hard as they could.

"Take that, Mucous!" said Graham. I fell to the grass and writhed. My glasses slowly fell off. Tears of embarrassment at the corners of my eyes. When I got to my feet, I decided that was enough of the Joe Flynn act. I put the glasses away and blended in. The toothy grins on Flaherty and Graham's faces grew wider. My shins hurt so much that they stung to the back of my legs. Bennett blew his whistle to end the game. We had lost, and I didn't know the score.

The next day was the same, only now the small Graham kicked me harder than the Neanderthal kicks of Flaherty. Dominance lay in the tan swell of his muscular legs.

"Take that, Puke-ass!" he said. The pair of them planned their strategy each morning as class got underway. They charged at me from behind and from other directions of attack. It went on like this for the rest of soccer season. After I was on the ground, Graham always turned with a sadistic smirk and a comment as he walked behind Flaherty.

"Take that, Leukoplakia!"

Nobody beat up Frank or Pringle like that, ever. Coach Bennett never seemed to notice. He made sure every minute of class was put to good use. I was chosen last on each team. I was so bad at every sport that it defied imagination. If you picked me on your team, you would lose.

What Hump?

"Can't I just play handball, Coach?"

"No. Handball is for second-graders."

At least Pringle had pretty good endurance. When I ran on the hard track in that useless circle, I would always tire out ahead of the others. It didn't help that I felt depressed. The rat tail towel whip was what shower time was all about. I managed to weasel my way out of that most of the time. There were easier targets than me. Pringle got the worst of those. He just wilted against his locker as they whipped away at him until they were satisfied.

Tommy and I saw the movie *Young Frankenstein*, and we both bought the soundtrack album. We walked home and reminisced about being on the set.

"I think *Young Frankenstein* is symbolic of our friendship, Tommy. You are the Frankenstein creature and I am Doctor Frankenstein. You know… if I should make it in Hollywood some day when we grow up… that I'll take care of you, right? I don't want to think of what the world might do to you if I don't."

"Okay! It's a deal!" He grinned widely and clasped his hands in prayer fashion. I laughed.

In my math class, they treated me like I was mentally retarded. The teacher didn't know what to do with me and pretended I wasn't there. In arts and crafts, Mr. Rickard asked me every day what his former star pupil, Steve, was up to. Steve sculpted and drew in all his free time. I couldn't get it. When Mr. Rickard asked us to make plastic scoops, I glued all my fingers together. My hands looked like seal flippers for the next three periods.

The best part of school so far was the cafeteria's hot brown-sugar cookies that melted in our mouths, for fifteen cents. They were as big as an adult's hand. We ate them on cold mornings, served in greasy wax paper bags. They had been ten cents when I was in sixth grade and had to sneak over to buy them, but they were fifteen cents now that I was in seventh.

Seven

Autumn 1974 to August, 1975 thirteen years old
THE SUGAR BLUES KID

My biggest problem was a small card in an envelope with sharp, hard corners called the D notice. The policy at Malibu Park was to allow every student to pass to the next grade. There were no F's. D's were as shameful a grade as they gave out. The D notice required a parent's signature, and the school dean drummed it into us that this signature had better not be forged. My father refused to sign it and kept it for a week or more on his dresser. He waited for when Steve and Jenny were out of the house so he could have me all to himself.

Stubborn arguments were flaring up between the two adults in our house. One argument was whether butter or margarine was better for your health. My father chose margarine. I felt like an elephant under the carpet with them.

"Do you want to make a bet?" asked Jenny crisply.

"Yes," he said, hunched over at the head of the table. They

stared each other down.

"All right then, the one who loses must leap into the ocean on the first day of winter," said Jenny.

"I say… good show," I did my Terry Thomas voice through my gapped front teeth. My father shot me a look.

"We'll shake hands on it, then," said Jenny. She held out her hand and my father clacked his sheepish tongue and shook it.

Jenny went to work at UCLA and looked it up. She laid out the papers with the facts on the table as we dined on an extra rabbit that she had brought home from the UCLA experiment laboratory.

"The rabbit supper is free, and here are my findings."

"Well, I guess that settles it then," my father said through his shit-eating grin.

"Don't worry, Dad, Steve and I will jump in the ocean with you on the first day of 1975," I said.

"We will?" said Steve. My father glanced at me and rolled his eyes. I knew he wouldn't dive into a cold wave in January because he lost a bet. Jenny would have gone into the sea if she had lost, but not my old man.

He found me standing at the edge of the canyon, mulling over what thoughts my friends might have. His massive frame came up behind me.

"I want you to accompany Jenny to watch a film series at U.C.L.A. It will be something you can do together." He looked at the ground as he talked.

"What is the film?"

"I don't know. Something about Africa. It's a series so you'll be going a few times together." There was a pause. He started to speak but breathed unevenly, closed his grim mouth, and gathered his thoughts.

"I would like you two to try getting along better with each other, if at all possible."

"Yes, I would like to get along better. I didn't know there was much trouble between us, maybe a little trouble but not much. Is there?"

He was tight-lipped as he raised his head and glanced off to his left, hands on hips.

"When do we go? I'm all for it." I said.

"I don't know. Why don't you ask her."

Jenny led me into a room at U.C.L.A with no windows, with rows of comfortable chairs facing a screen about the size of a slideshow screen. Jenny and I took our seats in the third row together.

We watched the film, "The Search For The Nile", produced by the BBC, starring Kenneth Hiagh as Sir Richard Burton and Michael Gough as David Livingston. Jenny and I both paid close attention to the hypnotic film which was about British involvement in Africa. The source of the Nile was the last great geological mystery in the nineteenth century. Burton and Livingston trekked in faith all the way to the source, with heroic determination. Greed and obsession took over the quest.

Memorable scenes for me was when David Livingston goes a bit mad and says to Burton, "All we do here is drink coffee!" That made Jenny laugh. And when Captain Sir Richard Francis Burton is attacked by a hostile tribe and is stabbed through his face with a spear. He gripped the handle of the spear with both hands as he walked down a hill and eventually pulled out the spearhead and he kept walking.

We drove toward home along the coast highway together in her two-seater car, the fancy stick shift between us.

"Did you like it?" I asked.

"Very much. What did you like about it?" she asked.

"I liked Sir Richard Burton. Is he related to the actor Richard Burton?"

"No. No relation whatsoever."

"Oh. Sir Richard Burton and his wife had a strange relationship, don't you think?"

"Yes, seemed all topsy turvey," she smiled a bit.

"I had anticipated that it would be a big movie theater. Is that the only place they show movies at U.C.L.A.?"

"Yes, that's all there is."

"It looked more like a screening room. Though I guess they wouldn't show that series just anywhere. Do they only show the more interesting films there like "The Search For The Nile"?"

"Yes. That's the idea," she said.

"Is this where you saw that Mark Lester movie?"

"Yes."

"What was the name of it? I can't remember the title right now."

She didn't say anything.

"I don't guess they will be showing that again, or will they?"

She didn't answer me. I watched her shift gears as we took off from the stoplight at Civic Center Way.

"Anyway, I know dad wants us to be closer. You know, as mother and son. Thank you for taking me to see this."

"Oh, you're welcome," she said, looking ahead at the road all the while. We did not speak the rest of the way home.

Matt Peckinpah phoned me from Sierra Madre, a town near Pasadena. He had abruptly moved there with his mom. "Are you ever moving back to Malibu?"

"No," he said in a sad, small voice.

The Winds of Malibu

Matt had his mother drive all the way out to Malibu just to pick me up so I could spend weekends with him there. The best part for me was when his mom played her 1920s Bessie Smith blues records as she cleaned the house. I became hooked on Bessie Smith. "Sing Sing Prison Blues" and "The St. Louis Blues", with Louis Armstrong shadowing her full voice on his muted trumpet, really got to me. After hearing that I had a place to put my sad feelings. Matt didn't seem to like his mom's records much, as he sat in a swivel chair, bored and out of place. I knew he missed Malibu terribly though he didn't mention that.

He invited me out there every weekend, but I didn't want to go after the second visit and I didn't know how to tell him. There was less to talk or joke about. I got in the back of his mom's station wagon on Friday evenings or Saturday mornings as he requested.

I would never see his charismatic dad again, for some reason. I didn't ask why. Friday would come around, the phone rang in Malibu, and there would be another Sierra Madre weekend to get through.

Frank began spending his weekends with Chuck Cruise in Sycamore Park instead of me. Chuck was lanky, with long hair and a nose that showed extra nostrils. We were friends, but we were opposites. Frank had motorcycles in common with Chuck. Being out of Malibu was like being a fish out of water.

Matt and I threw eggs at cars on the small Sierra Madre streets at night. We accidentally threw one at a police car, but we ran a zig-zag up slopes and along dark fences on a hillside away from the searchlight and got away with that too. I wanted to end the visits before I had an anxiety attack over there. The dullness of the Sierra Madre neighborhood closed in on me like an Iron Lady Torture Chamber. I didn't even know how to describe my panic attacks to anybody except psychologists, and they never listened.

On a Saturday night, he played a *Haunting Sounds of Halloween* album over and over as I paced the room and he yawned in the swivel chair. He twisted back and forth hundreds of times. He played the Halloween record one time too many before we went to bed. My pacing across the floor quickened in the living room. I stopped and braced myself, hiding my pained face from him. I knew the signs. I shook with tremors and was turning pale. I went to bed in my clothes. He had the bed to the left and I had the bed to the right. The door was at our feet, the window was at our head.

The deep night became alive. My toenails and fingernails scraped the sheets and the bed frame shook a bit. I could barely breathe. My body temperature dropped.

"Are you okay?" asked Matt. He sounded irritable.

"Guess so," I could barely say. I fell into a nightmare while awake. I had to escape from my bed. I sank to the floor and leaned onto the side of Matt's bed.

I had somehow slept. I awoke to a sunlit room in my bed on the right. Matt stood up, got out of the room, and didn't come back. I stepped out into the back yard. Matt followed me.

I tried to act like I was normal last night.

"What is on the agenda today?" Matt stepped up to me and got in my face.

"*What happened last night!*" he screamed.

"Well, for starters…" I began. He cut me off.

"*What happened last night!*"

"I…."

"*What happened last night…what happened?*" he screamed. He was four inches from my face and his eyes bulged. An alarm had gone off in his head. I looked away.

"I don't know." He stared across the yard with his arms folded. He dashed into the house and spoke quietly to his mother. They both got into the station wagon fast and started the motor and waited there.

    I slowly went out to the driveway and got into the back seat and lightly shut the door. We left right away for Malibu, much earlier than usual. It was a long, slow drive and no one said a word. Matt sat there like a statue that blinked once in a while. He stared out the left-side window. I glanced at his motionless figure as we turned right onto Deerhead Road. I got out of the car and shut the door.

    "See you," I said.

    "Go!" Matt told his mother firmly. She didn't move.

    "*Go! Go!*" he yelled. Mrs. Peckinpah drove off and they didn't look back. My bad nerves shook me all over. I turned slowly and walked with exhausted small steps up the driveway.

    I stopped Emilio in the foyer of the school.

    "Are you going to try out for the talent show? There are only two more days left after Christmas vacation." Emilio looked thoughtfully at the ground.

    "No."

    "I'm going to see what I can do," I told him and sprang ahead.

    I spent my Christmas vacation in Malibu. I listened to the Big Band era and thought vaguely of the talent show. My father didn't like Glenn Miller or any of that 1940s bunch, so I could only listen to this when he was out of the house. He had been my age when big bands were the new popular sound, and he shunned it then just as I now shut out my own era. My father and Jenny spent most of Christmas vacation away from Malibu. They were with my father's mother, who had recently informed them that she had advanced cancer of the uterus.

    Rule number one for me was not to bore my audience. A good sense of timing was my only hope. I decided to audition with a big band song from the 1930s, "The Sugar Blues" by Clyde McCoy.

I watched the black record twirl on the turntable and paced across the green rug. I had never danced to music in my life. There was a continuous wah-wah muted trumpet. I pantomimed every wah-wah with my lips. I studied my wah-wah's in the bathroom mirror and planned my lips.

I entered the school auditorium and noticed how vast it was. I didn't understand why the ceiling had to be so high. The stage was big and beautiful, made of strong, smooth, glossy, yellow wood, and the gray curtain was velvety and heavy.

Only a few seventh-graders auditioned. Mr. Thacker and a couple of ninth graders were seated at a table with pencils and notepads.

"I am going to dance to a jazz record," I presented the big band album on my chest that had Benny Goodman's face on the cover.

"Okay," said Bill Thacker. I didn't want to waste his time. His assistant took my record and carried it to a record player in an upstairs room in back of the auditorium.

"It is the third song on side one!" I shouted. I sprinted up the steps to the stage. I immediately fell in love with that stage. The music came across rich and beautifully crystal clear through powerful speakers. I glided along better than I had in my living room. I imagined I drew everyone into the theater from outside, as I skipped, leaped, strutted, and spun to the syncopation. We waited two days on pins and needles to find out.

"Mr. Thacker told me to tell you, you passed the audition," his assistant told me.

I wanted my dad to attend.

"I would really like you to come to my school and see me in the talent show."

"Okay. Let me know when it is."

"February seventeenth."

"Oh, that's more than a month away."

"That's why I'm telling you now."

Straw Hat Pizza, next to the Malibu Cinema, sold Styrofoam skimmer hats for $1.25. I tore off the advertisement and glued a cardboard black band around it. It weighed one ounce. I wore a dark suit with a white dress shirt and a tie that had designs of Fred Astaire on it. I bought a straight black cane with two white tips at a magic shop in Santa Monica.

After the first run-through, I saw a slight, rare smile and even rarer kind eyes from Mr. Thacker. I left the auditorium in costume. I walked past the lunch area and crossed the big parking lot. I held the Styrofoam hat on my head as the breeze picked up. A yellow school bus full of ninth graders circled on its way back from a field trip.

"It's a gay lizard!" someone bellowed out of the bus window.

"Hey lizard!" His voice roared across the parking lot.

"You are a lizard!"

"I'll kill you. Fucking lizard!" I took my hat off, and with a manly walk, made it to the gym for the last twenty minutes of PE.

"My school's talent show is this Tuesday," I reminded my father.

"Is your mother going to be there?"

"Yes."

"Okay. I'll go," he said gravely.

Eight hundred wall-to-wall metal chairs took up the floor space. Halfway through the show the curtains were drawn, and the light was on me in center stage. The music began, and my body became rubber with rhythmic sensitivity. Halfway through the record, there was a pause where the trumpet played a spastic wah-wah. The audience stood and erupted in a cheer, and I thought something had gone wrong.

The entire audience whooped and applauded and stood for minutes on end. I had delayed a tightly timed show. I made all the students late for their classes.

I went down the steps on stage left. One of the first students who walked up to me was the ninth-grade class president, Sean Penn. Sean was blond and tan, and outside of school I had seen him carrying his surfboard. He was the most popular student in our school. He looked at me with a serious expression.

"That was really great. I really enjoyed that," he said, articulating his words well.

"*Thank you*, Sean."

I got out of the auditorium and squinted in the sunlight. My mother waited in front of the school. Her eyebrows puckered a bit.

"Wow. They sure like you here!" she said over the droning of the surf.

"Today was a good day, in that category."

"This is a nice school. I've never been inside it."

"Yes, it is! Hopefully after today, I'll have more friends."

"Well, I had better go." She glanced around nervously.

"Yes, you better. Dad is here someplace. It's only a matter of minutes before he spots us."

"He probably still hates my guts, right? Bye, honey. Love you." She hugged me, waved, and walked to her car fast. I rounded the northwest corner of the building and found my father, identifiable by personality and dark clown hair.

"Hi, Dad," I said cheerfully. He didn't smile.

"Did you talk to your mother? Did your mother say anything to you about me?"

"Yes, she guesses you still hate her guts." His eyes got big as he looked at the ground. "I have to get back to class. Bye, Dad." I walked away, glanced back and left him in his sick search. At least they had both shown up.

An announcement came over the intercom the next morning:

"Students, see your teachers regarding making up time in your studies because of yesterday's talent show running way over time." The whole classroom stared at me at once. Students from

all three grades complimented me. Rather than just compliment me, Emilio Estevez took an interest in my artistic endeavors.

"Come here." I followed him, and we snaked through a crowd in the lunch area. He got me alone in front of the student store and looked me in the eyes.

"What are you going to work on next?" he asked seriously.

"That's a good question. I guess we have to bide our time

"The Sugar Blues. Malibu Park Junior High, 1975." Photos probably by Paul Younis.

together until we can get in Thacker's workshop."

"Let's try to stay focused and find projects we can do," he said emphatically.

"Yes! Good idea! We will." He waved an adios. I headed down the ramp with half a smile.

Mr. Thacker paused in front of me.

"Honestly, in a school, I have *never* seen an audience *reaction* that wild before. Were you ready for it?" he asked, hands on hips.

"No."

"Well, whatever it is that you were doing, keep on doing it," he beamed.

"Thank you, Mr. Thacker." I blushed. I adjusted my invisible glasses like Frank Kratovil.

And Frank Kratochvil examined me curiously when I met up with him, as though he were seeing something new and valuable.

A girl in back of me put her hands on my shoulders and we went down the stairs together. I walked stiffly

"Jeff, that was *so* good!"

"He knows it!" a girl a dozen steps up yelled. I spun around.

"Who said that?" She tried to blend into the crowd. I had only mouthed along to a record and bounded around the stage. None of the other talent show acts got recognition. I had thought the others would be more acceptable to school tastes.

There was a "Best of the Talent Show" night. My father looked at me in the kitchen as he fixed his tuna salad. I amused him.

"Musically speaking, I can see you liking today's crap, but to reach back in time and enjoy listening to that *old crap*... that I cannot understand."

I held on to my Styrofoam hat in a heavy drizzle. I wiped the mud off my shoes and let myself into the back of the auditorium. It was pitch dark backstage. My signature dance outfit was now complete. A deep red sweater without sleeves, tuxedo shirt, wrap-around bowtie, dark slacks, dress shoes, black socks, and my Styrofoam straw hat, and my face of course, particularly my mouth. If my mouth wasn't shaped like it was, I don't think any of it would have worked.

My standing ovation for "The Sugar Blues" was more reserved. I shook parents' hands. It was raining heavier when it was time to leave. I left my hat in a careful part of the stage, pushed the lever of the auditorium doors in the back, and let it close behind me.

Malibu alone at night in the moment was a challenge all its own. I walked out seven feet and gently stopped, turned my palms up and my face to the clouds, and looked directly into the raindrops, feeling the power of the Malibu moment. Muffled thunder rolled from left to right. I peered straight up to the clouds into piercing raindrops, into my hands I felt them, into my face, my Sugar Blues clothes drinking it up. I shut my eyes tightly and felt the Malibu rain in my hair. I put my head down and let it get the back of my head. When I felt directly in tune, I hiked home through wet branches.

I took Frank to see *Paper Moon* at Cinema-on-the-Mall in Santa Monica.

"I'll show you where they've got the best soup," he said afterwards. Across from the theater was a small, fancy restaurant called Sardi's on the Promenade. The soup was dark and good, minced garlic in a beef broth of some sort.

"Did you like the movie?"

"I loved it," said Frank.

"And what do you think of Tatum O'Neal?"

"I love her too."

Grandma Lucas was thin and pale on the couch. I sat on the floor beside her.

"Do you know what I want to be when I grow up?"

"No, what?"

I licked my lips. "An *actor*."

"…oh…" she barely said.

She stood up and disappeared into the kitchen. Chemotherapy had caused her hair to fall out. Dressed in her satin robe, she came out without her wig.

"I'm Kung Fu," she said. I laughed hysterically. When she said goodbye to us, she didn't seem upset about anything.

"I wonder if I'll see her again," said my father.

"Oh, I think you will," said Jenny. He kept a vigil in the hospital at the end. He was in another room when they told him his mother was dead.

He went in and stared at her. Death had come twenty minutes earlier. Her mouth and eyes were open. Worst of all, of course, was her stare. Her cheery blue eyes stared up at *Zero* for the first time in seventy-five years.

Grandma Lucas cared about the people in her life, but she spent forty years with the wrong man. How she ever got suckered into that marriage no one knew, except it was the 1920s and she was an optimistic girl. Maybe she thought she could brighten up a terrible personality. She couldn't.

My father sat us down before school.

"I shouldn't have looked at her corpse," he said. When he was really depressed, he was a nice guy. Soon he would be angry again, and that would shake off his blues. He preferred to be angry, made him feel alive. As I sat there and listened to him mourn his mother, I couldn't help but wish he would stay depressed all the time. Not that I wanted his mom to die each day.

My brother and I were spared the funeral, and our life in

Jeff Lucas, seventh-grade yearbook picture. MPJHS 1975. Public domain.

Malibu returned to subnormal. I took advantage of my father's short-lived depression and got him to take Jenny and me to see Charlie Chaplin in *Modern Times* in a theater. It was my first Chaplin movie, and I got to see Chester Conklin—great-grandfather of my school friend, Craig Conklin—in a comedy routine with Chaplin. Conklin was Chaplin's favorite partner in his films. I could see the resemblance, except Craig had hair. Mrs. Bolton dragged him out of the classroom by that mane of his a few times.

I had been summoned to the principal's office. I walked past Mrs. Edgington and entered Principal Delkner's office.

"Oh hi, Jeff!" he said cheerfully. "Mr. Loyd, the band conductor, wanted to see you. He is putting together a program for the senior orchestra and he wants to collaborate with you on something. So…go see him."

"Thank you, Mr. Delkner. Did anyone ever tell you that you look like Franklin D. Roosevelt?"

"Oh thanks!" he beamed.

I stood in the band room to the right and front of the senior orchestra. Mr. Loyd twirled his baton with a flick of his wrist and blinked, and looked at me through his aviator glasses.

"We're going to play 'The Entertainer' for the spring concert and we all figured it would be a nice addition if you would dance to it just like you did at this year's talent show." He turned forward and glanced down at his sheet music. "Are you familiar with the tune from *The Sting*?"

"Of course. It's famous. It's by Scott Joplin from 1909, during the ragtime era."

He did a double take. "You are absolutely correct."

"Have you ever asked a student to do anything like this?"

"No, this would be a first."

"Because I have never danced with an orchestra." The orchestra laughed.

"Well, you wanna try it?"

"Sure." He raised his arms in his long-sleeved psychedelic shirt. The senior orchestra played it through, and it was more than a hair out of tune.

Rehearsals proceeded with what I considered unnecessary frequency. I was given permission to get out of classes. I wished that they could get me out of PE, but Ms. Merrill's biology class and my math class were miracle enough to avoid.

The violins played "The Entertainer" over and over while I tried to figure out a dance for it. Unlike "The Sugar Blues," there were no surprises in the arrangement and no break of the instruments: this was the senior orchestra, so it didn't get any better than this within the boundaries of the school. They droned along in a limp fashion and then it was over.

Syncopation was lacking. My straw hat strut wasn't enough for this number.

I drew on an eyeliner mustache and dressed for the part of Charlie Chaplin's tramp, with a nice black bowler hat my mother had bought for me. I had my part down but the orchestra needed more practice. At a break, I turned to Mr. Loyd.

"You don't suppose Charlie will be in the audience, do you?"

"I wouldn't worry about it. I don't think he gets into that costume much anymore."

On performance night, I waddled down to the school dressed like Charlie Chaplin. I saw my name listed handsomely in the thick-papered program and smiled. I was the only dancer ever... for something like this, as far as I know.

Jeff with Robert Mirabilio and timpani in the background, on the Malibu Park Junior High school main stage in the auditorium. Mr. Loyd's class, dress rehearsal for "The Entertainer." Spring, 1975. Robert is making his Harpo Marx face. Photo by Naomi Mirabilio.

Mr. Loyd introduced me awkwardly. He spoke softly, and then shouted out my name slowly. It was a freak thing to see. I tried to get interested in imaginary objects around me, because I had no props. The orchestra was in the pit and I was on the stage. In every other performance, they were on the stage, but they played the entire performance in the pit because of my one dance.

I just waddled around, examined my bowler hat, which I took off in different ways, and picked up imaginary trash on the ground and kicked it away.

There was a standing ovation that went on and on. I bowed and waddled off. The stage manager, Cameron Thor, pushed me out for an encore bow. I wiggled the mustache, lifted the hat and bowed. Cameron pushed me out again, hard. He got off on the applause more than I did, and I laughed.

"You're a ham! Again!"

Best of all, Flaherty and Graham backed off during PE. That was a miracle.

I sat in on the auditions for *Around the World in 80 Days*, away from the others. Mr. Thacker did a double take when he noticed me.

"I'm just here to observe. I know seventh-graders are banned."

"Okay," he smiled. I was there for every rehearsal. Mr. Thacker knew what he wanted out of the production. I imagined what I could do with all of the roles.

"Is this a comedy or a drama?"

"Well, it's got elements of both," he said.

After rehearsal, we all had to leave, and the auditorium was locked. I strolled out to the big, grassy area near the flagpole. The busses had all left an hour and a half ago. Just a few students stood around. I noticed Sean Penn with some friends. He interested me somehow.

I silently walked toward him until I was just within earshot. It was always the same when I eavesdropped on him. He talked about the sport of surfing.

"Let's see what he is talking about today. It's going to be surfing, I bet. Yeah, it's surfing again," I laughed quietly.

"*Whoa!* Over the weekend, the waves at Little Dume were *gnarly rad*, dude. Oh, for sure! I *know! Awesome.* Totally gargantuan waves! No, I haven't seen John Kelly. Have you? I don't know. So gnarly. No *way*, really?"

I would like to do a better imitation of it, but I can't even talk like that. He sure could! He had a voice that carried. He paid me no mind as I stood and watched him. He had a book in his hand by his right side. I rarely saw him around the same person. I never saw him around Emilio, and Emilio never brought up his name to me.

If you wanted to be accepted at this school, being blond and tan were big advantages, because you were either a "Local" or you were a "Valley Kook." I had seen dark-haired students dye their hair blond with peroxide or something, and it was always a bad dye job. I had never seen this in any other place I had lived. All the black-haired kids had a more insecure look on their faces, even in the yearbook pictures.

Sean had a kind, likeable face. I guessed that he couldn't have become school president without good grades. He was certainly self-assured. The winds of Malibu would not whisk away Sean Penn any time soon, I could tell that. I bet his parents gave him plenty of confidence. He reminded me of a healthy young bird adapting very well in a strongly built nest.

The ninth-grader who played Phileas Fogg, the lead in the school play, was taller than the rest of us and thin with long brown hair, a large pointed nose, and much acne on his face.

Fred Grossman was a shoo-in for this year's drama trophy that Mr. Thacker presented.

"My name's Fred." I shook his hand. "You must be the seventh-grader who stole the talent show."

"That might be me. Shh… they don't allow seventh-graders here."

"Oh, nobody cares. Great job, by the way!" He headed back, dressed in a long, dark coat and 1800s-style bow tie and vest.

A student quit that had a small part near the end where he sits at a card table, with one minute to go before he wins a bet with Phileas Fogg, and his only line was "That's it! Time is up!"

Mr. Thacker motioned me up on stage into an empty chair.

"And action!" said Mr. Thacker.

"That's it! Time is up!" Phileas appeared behind me. With my back to him, I acted like I was the only one at the table who didn't notice him. I broke with the script and I leapt up out of my chair.

"I WON! I WON! I'm rich! I won is what I did!" I built the comic fire *"And I won!"* I said eight times before I turned and told Phileas Fogg and then froze with a Looney Tunes Daffy Duck face. Mr. Thacker fell out of his chair and laughed so loudly it scared me. He came up to the stage, excited.

"We are going to keep that. It's *in!*"

When performance day came, the school roared out and I received more applause than anything else in the play.

(MPJHS 1975 Yearbook)

"Jeff, This year has been really fun knowing you. Your such a kick in the butt, I think your gonna have a great future in comics. Keep up the great work, Love, Bean."

"My best, to a bright, talented, & most enjoyable young man with whom it has been a pleasure to work. L. Vincent." (Leonard Vincent, teacher)

"Jeff- All I can say is Whoop-Whoop! (only you would get it, right Stanley?!) David Knight."

"To Jeff – THE STAR!!!!! I'm very proud of you! Mrs. Donna Dutton."

"Best wishes to a fantastic actor! Happy summer, Mrs. Glass."

"The best of luck next year, Mr. Sheets."

"Jeff, You are really a talented kid. Keep it up. One day you'll be a star & I'll see you & say, 'Hey, I went to school with him.' Well, anyway have a great summer. See you next year. Good Luck. Luv, Avril."

"to Jeff, who's Laurel & Hardy in one kid. Hi! Hi! Hi! Hi! Hi! Again. I'll see ya next year. Glenn Newcomb."

"To Jeff – May your sense of humor never cease. Best, Glen Fergeson."

"Jeff, have a real hot summer. Maybe I will see you down at the beach and next year. Erik."

"To Jerry Lewis JR. (Jeff Lucas) Good luck on your acting carrer. I'm sure you really don't need it *because your already at the top. Have a great summer. See you in summer school. Emilio."*

"Jeff, I've only none you since 6th grade. You will be a great actor when you grow up because your good now. Mike Warnes (Pickle)."

"Jeff, You were a real kick this year I enjoyed you in 2nd period. P. Rolie."

"To Jeff, hope you'l have Tatum O'neal for a wife and you will have a very good actor. Robert Merabilio (Hillbilly). Jeff + Tatum."

"To a great comidian and actor, the great JEFF LUCAS. Have a great summer, Tom Knauer."

"Dear Jeff – I've enjoyed our visits this year & I'm forward to 2 more great years from you. Mrs. Behail."

"Dearest Jeff (rubber-man) Have a marv of a summer! And have a happy '75 – '76 school year! See ya later alligator. Love & Kisses, Kari Blayer."

"Dear, Jeff Best of luck with your acting. P.S. Have a good summer. Craig Conklin."

"Jeff, Hope you have fun acting in summer school and have fun this summer. Pat Bader?"

"Jeff, hope you become a big joke next year. The Cayote."

"Jeff, have a ~~rotten~~ good Summer. Dan Silliman."

"Jeff – It's been fun with you in Drafting. You make the class forget about Mr. Shits easier. Thanks for all you have done. Have a hot summer. Love, Terri."

"Blfye Jelfff Lulfgie (ha, ha, ha) Selfe youlfu nelfxt yelfr. Chrilfs Tholfmas."

"Well, here I am; 2ⁿᵈ. Per. June 20, 1975. My math class has been my most hectic class."

"I'm sitting here in 7ᵗʰ per. There is 8 more minutes to go here until summer but I have to go. 1:20 June 20, 1975. The end, Jeff Lucas. Be Alive in '75."

There was the bell. Frank and I headed up the hill beyond the gymnasium. We took our time up the steepest side of Fillary Heights. I glanced back down at the school and out toward the sea.

"Do you know who I think is the most opposite guy from me out of anyone in the entire school?"

"Who?"

"Sean Penn."

"Why him?"

"What do you think of him?"

"I don't know. He has got the second - biggest nose in the school, next to Mickey Rasgon."

"I am not talking about his nose. Think about it. Sean Penn is everything I am not, like good grades, he surfs, he doesn't act in stuff at school." Frank thought it over.

"I kind of know what you mean… when you put it like that."

"Wait until you hear the Paper Moon soundtrack album! There is no dialogue. It is only *original* songs from the movie from the start to the finish! I love it *so* much."

"Okay, good."

I put the needle on side one. Frank liked the first song because it kicked off the movie. A few songs later, he frowned.

"What's the matter?"

"Is that a *violin?*"

"Yes."

"I don't like it." I took the record off abruptly.

"That is all for now. I don't want you getting set on your opinion."

I got to class early on the first day of summer school in the auditorium. Emilio and I waved to each other.

"Welcome to our summer workshop. Before we get started on scene work, I would like to hand out a couple of sheets of paper. These are awards for the school play." He handed a sheet here and there and I was the only one who got two yellow slips of paper for "Best performance in a small role" and "Most polished performance." They were designed by Mr. Thacker: the Bachaues Bacheau Award. I memorized stage direction in five minutes. He let the class go early.

My father entered my room.

"I just spoke to Stevie. I am sending both of you to your mother's for the rest of the summer. I will drop you off there tomorrow."

"But I am in summer school! I'm enrolled!"

"Then I am taking you *out*."

He parked in front of our mother's house and turned to me in the back seat with a closed-mouth grin.

"Make sure to give your mother a big kiss for me, and you know where."

"Yeah," I said.

"Where?" said Steve.

"Nothing." I said. Our dad laughed bitterly. We got out and went to the porch.

"Where does he want you to kiss Mom?"

"On her asshole."

"Shut up!"

Terri just had her appendix removed. She was weak and bandaged, and we let her rest.

"Don't make me laugh. I have stitches."

"I won't. I have a stomach ache. It's probably just gas pains,"

"That's what I thought, and I ended up having my appendix taken out."

"Well, that sure doesn't help my hypochondria."

"Watch out for the symptoms. It's no joke."

TIME *Magazine's* cover said, *The Summer of JAWS*. We saw the movie and got caught up in shark fever. I bought a shark tooth necklace and we all had pukka shell necklaces. As we sat around swimming pools together, I fidgeted with my shark's tooth and dreamed I was a rich and famous Hollywood movie star.

Terri won at a game of checkers. I would never be a very good chess player or even a very good checkers player. I flipped the game board against the ceiling and checkers flew. She dug a gash down the left side of my face with her long fingernails. I ran to the bathroom with blood down my left cheek, and Terri stood outside the door.

"I'm sorry! I felt bloody skin under my nail!" She apologized for hours. I had never been apologized to like that. I came out of the bathroom.

"I don't mind the scratch. I think it looks kind of cool." We hugged.

"To make up for it, I want to give you a manicure!" she said.

"Okay, do my nails!" I held out my claws.

Jack and my mother were in competition with their insults lately. We strolled through a mall and saw a T-shirt pinned to a wall that said BITCH in glittered letters.

"There is a T-shirt for you, Reba."

"Yeah, right, Jack. Go to hell."

Terri stayed up late with me in front of the TV.

"What's your favorite song?" I asked.

"I love a song called 'Where Have All the Flowers Gone?'"

"I don't know that one. How does it go?" Terri sang the first verse almost on pitch.

"I bet that's a good song."

"It is. I miss my boyfriend. I've thought about giving myself to him this year after we've gone out a while." The TV droned on quietly, and Terri tapped her hand on the couch.

"He's a lucky guy."

"I think a baby is the most beautiful gift two people can give each other. What I really want is to be a mom someday."

I grabbed my forehead with my right hand. "I am getting a nervous stomach again," I said.

"Relax with me, and breathe slowly." I breathed slowly and peeked sideways at her, and noticed her straight, white teeth. She sat to my left and her right leg lightly brushed against my leg, I casually slid my left hand down the inside of her thigh. She calmly removed my hand and put it back in my lap.

"I admire how patient you are with me," I said. She laughed.

Terri gave me the long-awaited diary and also a fancy autograph book. I asked each of the three girls and Steve to sign my autograph book.

"You can only use one page because I intend to get autographs from famous people!" I passed it around.

Jeff and his brother, John in Mar Vista, California on summer vacation, 1975. Photo by John N. Dick

Autograph book entries:

-Jeff- You're a great actor and will become a greater one as time goes on… Love ya always, Kelly

Jeff – Well, after waiting for this book for two years, here it is. I just don't know how to put my feelings into words. I will agree that you're different than most people, but it's a good difference. We've known each other for 5 years. 5 good years. We've gone through good times and bad times. But no matter what happens, to me you'll always be my brother. You've got a great career and future going for you. But to get it, you're going to have to work hard, which I know you will. I LOVE YOU VERY MUCH and I want you to write me and tell me how you're doing. Look at me, just like a big sister worrying about her younger brother. Do me a favor, don't spank John too often. Love ya always, Terri

Jeff – I think you're a great actor. If you ever become a actor I think you will have lots of fans. Love ya Michelle

JEFF,
Although we're Totally Different, it doesn't mean that we can't be good friends. I truly think that you will be the best that movies have to offer when you get older because you have a talent that only a few people have,
Have a good life
Your brother,
Steve

I sank in the heavy, grey velvet swivel chair that Terri had spent most of the summer in and wrote my first diary entry in pencil.

(Journal entry)

1975
July 26
6:40
7:8

Today was a hell of a depressing day. Jacks girls; (Terri, Kelly, and Michelle) left for Texas and I probably won't see them again – or until many years from now. This is the first day that I write in this diary. I'm going to try to get that letter to Tatum before school starts. I'm at Jacks house and scared to go home tomorrow because I received a record—among other things. Jack and Mom are going to split soon—but I don't know when. We got our pictures taken in old style yesterday.
blah!

(Journal entry)

1975
August 2
7:40
8:4

Not much happened today. Just another boring Saturday I guess. I went to Tatum's house with Frank on the 29th (only to find however that she doesn't live there) but we did climb up a bank and go underneath their house. We looked inside their storage but didn't take anything. I don't know if I should believe him or not but Robert said she's living in Beverly Hills. Summer school ended yesterday. Ho Hum!

⇶⇷

My mother phoned.

"The Air Force has relocated Jack to Maxwell Air Force Base in Montgomery, Alabama, honey. I want to see you before we move." The wheels turned in my dad's mind as he nodded his head and slowly paced the green, living room rug in his black stinking socks.

(Autograph book entry)

>   *Aug. 11, 1975*
>   *To Jeffrey –*
>   *My sweet dear son –*
>   *Charlie Chaplin, Laurel and Hardy and you are my favorite comedians. Keep up the great work and someday you'll be among the famous people of our time. You have the talent, the stamina, and most of all, the personality to carry you through the whole way… Remember I love you very much. Be a good boy and we'll see you for sure next summer….*
>   *Love always, mom*

(Journal entry)

1975
August 11
Here I sit with my mother in the car. I'm very depressed.

*Today had been some day. First, I went to the mall to see a movie, The Apple Dumpling Gang. Then I messed around in an apartment with Frank and caught the 6:30 R.T.D. and after I arrived home, I got a phone call from my mom. It appears now that she is going to Alabama with Jack and they are not getting a divorce. I went with mom to the coffee shop and ate with Jeff Ball. I got a check for $25 from mom and then she took me home...a few sentimental words...and that was it. Just it! Just one quick phone call, a quick night...and before I know it, I'm not going to see her for one year! Oh boy will I miss her. Think of it... ONE BIG YEAR!
I'm so depressed
Yours truly,
Jeff Lucas*

⋙⋘

New movies were how my father attempted to keep us together as a family doing something as a unit. It worked less and less. So we went to the cinema "in town," as he called it. He drove us into Santa Monica or further inland to some Wilshire Boulevard theaters. We saw *Alice Doesn't Live Here Anymore, The Front Page, The Pink Panther* sequels, *Romeo and Juliet, The Valachi Papers* (I hated that one), *The Eiger Sanction, Our Time, One Flew Over the Cuckoo's Nest, A Man Called Cat Dancing,* and *The Omen. The Omen* made me feel better because I liked the control Damian has over his father.

Eight

September, 1975 to March, 1976. Fourteen years old.

THE MOST REFINED ASSHOLE

Jenny left us suddenly one morning.
"Jenny and I have split up, and it will be permanent."

She had taken her African tribal masks and statues with her. All she left were large framed brass rubbings of ancient English graves.

The phone rang, and he picked it up. It was her.
"How is Stevie?" she asked.
"Stevie is fine."
"Good. I always liked Stevie," she said.
"Good riddance to you," he told her.
"You are an *asshole!*" were Jenny's last words to him in life.
"Well, I must say, that is the most refined asshole I have ever been called," he said. She hung up on him, and I watched him let out a horse laugh.

I didn't get along with my stepmother, but I never wanted this to happen.

It seemed like Malibu would remain mine. He bought me a nice tape recorder for my birthday.

"It's just going to be the three of us men now," he said. One week later, I saw him stare out the windows at the horizon for hours. He walked up to me.

"Do you want to go into Santa Monica with me?" he simmered. I looked at him. He had his dangerous face on.

"No. Thanks anyway."

"Come on. I *want* you to go with me!"

We drove down the coast. The radio played "The Way We Were" by Barbara Streisand. He switched it off in mid-song as we entered Santa Monica.

"Why'd you turn it off?"

"I can't take that right now."

"I know a good place to eat that might cheer you up. It's across from the movie theater. Frank told me about it." He parked at the promenade and I led him into Sardi's. We were seated by a grouchy host and I ordered us the dark soup. My father didn't touch his.

"It's *your fault* Jenny and I split, if you really want to know."

"I think she had a problem with certain children who are interesting," I said. I looked down at the table and took another spoonful.

"No, she thought you were the worst person in the world."

"I thought you said my mom was the worst person anywhere in the world."

"You really are just… worthless to me… you are just a worthless dreamer," he said quietly, so only I could hear. Most of the other tables were occupied. I had half a spoonful.

"You really are just…." I put the spoon in my mouth. "…rotten," he finished. "Just a real… *nothing*," he said on cue with the spoon in my mouth. I put the spoon down and did not lift it again. The bowl was half full.

"Let's go. Let's get outside of here. I can't stand being here with you. I love this place, and you are turning this restaurant ugly!" I told him, and not too quietly either. I stood and walked to the entrance. He paid at the register.

I had become afraid to sleep by myself, and I woke up Steve.

"Can I sleep with you?" I whimpered. This worked out for two nights. I shook with anxiety spasms in his bed.

"*God*… leave! Get the fuck out of here!" I limped out and stood in the center of the white painted dark hallway as the walls closed in. I trembled until I was exhausted enough to go into my own room.

"I need to control my dad like Damian does, in *The Omen*," I said to a lizard in the breezeway that stared at me.

It was next to the weed can that he made me fill up weeds with. Unlike spiders, I was drawn to lizards. We got some big ones in Malibu. I was usually nice to them.

I caught lizards easily. They seldom got away from me, and they rarely had to lose their tails. I held the lizard close to my face and leisurely sat cross legged on the cement in the breezeway. I spoke to the lizard in an English accent reminiscent of Jenny.

"Your name is Paul Lucas, isn't it? Yes, you are. Of course it is." I diddled its tail with my left index finger. "Why do we have kerosene in the garage? I don't know why we have kerosene in the garage but we have kerosene in the garage." I held the lizard in my right hand. It bit my thumb, but that didn't bother me. "In with you Paul Lucas." I dropped the lizard in. I sat up and lifted the kerosene.

It stared up at me up on its hind legs. I squeezed kerosene into the bottom of the can but not on the reptile. The lizard did not react.

"We have wooden matches to light fires in the fireplace. Off to the fireplace, then. Necessary is necessary." I danced to the fireplace and back. The lizard hadn't moved.

"*What the Peeper Saw,* eh, Jenny? If I could only see that movie once, then I could win every fight with my dad." I lit the match, dropped it in. The flame almost reached my eyebrows. I held up my unoccupied hand. I barely saw fire, just half invisible blue flame at the base of the can. The lizard danced up and down for five seconds, then was still and crisping up, its mouth opened slowly into a yawn. I smiled a Mona Lisa smile.

My favorite yellow blanket had been slowly cut up into ribbons when I was four by my parents to wean me away from it. I got another blue one when I was five, but it wasn't the same.

Alone in the house, I paced from room to room in the night with my blue blanket around my shoulders sliding along the walls. I held my head with both hands and clutched my hair and moaned faintly. I glanced in my father's bathroom mirror and my lips were pale; the rest of me was white as the walls. I whimpered into the mirror.

"I need an exorcist. Help me."

I put some clothes on, picked up the phone, and dialed Mrs. Allgreen. She answered and drove up straight away. She hugged me, and it felt good to be held.

"I feel awful. Can't I come live with you? Can't you adopt me?"

"It's all right. There, there, Jeff." She had brought some tea with her and heated it on the stove. I sipped it. The caffeine didn't help. "Come down with me to my house then," she said.

Andrea was there with the rest of the Allgreens. The TV was on. They looked so calm. Mr. Allgreen sat in his chair and slowly ate a cantaloupe with a spoon.

Andrea crossed the room and sat on the floor next to me. "Hey, I never congratulated you on all of your performances. You're really good. You are great, in fact."

"Acting and performing is all I have."

"Well, one day, when you're famous, don't forget me, okay?"

"I'll never forget you. Remember when we used to pretend together? When we used to play 'our game'? That is where my talent started."

"That is so neat." We spoke softly. Andrea went off to bed and I went to their couch and dozed off.

The phone rang. Mrs. Allgreen had left a note for my father.

"Your dad is coming down to get you, Jeff." That woke me right up.

He was at the door in two and a half minutes. From the kitchen window, I saw his headlights stop abruptly. He knocked very politely, and Mrs. Allgreen let him in. He glared at me and talked with Mrs. Allgreen for three calm sentences. He grabbed my arm and yanked.

"*Come on!*" he growled low. I hit the ground outside.

"You really embarrassed me! You went way too far this time! I've *got* to find the right punishment for you! Hmm…I'm really going to have search within myself to find a way to punish you for this! And don't worry, I will!"

We entered the house. and he slammed me against the refrigerator.

At 6:30 a.m., my bedroom door banged against the wall.

"Get up! I'm not letting you sleep today!" I got ready for school fast, didn't eat, and left him seated at the dining room table.

The school was empty and quiet. With math book in hand, I waited for classes to start. Two hours later our old, black custodian, Teddy, slowly approached me.

"School start tomorrow... school don't start today," he said with his great smile.

"It does?"

"It does." I looked at the landscape, kept still, and zoned out for the rest of the day.

Eighth grade began at last, and I do believe I was happier about it than anybody. It was especially good to see Emilio. Emilio had a curious laugh, rather like the bray of a donkey. Everyone around him stopped laughing to listen to him. I changed my laugh every three months.

I walked a line along the edge of the school parking lot in the early fog, I saw him catch up with me.

"*Jeff!* I was talking to my dad and he's gonna do this movie and I mentioned you. There might be a part for you."

"What's it about?"

"It's about a trumpet player in the twenties. There's a part for a kid in it and I mentioned you."

"Thank you! That's really terrific!" I picked my head up. "But why don't you do it?"

"I think you'd be better for it, but you'd probably have to cut your hair though."

"I'll think about it."

"Okay." Then we walked separate ways.

"I shouldn't have said, I'll think about it. I should have said, I am so grateful," I undertoned.

I entered my new math class. The student behind me each day was Joseph Winter, a big black fellow who talked like a five year old, and leapt and danced in the halls, bumping into people. Always smiling at everybody, he had a heart of gold. He wore a bright red Spider-Man mask and his afro was wild and unkempt. The teacher, Mr. DiGarmo, with the long gray beard, was patient and nice, and his breath could kill an elephant, or so we imagined. When he bent over our desks to help us, we found out how long we could hold our breath.

(Journal entry)

October 8, 1975

It's been a long time and a lot has happened. First, my dad and Jenny are getting a divorce. I think it's my fault because we didn't get along well. Second, School has started. Things haven't been too bad in that area except I broke, or tried to, into a locker, trying to get revenge on some kid for punching me in the stomach. I got caught at it and I have to pay $3.00 to have it replaced. I haven't told my dad yet and I don't know what to do. Oh no!!

⟫⟪

Frank understood better than anyone my relationship with my father, and he took me away from him when he could. At night, we went down to the school and climbed on the roof and ran across the entire length of the rooftops. There were different levels on the rooftops. Frank was too short to make it up by himself, so I went first and gave him my hand, and spoke in exaggerated German.

"One, two, sr-ree… *UND!*" The "UND" was a loud falsetto. Frank laughed so hard he lost his strength and collapsed breathless on the pebble rooftop rocks. The scene repeated six times until I stopped being funny, so he was able to breathe. I got him up and we ran across the length of the school again with unquenchable oomph in the dark and yelled in comic German accents as the waves fell on Zuma beach.

I was able to spend many nights with him in Sycamore Park. The condominium was always the best place to be. For Frank to like you, you had to be up to snuff.

"Frank, do you ever ask any girls to dance at school?"

"Why should I? They make me sick."

"I wish I felt like that. My brother's friend, Ron, big guy, long hair, we listen to his Elvis records sometimes. I asked him, 'What do I say if I ask a girl to dance and she says no?' He said, 'Just look her right in the eye and say, 'That's okay, I had to take a shit anyways.'"

Pringle sometimes joined us with a toothy grin frozen on his face.

"Pringle, what the hell is wrong with you! You look like an idiot!" said Frank with a straight face. He stomped, and his arms went up and down. I leaned against a tree and laughed.

Tommy liked to talk about James Bond.

"I have read every Ian Fleming book!" he told us.

"Do you want a cookie?" said Frank. I braced against the tree. I saw enough of Tom Pringle next to me in my special math class. I wondered why it had taken so long for him to be placed in there.

Frank and I were on a frenetic obsessive Big Band Era discovery together. We scoured record stores separately. He found "Boogie Woogie" by the Tommy Dorsey Orchestra and presented it to me at his Dad's place. I found "Let's Dance" by the Benny Goodman Orchestra and sat him down and presented it to him at my dad's place, one after another. Of course, Glenn Miller was our hero when it came to Big Bands. We loved his hits, "String of Pearls" and "American Patrol". He found obscure ones though that I was delighted to be introduced to, like "Sliphorn Jive" by the Glenn Miller Orchestra. Frank pronounced it "Sliffern Jive" until I corrected him.

Then we got into Scott Joplin's music, both when it was played like it was on *The Sting* soundtrack or gently on piano recorded by Joshua Rifkin. We listened intently to entire albums together.

"I want the theme song of my life to be 'Solace' by Scott Joplin," I told him. 'Pineapple Rag' was his favorite. 'Solace" is the most haunting of Scott Joplin's compositions and 'Pineapple Rag' is the most upbeat.

On Halloween, I met Frank, Vance and Frank's neighbor, Rodney, in Sycamore Park. We prowled the dark streets and were found by Frank Weatherwax, who was over six feet tall with a big Adam's Apple, and his gang of eight older teenagers. He spat on the asphalt and recognized us with a grin.

"You fuckers are mine!" They had plenty of eggs. When they recognized us, they hurled eggs, and we ran down an embankment to the Kratochvil condominium. Frank took one carton of eggs out of the refrigerator.

"We have to aim carefully, because they have five cartons," I said.

"We will."

"I don't feel like getting egged. You know what I heard today? My parents have a record of two people making love," Rodney said nasally and blushed.

"Rodney, you look like a pig!" said Frank. That wasn't meant to be mean. It was simply true.

The Weatherwax gang chased us down for hours and they never hit us. They wasted egg after egg. We were outnumbered, and they ran faster and threw harder, but Frank was a natural strategist. He led us wherever we went, and it was always in the correct place. He kept us quiet, and the Weatherwax gang was noisy.

"Find those dweebs!"

"They're not here! Where the fuck did they go?" Our tidy little gang ran up a slope after they walked past, and we nailed them from behind, a direct hit on the back of their heads. Frank Kratochvil got us out of there with clean clothes.

I came back on Sunday. Frank and Vance had just finished a game of tennis on the Sycamore Park tennis court.

"You wouldn't believe what we found on the tennis court today!" announced Frank. "What?"

"It was a porno book about fags! We read part of it. One guy licked another guy's asshole!"

"He licked his asshole?" I asked.

"Yes! And he kept on licking it!" yelled Frank.

"Who left the book on the tennis court?"

"We don't know," said Vance.

"A fag did," said Frank.

"I can't believe it. What did you do with the book? Can I see it?"

"We threw it away! It was disgusting!" said Frank.

"Yeah, that's disgusting. Let's get the hell out of here!" I said.

"Yeah, let's get out of here!" said Vance.

We strode through Sycamore Park like we owned it.

"Where are we going, Frank?" I asked.

"To Rodney's house. He has a BB rifle I want to shoot!"

Rodney answered the door.

"You probably shouldn't come in right now," he grinned sheepishly. We could never quite tell whether he was blushing, because his complexion was always bright pink.

"We don't want to come in, anyway. We want your BB rifle," said Frank.

The Most Refined Asshole

"Okay." Rodney handed the rifle over to Frank quickly.

We headed for the foundation of a house under construction.

"Let's shoot it at each other! One of us stands on top of the slope and shoots, and the other three have to dodge it!" Vance yelled.

"Okay, let's have a few rules. I will show you how to do this carefully, so we won't get hurt," I said. I took the rifle away from Frank and climbed to the top of the steep slope.

I peered through the aim to miss them and shot instead at the concrete. Frank, Rodney, and Vance ran around in circles and yelled and laughed. No one could get hurt unless a BB ricocheted. Rodney was a bigger formless shape down there

Then it was Frank's turn. He yanked the rifle out of my hands. He sprayed them randomly from side to side with his eyes closed and an impulsive frozen grin. I watched where the rifle pointed and got serious. Frank sprayed ruthlessly from side to side across the length of the foundation, his trigger finger accelerated.

"Frank, stop it, stop the game!" I shouted out over Vance's laughter. Frank was firing as fast as he could and even though he heard me, he kept firing.

A BB slammed me just below my right eye. My head whipped back. The BB pellet bounced off the bone of my eye socket. A half an inch higher and I would have been blinded for life. I put my hand up to my right eye and got dizzy.

"*Frank, fucking stop it!*" It hurt more when I yelled. Frank opened his eyes and put the gun down and descended the slope. I showed him what he did.

"As my friend and future manager, I have to tell you that when you aim at your friends with a gun, you aim to miss! *Got it?*"

"Well… yeah."

We went back to Rodney's house. I could still see out of my right eye.

"Hey, Dad?" oinked Rodney. Mr. Hudson came out and stood in front of us. His face was flushed, his eyes bloodshot, and he smelled of whiskey.

"He got hit with a BB from our rifle!" His dad put his hand on my forehead and took a look at it quietly.

"You're *lucky*. Damned lucky…you could have been blinded for the rest of your life so easily. You are damn lucky, that's all." He turned and went slowly back into his house and shut the screen door behind him.

(Journal entry)

1975

November 6th

I declare this Halloween the rowdiest that I can remember. Frank, Rodney, and I were ferociously outnumbered 8 to 3 but even though we were like fugitives, running and running, we gave them more hell than they gave us.

Saturday I walked my feet off, and Sunday I was shot with a BB near the eye.

Gee Whiz!

⋙⋘

I sat down beside my father on his bed as he slurped down a bowl of cereal with a big round spoon. Martin Sheen was on television again. I waited for a commercial.

"Martin Sheen's son and I are pretty much the leaders of our acting class at school."

"Oh yeah? What's his name… Emilio, you said?"

"Yes. He wants to be an actor someday as much as I do. We

act in stuff together as much as we can."

"Huh! No kidding. You two are really gonna make the big time together, huh?" He looked at me and laughed with a grimace. I studied his countenance.

"…Yes," I said.

"Yup… *sure* you will," he breathed uneasily and stared into the television.

A commercial about sinus colds came on. There was a diagram of a head in profile. Green fluid in the center sloshed back and forth. He switched the channel.

"God! They're showing more snot and puke and crap and everything else on TV these days! It is really getting to be too much!" he grunted. He slurped down a mouthful of corn flakes and granola. I laughed and went back to my room.

He was dating a cute woman named Janis who had short blonde hair. Janis had a daughter she wanted to introduce me to.

"I only like girls who look like Tatum O'Neal, or forget it," I told her.

"Oh, she looks like Tatum!" she said.

(Journal entries)

7:4pm

7:24pm

November 12, 1975

It has been a particularly "hot" day! The day I've been waiting for has come, in Beginning Winds the contest has begun to see who No. 1,2,3 trombonists were. Well, as I had hoped for, I was no. 1, Sean King was no. 2 and last but least was Arthur. I hope to God I will continue to be no. 1. We'll be having a contest every

week. I've almost given up on Tatum but there's a new girl around school who looks better! But unfortunately as usual, "No Go Joe"
Whew!

11:20 pm?
November 29th, 1975
1. That girl at school who was no go Joe is now go Joe. And I found out that her name is Lynn. I asked her if she would go with me to the dance, but she said she couldn't.
2. I fixed the house up special for Janis's daughter but she doesn't look like Tatum O'Neal at all. How dull!
3. (Bad News) I found out while playing Monopoly that I have a big bulk of some sort on the back of my ear. I told dad and he said to just wait and see what happens, but I told him I would like to see a doctor as soon as possible. He said "Alright," but he doesn't know when. If I should pass away, I'd just like to say I owe everything to my Grandma and Dad. God Help Me!

>>><<<

Frank got a job in the school office and I watched him from outside as he went through cabinet drawers beside the principal. I waited until he walked out alone.

"Would you just *happen* to have access to the locker combinations of every student in the entire school?"

"Yes."

The Most Refined Asshole

"How about a seventh grader named Lynn Craig?"
"Who is she?"
"Someone I am in love with."
"Oh."
"As my manager and possible future agent, could you perchance, would you perchance, Get me her locker combination?" Frank hesitated.
"Okay," he said with a slight smile. I wrote her name in my notebook, tore it off, and gave it to him.

At lunch the next day, he handed me a neatly folded piece of paper with a locker combination and local phone number written on it.

"This is illegal, isn't it?"
"You asked me to."
"I know, keep calm. I will take all responsibility."

Emilio walked into Mr. Thacker's class with a shillelagh. We all looked it over as he passed it around. It was black, gnarled, and about two feet long. Emilio looked up at me and back at the shillelagh.

"Aye, it's a shillaylee," he said, in an Irish accent.
"Let's do a skit about a shilaylee," I said. Emilio smiled.
"Okay."
"Let's see... I'll be a bank robber who walks into a store and wants to buy a shillelagh."
"Okay, and I'll be the guy who sells you the shillelagh and I'll be Irish," said Emilio.
"I'll buy the shillelagh and start to hit you over the head with it whenever your back is turned. But you keep turning around just when I'm about to hit you and then I'll pretend that I'm just scratching my hair," I said.
"Maybe I should sell you more stuff."

"Yes, that would lengthen the skit!"

I still walked home with Tommy Pringle on most days. We were a familiar sight.

"My mom says that eating an apple is better than brushing your teeth."

"An apple is good for your teeth, but it is not better than brushing," I said.

"*It is so!* An apple is way better than brushing!"

"Is not… no way," I said. He got in my face, his eyes wild.

"If you ate apples every day, you would not ever have to brush your teeth!"

"You mean you never have to brush your teeth?"

"That's right. I never do!"

"Well, maybe you should eat more apples then." Pringle stared at me from out of his new, horn-rimmed glasses as we walked. I was used to this. I glanced at him and laughed.

"Okay, Tommy. You win, but look forward where you are walking, please. Those glasses look expensive."

(Journal entry)

December 9 1975

Glum days in store.

Good- Miracle of miracles Lynn showed up at the dance. I was on the miserable side, up till I saw her. She seems to want to avoid me. Well, at least I know her address and phone number thanks to Frank.

I went into the doc about the lump, "Seymore," and they said if it doesn't go down in a month to go for a blood test! There's not enough room to tell of the

The Most Refined Asshole

suffering I'm going through with doctors. The wart being horribly sizzled off, "Seymore" behind my ear which might be removed. All this and more!!! It's all happening too fast!!!

"I'm Nervous"

⊱❋⊰

Six Great Trumpet Artists was a small album for 35 cents I bought at a community yard sale in the school auditorium. "From Monday On", was a track that featured Bix Beiderbecke on cornet. Bix died at age twenty-eight. There was a picture of him on the cover. My head swam, and an obsession took off.

I awoke when my bedroom door crashed open. My father took up half of the room. It was 6 a.m.

"Pack your things, and fast! You're leaving tomorrow morning!"

"*Where to?*"

"Your mother's… as if you didn't know!" I got out of bed in my boxer shorts.

"In *Alabama?* I don't get it!"

"I don't care what you get, Jeff!" he screamed.

Emilio forgot his shillelagh at home. I sat next to him.

"I won't be able to do the shillelagh skit. I am moving away." Emilio folded his arms.

"Are you coming back?"

"It doesn't seem like it."

"Well, I hope you do."

"Believe me, so do I."

The Winds of Malibu

(Journal entry)

December 19, 1975
This day marks the turning point of my entire life. For better or for worse, I don't know. All that I know is that yesterday I woke up thinking a normal day ahead and my Dad walks in and tells me that I'm going to Alabama to live with my Mumsy! I was shocked out of my mind and still am! Today I had to say goodbye to everyone. And I do mean EVERYONE!!! And each and every one person I said goodbye to, took a piece of my heart away. I brought my tape recorder to school and taped everyone except Lynn Craig, the person I'll miss the most, who refused!?

※

"Dad, what happens if I miss out on a movie career in Malibu?" I stared at him.

"Well, you can blame me then."

Christ, I hated him.

I walked over and hugged him.

"Dad, I love you more than anyone in the world," I lied. "Please don't do this."

"Well, I hope that's true. You are not getting out of this," he said coldly.

There was a whirlwind of movement. On the flight to Montgomery, I played Big Band tapes at maximum volume on my little tape recorder which ran on five C batteries. A middle-aged black man sat next to me. He ordered a whiskey from the stewardess.

"I like that. Keep them playing," he said. "What's a kid like you doing listening to all that?"

"It's all I like."

"Oh yeah, now we're talkin!'" he smiled as the Duke Ellington band played "Take the A Train." As soon as I stepped off the airliner in Montgomery, I breathed in air so cold, my lungs went into shock. I came down with laryngitis and couldn't speak for two weeks.

(Journal entries)

December 22, 1975
Today was my first day in Alabama.

8:05
December 30 1975
It rained all day today. I spent the day down in the garage, listening to records. I never do much around here. I truly miss everybody back home, particularly Lynn, for everything I see reminds me of her. It seems like I've been here months, but it's only been a week. I have an unpredictable future, but I imagine there will be good times along with the bad.

(An essay)

Eull Gibbons died last night of a heart attack. In his days he was a successful writer on natural foods. He wrote many books and did interviews on TV in his later life. However I and probably

The Winds of Malibu

a lot of people didn't hear of him until into the 70s, when he started doing commercials for Post Grape Nuts. From then on out he was kidded, teased, impersonated and he became a household word very soon. His legend grew and grew, and soon he was being impersonated by many comedians in shows like "Carol Burnett Show," "Seymore's Fright Night," and the like. It became this way in 1973, overboiled in 1974 and was big for months into 1975. But then slowly, comics stopped impersonating him. The jokes were getting stale, but he was still a household word. He was thinking about retirement when all of a sudden on a stormy night in December the 29th, Monday, Eull Gibbons, the man who was supposed to be the healthiest person alive, died of a heart attack, of all things at the reasonably young age of 62.

(A letter sent to the MPJHS band class)

Mr Loyd and gang,

I feel really strange here in Alabama. The people are nice but my school is lousy. It seems a lot of people around M.P.J.H.S. take it for granted what a fine school they have, I know I did, but it isn't until one goes to a school that is truly the dumps that they realize it. I came to that school with an open mind. At the office there, they told me I only had one elective and only six periods. Of course, the elective I chose was music. Well, they didn't have a trombone to lend me and with money they cost nowadays, we couldn't afford to buy one. However, that didn't stop me. I thought about renting one and looked into it but they told me that we could pay $25 for 2 months but then we would either have to buy it or give it up. So unfortunately the trombone was out, but even if I could have gotten a hold of one, I'm not at all sure I would have stayed with that class. 1st, the room is at the most ¼ the size of yours and there is 26 people in the class. 2nd, there is no carpeting on the floor whatsoever, just wood and when you want to empty your instrument you have to practically put your feet in your pockets to keep them out of the puddle. 3rd, I didn't realize what a know-it-all musician you really are until I got a load of this guy. He was such a simple minded Polish pickle. I doubted if he graduated from the Alabama nursury school.

-Martha Washington Junior High had a good music section in its library, and though the books were dated, they were clean. I preferred old things anyway. I found a 1950's book titled, "Giants of Jazz" by Studs Terkel, and I couldn't believe my luck when I discovered that Bix Beiderbecke had a chapter to himself. I looked at the library card and saw that the book had never been checked out to anyone. I asked the librarian, who told me the book had sat untouched in that library for fifteen years. I checked out the book, and few days later, walked out with it hidden under my coat and she didn't stop me.-

(Journal entries)

Feb. 10, 1976
Times is hard here in Montgomery. I'll never enjoy California more than when I first come back. Seems like I write in this thing only when I'm depressed. Which is'nt very good although while I'm here I might as well make the best of it. Jack just walked in and is telling Mom how Terri is. I know how she is, on her death bed. She's getting better and worse quite frequently. I hate to say this, but I think her time is limited.

The Winds of Malibu

Tue. Feb. 17, 1976 Bicentennial
It seems strange now to think back about 2 months ago, for not a single thought went through my head about coming to Alabama. I'm torn between staying here and going back there. If I do stay here (which I imagine I will) I'm going to demand two things! No.1 A new school! No.2 Piano lessons! I absolutely dread this school and I think if I were good enough at piano I could and will easily compose a rhapsody, a "Sycodelic rhapsody." Pat, a girl down the street who is built like a football player, is in love with me But I'm not wild about her. On the bus today she said by mistake, as she pushed my books aside, "Sorry I have to move your books but I have to spread out!" I died laughing.

Wed. Feb. 26, 1976
One of the most tragic episodes in Jack's and Mom's and mine and Grandma Eda's and just about everybody else's life occurred today - Wednesday, Febuary 26 1976, 4:00 pm. Terri Dick, my stepsister whom I admired and respected so
DIED.
Exactly 8 hours ago. I guess her lungs gave up. I always looked to her as someday being such a fine mother! But so much happened in such a short time. 2 months ago, life was fine for the 15 year old child. Then it started with dizzy spells. She was brought in for a checkup and

The Most Refined Asshole

I'm kind of lost as to what happened while she was there. But I believe they ran a test and somehow fluid got in her lungs. She was taken to the hospital. They couldn't find what was wrong with her — so they threw her in intensive care and harpooned about 7 tubes leading into her lungs. Her condition went from better to worse quite frequently. Jack and Mom drove the car up their yesterday — and she died today.

Grandma Edith, my brother John and I will fly up there for the funeral.

I'll keep you informed.

7:10 am
Feb. 26, 1976
This is the first time I'm writing in the morn. I'm not going to school today. We're getting a call from Mom sometime today about flying to the funeral.

9:22 pm
Flying to Texas for funeral. I'm on the plane. We should be landing in a few minutes. I wish I could fly at night more often. It's so beautiful and I working on Sycodelic Rapsody in my mind, but I know this joyousness won't last. I'm going to hate to see Jack & Mom for I bet they and everybody are going to be so depressed and for some unknown reason — I'm not!

The Winds of Malibu

Feb. 27, 1976
We are getting ready to go to the funeral. It's the rush hour. I really hate to go through with this.

Feb. 29, 1976
It was worse than I thought it would be! 1st, I did my best to keep from crying in the church. 2nd, I saw Terries grossing out figure in the coffin. 3rd, We stood there before they planted her with about 350, it looked like, friends standing around. 4th, I busted up into tears. It was the worst day I've ever had.

March 1, 1976
The first time I write in pen here. I say, good news, and I could use some. Today was my grandmother's birthday and she granted me a hell of a good wish too. Somehow, Mom and I convinced Dad that I should go home. I'm going to hit Malibu like a bomb. Wow! I'm so excited I can't write straight. I know before I wasn't half trying at things, but now I'm going to give it the full juice. I'm so glad to get out of this hellhole, and when I do, things are going to change.

›»«‹

    He had kept my room as a guest room. I put my Hollywood memorabilia back on the walls and sat on my bed and gripped

Terri's grave in Texas. Photo by Reba Dick.

the edge of it and vowed to stay in Malibu until I was at least eighteen. I stretched delicately.

I went into Steve's room. We stood at his dresser.

"That was heavy, what happened to Terri," he said.

"You missed all that. It was horror. Real horror." He put some marijuana in a pipe and lit up.

"You wanna hit?"

"No thanks."

Nine

March to May, 1976. Fourteen years old.

PRODIGY

I hid behind a column and waited for Mr. Thacker's yellow Volkswagen Beetle, and I ran alongside the car in a Groucho Marx duck walk. His face brightened.

"Are you back?" He smiled as he stepped out of his car.

"Yes! I am back now!" I watched him go on his way with a spring in his step.

I put my arm around Frank's shoulder and walked him in several small circles around the flag pole.

"Are you glad to see me?"

"Yeah! I thought you were gone for good. I am glad you're back."

"I was gone for bad… and I am glad I'm back too, for good. I think I am!"

Everyone was glad to see me. I walked into our acting workshop as if I had never left and sat next to Emilio. He had this slow grin that turned into a full smile.

"Did I miss anything?"

"I had a feeling you'd be back." I went up to Mr. Thacker and spoke quietly.

"*So*, what's going on now?"

"Well, you missed the Talent Show."

"Yeah, I missed it all right… badly. Do you have a 'Best of the Talent Show'?"

"Well, yes… but that is already cast, and we can't squeeze any more acts in."

"That's okay. I'm going to hit the stage as soon as I can." I went back to my seat.

The next day, Mr. Thacker handed out programs for that year's Best of the Talent Show and I was on the list. He had removed a performer to put me in. The poor guy was upset and came to me for an explanation.

"That's just show biz, I guess. Sorry. Talk to Mr. Thacker about it."

I danced to "The Charleston" the *Great Gatsby* album and got a long standing ovation even though the performance wasn't as good as "The Sugar Blues." It did wear me out, though. It was nonstop fast jazz. I lay down on the boards against the back wall afterwards and just breathed.

"Jeff, are you okay?"

"Oh yeah."

"*Emilio!*" I ran up to him and we walked up a steep slope together at lunchtime.

"Do you remember that movie you told me about that your dad was going to be in, about a famous trumpet player in the twenties… and there might be a part for me in it?"

"Yeah, but now they don't know if it's going to turn out."

"That doesn't matter. What matters is… *who* was that movie

about? Can you remember the name?" Emilio stopped to think.

"Something like 'Blix' or…."

"Bix Beiderbecke?! It couldn't possibly have been Bix Beiderbecke of the twenties, could it?"

"Yeah, that's it," Emilio smiled calmly. "My dad has some stuff on him because he was studying for the part."

My heart dropped to my toes in delight as I caught my breath. "That is the neatest thing I have ever heard in my whole life!" Emilio watched me fly back down the slope.

Endless weeds were pulled up on Saturdays and Sundays and placed in our cans, for our allowance. We were paid one quarter per can. To expand our income, the cans were loosely packed. We showed each refill to our father, and he packed it back down and ordered us back out there with his pointed index finger.

"That's not a full can," he said.

Steve's long hair and red bandanna, laid flat across the top of his head, left little doubt as to his musical tastes, which were whatever was current. He pointed the speakers toward the open windows and let the volume rip. The number one new rock song in the United States blasted.

"♪ *Play that funky music, white boy!! Play that funky music right! Play that funky music, white boy! Lay down and boogie and play that funky music 'til you DIE! TILL YA DIE!!*♪"

Our dad ate his tuna salad in his bedroom and drowned out the music with a tennis match on TV. He came out and laughed his head off. I hadn't seen him laugh that hard in years.

"Oh, that is funny! That is so funny!"

"What? That's a *good* song!" Steve rotated his neck in circles to the beat.

"Shut up. You look like Aunt Jemima!" I said. We yelled over the music.

"You look like a dickless wonder," he said. We stood there in our torn, stiff leather gloves and held our rusty coffee cans. The weeds around our house were healthier than we were, and each was a tug of war to get them out of the hard soil. The root stayed in the ground. Our dad listened to the rest of the song carefully, and then went back inside.

"That is too funny," he said and closed his door.

A week later, my dad and I drove home from the bank together when I tried to make conversation.

"It is surprising how many movies are rated 'R' now. I wouldn't mind seeing some, just to see how they are made from an artistic standpoint. Would that be all right with you?"

"No, I refuse to let you." He reached to check what was on the radio. There was that song again. He grinned. I liked it when my old man smiled. I sang along.

"♪ *Play that funky music, white boy.* ♪"

"Don't say that, Jeff." He switched the radio off.

"What happened? What's the matter now?"

"Don't say that *word*."

"What word? What *word*?"

"You know what word, Jeff."

"Dad, I really don't know what word. I really don't know."

He sighed, glanced around and said it. "Fucking."

"Oh my God! You think they are saying fu… that word? They are saying, Funky. F-U N-K-Y. *Funky!*"

"No they are not, Jeff. I hear what they are saying. I have been around a lot longer than you have," he said seriously.

"You don't think there is such a word as FUNKY? *FUN-KY?*"

"No. There is no such word as that and you know it, so don't argue with me, Jeff. You won't win… and I know what they are saying! I have been alive a lot longer than you have! Do not say it again, please!" I stayed quiet the rest of the way up Cuthbert road. We got out of the car and the doors shut.

"Have you got any homework?"

Night time. No one home. Steve had Thai Stick in his top dresser drawer. He also had porno magazines under his bed which I helped myself to. He had some smutty ones. I put them back where I had found them, dotted some Chap Stick on and turned off all the lights.

I tore an inch off the stick and packed it into my brother's pipe. I smoked it all, not wasting it. I ran my hands through my hair and my mouth dried up. I darted my pointy tongue out and licked my chapped lips.

I had to run! Out the kitchen door, through the neighbor's back yard, through the swamp and its faint shadows where I watched Frank kill baby frogs by slamming them to the ground.

We were with Pringle that day, and baby frogs were everywhere. I guess they got on Frank's nerves. First we played catch with them. Frank got bored and laughed and picked them up and slammed them to the ground one at a time. I shook my head and followed suit. Pringle dropped them gently on their backs.

Into our school, running like a wolfman, I stopped at Mr. Thacker's classroom. I put my handprints across his windows, pressing.

"I'm back Terri, I'm back Terri, I'm back Terri, I'm back!"

I opened my mouth, put my face against the glass and rolled my face on the window, and leaned back. The imprint spoke.

"Jeff," it whispered. The imprint's lips moved. I smudged the imprint with my sleeve, ran out of the school toward the sea. The darkness was smothering except for the retarded Milky Way through the haze until I came to the headlights of cars on the Pacific Coast Highway. There was no way I was going to be in this condition on Zuma Beach. My heart had never beaten so fast. I crossed the PCH, no problem with the oncoming cars.

I ran along the Pacific Coast Highway at eleven o'clock at night. Lots of wind on me. Cars raced by, but no one slowed to watch me, and that was the best part. But at the top of Point Doom, civilization loomed.

I looked at my watch on my slim left wrist in the light of the gas station. It had been an hour and twenty minutes since I smoked that shit. Bushes, foliage, bushes. I bounded in back of the market into the thickest mass of bushes and stood there. My tongue was numb.

"Jeff!" The loudest whisper in my left ear. No one there.

"JEFF!" Same thing in my right ear. I peered deep in the branches. Only more leaves, and a spider in its thick, well spun web.

"JEFF!" Now the loudest whisper was in front of me.

Now on all sides, "JEFF, JEFF, JEFF, JEFF!" Crystal clear. Whose vocal cords were those? I backed out the same direction I had climbed in to the bushes, brushed off for spiders, and looked at my watch. Eleven twenty-seven, big hand and little hand and a little brass winder on the side that had to be wound every five days.

I headed home with the steady Malibu walk, on the streets only. As I had hoped, just as I got on to Deerhead Road, the Thai Stick subsided, as had my anxiety, and I got in our house, to bed and to sleep, with no one home.

"I am going to present a twenty-minute afternoon showcase," Mr. Thacker announced. I sat in the back of the class. He found me and motioned me over.

"It is only going to be you in this, so whatever you've got, show them," he undertoned.

Jeff on the Deerhead road property in 1976 in 3-D. The view from the front yard down the mountain. Photo by Steve Lucas.

I danced to "The Sugar Blues" and also a classical piece from *Carmen* that was featured in Tatum's movie, *The Bad News Bears*, and another Charleston song from *The Great Gatsby* album with a vocal in it so that I could mouth along to words. I wanted to pound the 1920s into their minds, and what better introduction than the Charleston? The auditorium speakers sounded better than ever. These Pink Floyd and Led Zeppelin fans heard my music crystal clear!

The curtain drew open and I wondered if I had forgotten to tell my friend John Ufland, in back of the theater, which selection to put the arm of the needle on.

"You'll pardon me just a moment." I jumped off the stage and scrambled through the audience to the back booth. I saw Thacker's eyes follow me as I ran past him.

"It's the first song on side three, John!" John's dad was the most successful talent scout in Hollywood; at least that's what I was told.

"Okay. I was going to be put it on the first song on side three anyway." We laughed together. His hair was dark like mine but curlier. I ran back up through the audience, jumped onto center stage from the floor in one leap, and strutted "I'm Going to Charleston Back My Way to Charleston."

I sat low on the ground after school and caressed Lynn's locker. I waited until no one was around and let my eyes rest on how neatly the books and pencils were stacked in there. I placed the most beautiful flower I could find on top of her books before gently closing it, and I made sure it was well locked. Only one other boy was interested in her; a cool Latino student who sat next to her. He grinned and couldn't take his eyes off her. It drove me up the wall.

A delightful daydream about Lynn and I played out in my mind to the movie soundtrack of Gershwin's *Porgy and Bess*. I sang out loud the name Lynn every time the record sang the name "Bess" and the name Jeffrey every time the record sang the name "Porgy."

Together we sing. She rides her beautiful garnet horse, her luscious hair and the horse's mane flow in the wind along the streets of Point Dume. Lynn pities me and we sing, "Lynn, You Is My Woman Now" as we look in each other's eyes; the sprawling Malibu sunset, spilled out, is our backdrop.

Along comes the ridiculous, trendy surfer dude and he sings "It Ain't Necessarily So," in that lazy surfer dialect. The surfer has affluent parents, and Lynn accompanies him on luxurious dates. A terrible storm hits Malibu and destroys Lynn's house atop Dume Road. The arrogant surfer dude smooth talks her and she runs away with him to New York, to wine and dine and live the high life, and snort much cocaine. The house I live in is also destroyed, and my controlling father demands that I go live with my mother again in Alabama.

I can't find Lynn anywhere, and none of my friends want to tell me what happened to her, so I sing, "Where Is My Lynn?" My best friend, Emilio Estevez, finally tells me the awful truth, and I set out for New York alone. Barefoot, I trek over the Santa Monica Mountains as I sing, "Oh Lord, I'm on My Way." The needle on the record lifted on its own, moved over and rested in the cradle, as I lay on my bedroom floor and stared up at the cracks in my father's ceiling.

The Lucas residence housed three crazy males. That was fine with me. My father had just broken up with Jill, whom I liked better than any of his women. She was nicer than the others. It was him who had dropped her. She didn't meet his standards somehow.

I was at home by myself when there was a knock on the door.

It was Jill. She stood there and didn't say anything.

"Hi… um… my dad is not here right now."

"I know that. I came by because I wanted to see you and talk to you. Can I buy you lunch?" We got in her little Karmann Ghia Volkswagen and chugged up to the Point Dume Coffee Shop. We sat by a window that faced the Pacific Coast Highway. I ordered a club sandwich with onion rings and a Coke. She didn't order anything, just a glass of water which she didn't touch.

"Who is your dad seeing?"

"Someone who lives down on Broad Beach. She is really tan and has a lot of wrinkles. You are better-looking. I think he should stay with you."

"Who else?"

"Someone who made me laugh…a brunette. She was only over once. She said all of our silverware was so rusty we would get lockjaw. I don't even pretend to understand my dad."

Jill put her head down and cried. "I'm forty-six years old and suddenly, I feel like I'm thirteen again! Now that I'm divorced, I don't know what I'm going to do! It's too strange to find another man!"

"Can I bring you something else?" the waitress asked. Jill blubbered.

"No, we'll just have the check. Thank you," I said. She paid the bill, grabbed a napkin, and blew her nose loudly. People looked at us.

I left my half-eaten meal and followed her out. She sobbed in spasms on the drive back and clutched the napkin tightly in her trembling hand. When she dropped me off at the bottom of the driveway, she barely waved goodbye, and I never saw her again.

In the middle of the night, I played Bix Beiderbecke below my bed to calm my anxiety and kept the volume low.

"Turn it off, Jeff, now—before I come in there and really

smash you into nothing!" I turned down the volume knob completely until it was barely audible, like a mosquito, although Bix Beiderbecke's cornet was piercing even at mosquito volume. Twenty seconds passed. His fist slammed into his dresser.

"I said I want it off!" I leapt into the air and scrambled to stop the record. The needle scratched across the record surface. He screamed and growled as I imagined a man with advanced rabies would do.

Mr. Thacker's assistant, Sally Emr, walked in and smiled at me. She was on the short side and lovely. Her husband, Art, was an aspiring movie maker, and was taught by Jerry Lewis.

"Do you want to meet Jerry Lewis on May third?"

"Do you mean it?"

"Yes! My husband is interviewing him at Webster Elementary school."

I walked into a congregation room and was shown to my seat in the front row that had my name taped on it. Art introduced Jerry Lewis and out he stepped in a dark suit. He was in his prime as far as handsome goes. I didn't blink my eyes and jarred them open. Jerry was hilarious. He wrapped his lips around his large water glass and let it hang there. It took an enormous mouth to be able to do that! Mr. Emr stopped to laugh along with the rest of us. He joked about a hotel he had passed on the way called the Ramada Inn. The sound of the name made him laugh. At intermission, Sally walked up to me.

"Here, I want you to meet him." I stood up with jelly legs and we approached him in slow motion.

"Jerry Lewis?"

"Yes."

"This is your act-alike, Jeff Lucas."

"It's very nice to meet you, Jeff." I shook his big, warm hand

and was speechless. I made it back to my chair. I felt gravitated to Jerry, as intermission had just started. Against my will, I moved back toward him creepy and slowly. It was okay. I knew Jerry understood creepy. He didn't look at me as I drew near. I stood in front of his face as he sat in his chair.

"Are you going to make any more movies?" I asked. He frowned and closed his eyes and nodded yes with painful slowness. He nodded eight times like that.

"Well, that's what I was just wondering because… so… thank you… actually," I said. I got back to my chair and shut the hell up. I felt like I might have stepped on a tender issue with him. When the interview resumed, Mr. Lewis was in great form again.

"Do you ever think about dying?" Mr. Emr asked.

"No. I am fine, and I will be fine," he said.

(Journal entry)

May 3, '76

Everything has gone by perfect since my return here. I did the Charleston for Malibu Park J.H. Tonight was a night I'll surely remember the rest of my life. After going through everything to see my idol and image, I finally saw the one man that changed my life. I saw, shook hands with, and even held a halfway conversation with "Jerry Lewis."

⸻

The worst part of my life continued to be the legal owner of 5838 Deerhead road. I never had to go without food. Dozens of jars of Homemade Brand Chili Sauce and cans of Geisha Tuna, when they were on sale, were stored in the hot water heater

Instead of homework, Jeff drew this self portrait of himself while thinking of Tatum O'Neal. From 1976.

cabinet, stacked four feet high. We ate lots of Heinz Vegetarian beans with Colby cheese melted in. Cans of black olives, jars of Miracle Whip, many boxes of Quaker Granola cereal, (which was hell on my canker sores) plastic tubs of yogurt (he liked strawberry with cashews in his. I liked lemon) 2% milk, orange juice concentrate in the freezer. Iceberg lettuce and cauliflower were usually the only raw vegetables. He got mad if you ate his cauliflower. He crammed that into his mouth with gobs of Thousand Island dressing. Also he kept on hand chocolate chip ice cream and Nestle's chocolate chips that he melted with a teaspoon of water in a scratched-up Teflon pan, and poured over the top, which fed the pimple at the end of his nose.

My father's favorite lunch was his tuna salad. I watched him throw it together so many times.

The Paul Lucas Tuna Salad (one serving)

One entire jar of Homemade (brand) chili sauce

12 tablespoons of Miracle Whip salad dressing

One small can of Geisha tuna in water, half drained

A head of mostly white iceberg lettuce (throw out the base, try to make a basket from across the kitchen and miss the garbage pail by two feet). Tear into shreds with your bare hands vigorously.

3 full tablespoons of freshly ground black pepper

Mix it all together angrily, grind the pepper, slam all the kitchen cabinets and drawers closed, and stomp back to the television to watch the conclusion of a tennis match.

I found a friend in Mr. Loyd's trombone section named Arthur Mortell. He laughed at *everything* I did. He was a good boy, and always nice. Dark hair, freckles, he was small. He lived in a house halfway between the Lucas house and the Trancas. I got him to invite me over for dinner. His divorced mom cooked extravagant meals for him. I got chummy with the mom and I ate all the food left on the table.

"So, then, you want some more?" Mrs. Mortell asked in a New York accent.

"Sure! Thank you for being so generous." I ate dinner over there about three times.

As Arthur unpacked his trombone he stood there, sighed, and looked at me.

"My mom says she doesn't want you over for dinner anymore. She said you eat like two men."

My stomach hurt, so I lay down in the hay on my back on my way from school near the swamp of frogs, as long as I felt there wasn't a spider within eight feet of me. I remembered my dad told me when he was a kid, he jammed a straw up a frog's butt, blew into the straw and inflated the frog, and watched it race across a pond. I asked him if it was a paper straw or a plastic straw. He said he couldn't remember.

I had a zit on my left temple that hurt and a canker sore in my mouth. I felt growing pains in my knees. I was becoming more lanky, face a bit more chiseled from my imp look. I squinted up with one eye at the clouds until my stomach ulcers calmed down.

"Just think—those clouds have no spiders in them."

Ten

CENTERPIECE

I walked around Malibu dressed like Bix Beiderbecke. The classic Bix look was not very complicated. Basically, it was just an authentic 1920s Tuxedo, a smooth-shaven face, and well-oiled, slicked-back, brown hair, combed tightly back over the scalp and parted just off center down the middle. My hair was the right color but too thick to slick down. I did the best I could. There was no hat to wear and no glasses, and no rings on the fingers and no necklace. I didn't have a 1920s tuxedo, but I did the best I could. There was one more thing: Bix did not use a fancy case for his cornet. He used a brown paper grocery bag, which was just one of many signs that he was not normal.

I showed up for band class with the trumpet Frank had sold me wrapped in a big crumpled paper grocery bag. Frank stared at it as I sat next to him.

"You lost the case?"

"No, I still have it at home. Do you want it back?"

"No. I have this one. Is that how that guy carried around *his* horn?"

"Yes...Bix. Frank, say *Bix*."

"Bix," said Frank.

"That's better." When I took the trumpet out or put it back, it made a long crumple, which made the class and Mr. Loyd stare at me. It looked like a king-sized lunch sack. Frank checked out my wrap-around bowtie.

"I love the trumpet and the case you sold me at a good price... but if you ever see a cornet for sale, let me know."

"Okay."

"Lets warm up," Mr. Loyd announced. I slid three seats down from Frank, because in our weekly competition I was now in last place. We played our whole notes, and I couldn't believe how bad I sounded, like an animal in agony in the LaBrea Tar Pits. Frank, who was first trumpet, effortlessly had a good tone to his horn. His facial features looked more like Bix than mine did, but he didn't care. The hissing gurgle of Frank blowing out his spit valve sounded better than my best tone.

"Okay, let's play the theme from MASH," said Mr. Loyd. We set our sheet music on the music stands.

"Suicide Is Painless," the title read at the top of the sheet music. We played it through, and I imagined how Bix might improvise a jazz solo with it. The flute section played most of that arrangement with no surprises whatsoever, the brass took over for the chorus.

I sat next to Pam Gurak, who I had half a crush on and who resembled Lillian Gish. The song finished with a single wave of Mr. Loyd's baton. We put our instruments down in unison and rested them on our knees.

"And how painless is it?" I joked to Pam.

"How painless is what?" I pointed to the word, "Suicide," printed on the page, and she laughed quietly.

"*Jeff!*" sang Emilio in the foyer of the lunch area. I always felt honored when he called my name in a crowd because no one that popular ever called my name in a crowd. I walked over to him.

"I've been thinking. I think we should take tap dance lessons together."

"Tap dancing? Sounds interesting. I have never tapped in my dancing."

"My dad told me about a teacher in Santa Monica who is supposed to be good."

"Okay. We are gonna need tap dancing shoes."

"I already have 'em… and my brother is going too."

"Do you remember how much they were?"

Emilio paused and thought. "Forty dollars?"

"Okay. I will get tap shoes then. I will let you know when I have them."

"Okay."

"Dad, Martin Sheen's son wants me to take tap dancing lessons with him, but I have to buy a pair of tap shoes first."

"You don't say." He stood at the foot of his bed and folded his socks in the method he was taught in the army, where one sock swallows the other.

"The shoes are forty dollars… but it's with Martin Sheen's kid! Please? We are becoming really good friends, you know, he and I. We are!"

"All right… I guess."

"Thanks, Dad!" There was a basketball game on his small color television set. He watched with frustrated brown eyes.

"I'll be so happy when basketball season is over. You know, when I was a kid, basketball used to be a great sport. It was competitive. Now, it's nothing but a bunch of stupid shvartzes jumping up and down the gosh-darn court... it's all just niggers now." He appeared crestfallen. That meant I was going to get my way.

"Can I have the forty dollars now? I'll bring you back a receipt."

"No, on my next drive into town, come with me and we'll get them."

The two Estevezes and I rode the bus together into Santa Monica. Emilio got a double seat to himself and leaned back against the window. I was in the seat in front of him.

"Hey, I got a joke," Emilio began. "There is this island full of cannibals, and they're standing in a line, getting ready to eat dinner. So the first cannibal in line says, 'I'll have an arm... and a Coke.' So they give him an arm and a Coke. The next cannibal walks up and says, 'I'll have a foot and a Coke.' So, the cook gives him a foot and a Coke. And the next cannibal in line says, 'I'll have the face and a Coke.'"

"The face?" I said.

"Yeah, the face."

"And then what happened?"

"So, the *fourth* cannibal walks up and says, 'I'll have the thing and a Coke.' 'The thing?' says the cook. 'Why do you want to eat the thing?' So the fourth cannibal looks at the cook and says, 'Because things go better with Coke!'" I laughed.

"That's a new one on me, I'll tell you for sure," I said, trying to sound like Clyde Barrow. Emilio's brother laughed a little. I think he had been told that one a few times.

"Don't sell that cow!" I yelled out so the whole bus could hear. Emilio laughed. Big Al, the bus driver drove on steadily. He

was almost used to my outbursts.

We got off the bus, and Emilio led us to an old building and up a steep stairwell. The students at the Danny Daniels School of Tap Dancing were all middle-aged women who tried to keep up with the muscular Danny Daniels. The place smelled of sweat.

I was not a quick study.

CENTERPIECE

Jeff asked Steve to take another photo of him on the Deerhead road property in the garden. Photo by Steve Lucas

"And... step, ball, chain, step, ball, chain!" Danny Daniels instructed. It got hot up there on the second floor, and the tap shoes echoed loudly on the wood. The furniture dated back to at least the 1920s, so I got a kick out of the curvature and designs. After class, Emilio and his brother Ramon got picked up in a car and I took the bus back.

The Winds of Malibu

(Journal entry)

May 1976
Summer will be coming in about a month. I think I should prepare for it. I just got home from my last 8th grade dance. I danced with Lynn and for once she was impressed with my dancing! I jumped the stick with my 2 good legs and she gave me an affectionate and heart rendering smile. After the dance Lynn's friend came up to me and asked, "Do you like Lynn?" I said, "Why do you want to know" - "because I'm her friend." I just wonder who asked her to ask me that?
Jeff Lucas

⟫⟪

    I was at the dining room table with my father and Steve. Our dad paid us our allowance. We ate fresh bread that my brother had kneaded and baked with dirty hands after we picked dozens of weeds. When the dough was ready for the oven, his hands looked clean and the dough was dark. My father waited for a business call. He leaned back and sang a song to the tune of an old sports theme.
    "You've got a brown ring around your nose, and how it grows and grows and grows!" We laughed. He belched and puffed his cheeks out. My brother pointed at him and laughed.
    "You look like Richard Nixon! Do that again!" It was true. We all cracked up. He looked like a caricature of President Nixon. I had never noticed that.
    I glanced up at the clock. My tap dance lesson started at 1:00, and it was now 11:40.
    "I forgot my tap class! I gotta go! I don't want Emilio there

without me!" My dad did the Nixon face again and made peace signs with both hands. He shook his head back and forth like Nixon.

"I am serious! I've really got to leave! Can one of you take me into Santa Monica right now?"

"I can't take you. I am waiting for a phone call from Analog Devices. I told you," said my father.

"Maybe Steve can use your car."

"Not yet, he can't."

There was no time to lug around an extra pair of shoes. I jammed my feet into my white tap shoes and ran out the kitchen door. I sprinted in the direction that took longer but by the time I realized this it was too late to turn back and go the other way. Down the dirt path, the dirt clods and straw were slippery beneath my tap shoes and I half slid down the hillsides.

My arms were all over the place as I kept my balance. The dogs didn't bother me this one time, I think the sound of my tap shoes scared them away. I wasn't one to sweat very much but I began to. The noon sun was out as I got to the concrete part. The horses watched me go by. I sounded like one of them as I trotted along down a driveway.

I ran onto Morning View Drive, where there is no more shade from the trees and I could see the ocean. I ran past an old woman who trod slowly with a hat on.

"Top o' the morning to ya!" I yelled. If she said anything, I couldn't hear. When I got in front of the two schools, there was a sidewalk, and I decided to figure out if my tap shoes made more noise on the sidewalk or in the street. They made more noise on the sidewalk, so I ran the rest of the way in the street.

I made it to the Pacific Coast Highway and looked at the wristwatch that my father had given me for Christmas. It was four past twelve. Big Al was four minutes late and here he came.

The bus pulled over. I wiped sweat off my face and climbed in.

"Thanks for being late." I dropped the thirty-five cents in.

"I'm not late," he said like Humphrey Bogart with glasses on.

I didn't give a damn about the class; this was about not letting Emilio down. The city of Santa Monica got to hear my tap shoes echo down the sidewalks. I got to the front of the dance studio and the familiar black car drove up and let Emilio and his brother out of the back seat.

They looked immaculate, Emilio in his customary polo shirt and shorts, and I looked like hell, dressed like a scarecrow, in my weed-picking clothes. I leaned my back against the wall and caught my breath. We could hear the tappers upstairs.

"Is that the beginning class or the advanced class?" He leaned up the staircase as his brother stood next to him. I shrugged my shoulders, put my hands on my knees.

"That sounds like our beginning class. Let's go stand in back of the ladies," I said. We headed up the stairs and did just that.

Tap class ended and I walked slowly in my tap shoes to the bus stop. I stepped lightly, and it still clacked loudly. I sat alone on the bus stop bench that overlooked the Santa Monica bluffs and the park with cannons in it. I crossed my legs and fidgeted. A white Cadillac pulled up to the curb in front of me and the window rolled down. There was one man in the car at the wheel with a red beard and white hair. He paused.

"You want a ride?"

"Um…no thanks. I'm gonna wait for the bus. I've got nothing but time."

"Do you live in Malibu?"

"Yes."

"I'll take you anywhere you want to go. You'll enjoy it." I uncrossed my legs so the bottom of my tap shoe didn't flare.

"Well, thank you, that is generous of you but…no."

CENTERPIECE

"You could show me around Malibu. I am sure there are lots of secret places. Are you sure?"

"No! I am waiting for the bus. Come on, bus."

"Be that way." He drove away, and here came the bus.

(Journal entries)

Bicentennial
June 14, 1976 Monday 7:30 – 7:40 am
This is the last week of school. I will write in here every day this week. I finally wrote a letter to Lynn last night. I think the time is ripe. I have to give it to her today and I'm scared shit! To be continued.

Monday 9:00 – 9:30pm That beaner sonofabitch sat next to Lynn and I made a sign that showed Lynn I was jealous as hell. She got up from her seat and started mocking him behind his back. I took a picture of her and she got both startled and embarrassed. I finally, with help from Mr. Newcomb the music teacher, got the note to her. Things are good now, but I'm scared about tomorrow.

June 15, 1976 bicentennial Tuesday 10:9 –
I think I scared her away. She's backing in her shell again. The picture and especially the note of course, was a little too much. She didn't face me once today,

The Winds of Malibu

She was too damn embarrassed! So goes by one more day without knowing. But who knows. Maybe tomorrow things will look up.
Jeff Lucas

June 16, 1976 12:15 - 12:20 am
She wasn't there today. I'm beginning to wonder whether or not the note was such a good idea? *!¢/#

June 17, 1976
I don't know what to do! I'm going to pieces! Things are just getting worse and worse. I'm going to her house now. She still hasn't given me any kind of answer yet. However she was at school today.

June 21, 1976 8:20
I haven't written in here up till now because I was too busy. I'll tell you what happened. Fri. I kissed the best trombone player in our school, Margaret, goodbye. More like she kissed me! I only told Lynn to have a good summer. Sat. I was at the beach all day. Sun. I went to Trancas and found out through her sister that Lynn couldn't come and work there because the last time she made an ass out of herself in front of me. Mon. ,

today. A week ago I gave a note to Lynn. Today I called her 2ice. I asked her to go grunion hunting and she said no but that she would go to a movie with me! I think I'll ask her next week. Boy, am I lucky this summer of '76. Jeff Lucas

⇒⇒⇒⇐⇐⇐

Emilio leaned against the auditorium stage to my left beside me. He paused and looked serious.

"I'm going to have to quit our tap class. My dad just got a movie, and it's being filmed in the Philippines."

"The *Philippines?* Is it a Filipino movie?"

"No, it's American. We might go with him." He looked me in the eye. The look suggested that maybe I should go too.

"My dad bitches about how much it costs to send me to Alabama. He would never pay to get me to the Philippines," I joked. He folded his arms and looked ahead.

"It's being directed by the same director who made *The Godfather*."

"Oh, *wow*."

I carried my tape recorder with me, angled with the speaker up inside my backpack. "Since I Don't Have You" by the Skyliners played as Lynn rode her red horse majestically within a few blocks of the Craig home on Point Dume. She kept her horse on the sides of the streets with the frame of a magnificent Malibu sunset behind her, incandescent with muted colors, ducks flying high in a V-line across the soft, waning colors; the various trees lifted in a slow dance under the evening winds from the Pacific, showing arches of horizon that were clear, clean, and deliciously blue. I had to rest against a telephone pole, she looked so beautiful, as the music from my backpack played, until at just the right moment with steady eyes on her, I reached in back and clicked it off.

Her father owned a supermarket near the Civic Center, and I took the bus there just to walk around inside the market. Lynn worked the cash register sometimes. When she noticed me, I picked up a small bag of Laura Scudders barbecue potato chips and read the ingredients. She had a lot of patience and was nice to me. After she took my three quarters, I would say something stupid.

"I always tell my dad to buy our food here to make money for your dad's store."

"Thanks," she smiled, and I left with my face red as a tomato. I just wished she would say my name one time. She never spoke the name Jeff.

I hid in bushes across the street from her house for hours. Frank, Pringle, or my new friend Joel stood with me sometimes, though they weren't interested in Lynn at all. Joel Anderson was the most patient of my friends. He was slim and had a face kind of like a blue-eyed reindeer with thin, long, tan hair. He was understanding, unselfish, and a good listener. What could be more entertaining than the view of a small, red house on a sunny, breezy day on Point Dume with a big horse completely still except for its red mane in the wind, in a small stable? We never saw anyone go in or anyone go out.

"You just have to be near her, huh?" said Joel.

"She makes Malibu so much more beautiful."

At night I lay trembling for a while, my teeth chattering at sporadic intervals. Terri's death weighed on me. I imagined her in the corner of my vision. I felt her eyes at the back of my neck. No matter how I turned, she was still behind my head. I couldn't close my eyes at night without her in my room. She floated toward me and asked for permission to appear. I wavered between yes and no. I was covered with chill bumps before I yelled, "*No!*"

I prayed at bedtime, on a bended knee that trembled.

"Just as Jesus is the son of God, so Terri is the daughter of Jesus!"

I sank in quicksand in my sleep. Or I was strapped by rubber bands to a post and forced to move forward, each forward step twice as difficult and if I gave in I'd be slammed and smashed on a mast behind me. I also dreamed often about a three-thousand-pound ball of assholes that rolled from side to side toward me slowly, and sagged under the weight. It backed me into a wall, and pressed, pinned, and smothered me.

I had ducked out of our junior high's end-of-the-year play for no apparent reason.

"I just don't feel like it," I told Mr. Thacker.

"I don't understand why, but I respect your decision."

I had too much time on my mind. I had two single beds in my room. One I used almost like a table to stack books and records on. The other was my bed. My bed was my friend. I stood naked at the foot of it. I had my imagination face on. I shaped my pillow into a pretty head, sort of. I sculpted my cover into the body I was after. My favorite blue blanket that I had since I was five was the centerpiece, and all my white stuff went in there, which I preferred to it flying all over the place. My brother jacked off in the bath tub. To each his own.

When I felt romantic enough, I slid my hand around my bare arm and gave it a squeeze, slowly got down on top of it all and dove in, missionary style. Afterward, sleep enveloped me like a cat's hallucinations.

When I awoke, I stomped on ants in the driveway. I danced up and down the trail and timed it to see how long it took them to forget their dead. I studied them on my hands and knees as I hummed Bix Beiderbecke cornet solos. I had made a tape of Bix solos and memorized them. The ant colony got the job cleared up in less than a half an hour every time and investigated what happened, but they didn't mourn their dead.

I pulled ticks off the back of my neck about once a month. There were so many on our dogs we couldn't keep up with it. They looked like grapes. Grapes loaded with dog blood. Greedy little suckers. They couldn't even crawl, they were so fat. The youth of Malibu placed them on the ground and ran over them with our bikes. They were grey, and the blood popped out thick and red.

We were taught to grab the tick, turn it counter clockwise, and pull it out. It hung in there as you pulled, its head burrowed in. Finally it snapped out and I rubbed my neck. Sometimes I would forget to kill it, and there would be one loose in the house.

Emilio had not enrolled in summer school.

"It's weird not having Emilio here," I said to Mr. Thacker.

"Have you seen him lately?"

"He is with his dad on a movie set."

"Well, do you have any ideas for class?"

"I was thinking of doing a skit about Adolf Hitler just for a geek act." Thacker laughed. I could tell he got a kick out of me.

Fred Grossman had overheard me.

"An interesting notion! Hitler, I mean! I think I could dress you up to look exactly like Herr Adolf, the crazy Fuhrer!" He grinned.

"Oh yeah? Marvy, simply marvy. How did it feel to get the school drama award, Fred?"

"Good. You will probably find out how it feels." I wrote the skit overnight.

Fred walked in with a black raincoat, impressive Nazi cap, and long, black boots in a bag. Hitler never wore a swastika armband, so at least I didn't wear one of those. I had randomly bought a paperback book about Hitler that had a creepy picture of his face on the cover and was a real page-turner. It made me feel crazy. I drew on a Hitler mustache with an eyeliner pencil, and my fairly short black hair already fit the part.

The curtain opened to the storm troopers yelling "Sieg heil." I sat in a chair and slowly stood up. I spoke softly at first and gradually raised the intensity. I quivered and got grotesque.

"Vee shall rrule zee vorld!" I fell back in the chair. The curtain closed, I messed up my clothes and slumped over, exhausted. The curtain opened, and Fred's bomb soundtrack played as the light flashed red. I stood up unsteadily and repeated my speech with a palsied arm and collapsed and slumped in the chair. That was the end. The curtain hurried shut.

I decided to stay in costume for the rest of the day just to get a reaction. I entered Mr. Loyd's music room. Mr. Loyd didn't greet me with his customary hello and he became tense as I carried on a cheerful conversation with a fellow student as if I had jeans and a T-shirt on.

"So, how do you like playing the timpani?"

"It's good! It's got a full sound! How do you like your new cornet?"

"It's astounding! I just love it."

"Get the hell out of here in that costume and don't ever come back with it on!" Mr. Loyd roared at the top of his lungs. He was red-faced.

"Okay," I said quietly, with my hand up. Then I remembered Hitler also put his hand up like that and I put mine down and got out of there. I walked home in full costume.

I wanted my father to catch me in my Hitler costume to throw him off from his usual tantrum. I only undressed when he told me over the phone that he wouldn't be home tonight. I took a hot bath. My eyeliner mustache smeared.

When I toweled off, I checked out my ass in the mirror. I felt cold and went to get my blue blanket. I switched on the light and there was a thick Wolf Spider on the ceiling. I could see the hairs on the spider from seven feet away. I ran with my blanket and got a can of Raid from under the kitchen sink and put the can within five inches of the spider and fired away. It dropped like a parachutist, hit the rug, and scrambled for the door. I leapt back with lame wrists, almost dropped the can, screamed like a girl, and came at it again on my hands and knees. The spider, covered in white foam, slowed down. It shriveled up and stopped within a few inches of my father's bedroom door. My trigger finger pressed the top of the can hard.

"You ugly motherfucker!" I screamed gutturally like Hitler.

On Saturday mornings, I was awakened by my father's mistakes on the piano as he played through the same two classical pieces that had been his repertoire for most of his life. First, he practiced arpeggios up and down the keyboard. Recently he had partially learned Joplin's "The Entertainer" and "Nice Work If You Can Get It" by George Gershwin. He usually couldn't get through five bars without an error.

"JESUS CHRIST!" he yelled, and laughed and pounded away. His blunt fingers crushed the keys like an invasion of privacy.

Or I was awakened by the sound of his rifle shot that echoed down the canyon. My father aimed his rifle and killed mockingbirds on top of our chimney because mockingbirds made the most noise during the night. It was the same gun that he had pointed at my mother's head for ten straight hours one day in 1969. He walked around the side of the house and shot every new mockingbird that perched there. I went in and looked contemptuously at my father.

"Was that a mockingbird?"

"I don't know what kind of bird it was, but he kept me up all night and he doesn't pay rent."

Neither do I, I thought.

Another time it was the Bergmans' rooster.

"You won't be hearing the Bergmans' rooster any more. He sang his last cock-a-doodle-doo." When Mr. Bergman knocked on the door and confronted him about it, he lied.

"I have no idea what you are talking about! Get your *ass* on the other side of the property line *now*, you damned Kraut!" My father was a good shot. He never missed his target.

He took me to breakfast at the Sand Castle restaurant. *The Rockford Files* was in production on the beach. Before we ate, we stood in the parking lot and watched. *The Rockford Files* trailer was always there even when James Garner and the film crew weren't. We never saw James Garner. We saw other actors from the show. The same crowd ate at the Sand Castle. There was Jeff Bennett with his coffee, a well-liked Malibu landscaper who wore a lumberjack shirt and a ready smile beneath a bushy mustache.

We both ordered California omelets, and then my father began.

"Jeff, I had a bad dream about you last night. You walked up to me, and your eyes were completely dull. You were dressed in filthy rags and you didn't have a penny in your pocket. You didn't even recognize me. I peered into your eyes and it was like you were dead. It was… like you pursued this acting thing and got nowhere with it. You were just… really pathetic, if you really want to know. And your mind was just gone."

"Is that how you really feel?"

"Yes, as a matter of fact, I do. You're just a dreamer, Jeff." He shook his head. I looked at him, difficult as it was.

"Come to my shows, then! You're never there to see them.

There are performers who are good. I am one of them! I know you don't believe that!"

"I'm not doubting your talent, Jeff, but there are *hardly any* who make it in that field."

"I am always asking people in school for criticism! I want them to tell me something is stupid, so I can fix it. All they ever tell me is how great it is! That's all I hear coming from a school with more movie stars' sons in it than anywhere else in the world."

He looked down in his plate, snatched the check from the waiter, and walked out with me following.

"I want you to call your mother up and tell her you're going back there to live. This just isn't working."

"No one can force someone to get on a plane," I snarled.

"Hmm…we'll see about that."

After breakfast, I accompanied him to buy groceries at Market Basket, or Market Bastard, as he called it. As we carried the groceries into the house, a gallon plastic jug of milk tore out of a paper bag I carried and exploded in the breezeway, across my shoes. He tensed up ahead of me.

"Don't get me angry!"

"That exploded like napalm," I tried to joke.

Just for that, you are not eating for the rest of the day!" he bellowed. I waited until he took a nap. Then I ate.

ALFRED A. ARTUSO
Superintendent
of Schools

WILLIAM J. DELKENER
Principal

SANTA MONICA UNIFIED SCHOOL DISTRICT

MALIBU PARK JUNIOR HIGH SCHOOL
30215 Morning View Drive
MALIBU, CALIFORNIA 90265

Mr. Jeff Lucas
Malibu Park Junior High

Dear Jeff:

I should like to take this opportunity to thank you for your participation in our Bicentennial program at the Civic Center Sunday, May 16. I was very impressed with your contribution, and it is indeed a pleasure to work with people who are interested in taking their time to contribute to such a community program. Thank you very much for all your extra effort.

Yours truly,

William Delkener

William J. Delkener

WJD:np

A thank you note to Jeff for performing in the Malibu Civic Center, from the principal of Malibu Park Junior High. From Jeff Lucas souvenirs.

Eleven

BICENTENNIAL

Only one student agreed to even try Hardy with my Laurel: a tall, thin Asian named Chris Pac. I had another friend named Robert Mirabilio, and we were close. He was hilarious in the halls. He was a blond Italian with an intense inventive streak. In fact, one night we really did "streak." I slept over at his house sometimes. It was always a good time. He was a real friend. The Looney Tunes cartoon characters and the Marx Brothers were what we went into as soon as we saw each other. But Robert refused to step on that big stage with me. He just became this shy, humble boy in front of Mr. Thacker when I dragged him out there, and I did. My other brilliant Italian friend, Chris LaCagnina, was sort of like that also.

I put a pillow under Chris Pac's coat. In the skit, Stan Laurel can't sleep, and his antics wake up Oliver Hardy. The noise wakes up the bully next door, who chases Stanley until he pulls a white, accordion-shaped, plastic container out from under his coat. Stanley squeezes the container and the cap pops into the bully who doesn't feel it. They run around in a clockwise circle. The bully knocks into a wall offstage and collapses onstage. Laurel and Hardy smile and shake hands and do their head nod.

My father showed up and he liked it a lot. He recognized the gadget I used as a rubber Cool Whip squeezer from our refrigerator.

"I can't believe how you hid that Cool Whip thing in your costume for so long until the end! That was really funny. God, the whole audience erupted," he said on the drive home. We went up the driveway. He just had it repaved and he could now shoot up the driveway with a vengeance.

"… but I think you smile too much as Laurel. You've always got that Laurel grin," he said as we entered the house.

"No, Laurel has a lot of good faces and I try to get them all in."

"No, I think you grin too much, falling around on the stage, but hey…."

My temper glared brightly. "Listen! Don't you criticize me in my act! That's mine! You do your job, and I'll do what I do! What do you know about me up there? You don't know a thing about acting!"

"I'm only offering a small suggestion," he said calmly. I frowned at him ungraciously.

"I can take criticism from everybody but I can't take it from you, not you! You make it hard enough on me already!" He made himself a tuna salad and I went to my room.

(Journal entry)

June 24, 1976

It seems now that the Lynn-Jeff relationship is practically declared. I called her last night with hesitation.

We talked for 45 min. The conversation went absolutely perfect! On the 22, I went to the beach with my T.V. Production class. I had to direct a film about a Seaweed monster that eats Vally clouds. Oh brother! Today we also went to the beach and I did my first starring role for this summer. It seems that Chris Pac and I will do a lot of films together.

Mr. Thacker walked the class down to Zuma Beach to make another five-minute film. He wanted to do this quickly, because he said something to me about skin cancer on his nose. He wore his floppy white hat to keep the sun off his face. The school's large video camera whirred along as I directed. He sometimes let me co-teach when my enthusiasm outweighed his.

When we finished, Mr. Thacker walked beside me ahead of the rest of the class back to school up the small hill

"I've been thinking. I really *believe* that you have an acting ability. You know what you are doing up there, and I believe that any other vocation other than the performing arts would be a great loss to your audience."

"Thank you, Mr. Thacker, very much. You know who I think is good, is Emilio. He is serious about it," I said.

"Emilio is very good to a point. Emilio is a film actor. He's kind of closed-in, with small movements, but he has a much harder time on stage than you have."

"Maybe I move around too much. I'm too big with my gestures."

"No. He'll have a more difficult time making an impression on audiences than you will. It's easier to tone yourself down than it is to have to bring yourself out. And you come across wonderfully on film, anyway."

He had a sincere smile as he walked on my left, and we didn't say any more.

(Journal entry)

July 2, 1976 bicentennial in 2 days.
The bicentennial is in 2 days and I'm not even excited about it like the rest of the world is. I've gotten too involved in Lynn. The thing that I have feared most seems to be happening. I think the relationship is slipping slowly. I know now that I need her very badly and I'm not aggressive enough to show it. All I've been able to do is call her and sometimes speak to her at school. I've decided to invite her some place. The only problem is "where"? I'm going to ask her to go into town with me and a group of friends when I can get in touch.

※

My demented but somewhat stable family parked along the Pacific Coast highway at Broad Beach on July 3, at night. Steve and my father shot off in opposite directions, and I was alone. One overhead light shone weakly across the sand, but I guessed that there must be fifteen hundred people that stood like seagulls at rest. I shuffled around in the crowd, and everyone looked through me like I didn't exist.

Steve McQueen and Ali MacGraw were neighbors of my father's new girlfriend. I had been there a couple of days ago with my father. I had looked out of bay windows as an old-fashioned black motorcycle with a sidecar rode by. The man who drove had more hair on his head than I had ever seen on anybody. His hair looked like a big ball of auburn dust.

"There goes Steve McQueen and Ali MacGraw!" said my father's girlfriend. It was the first time I had seen Steve McQueen, even though I was a slight acquaintance of his son, Chad. My brother had gotten a job at the Gulf gas station on Point Dume and had waited on Steve McQueen. He had never made a movie with his hair like that. The man on this bike looked more like Bigfoot or a caveman.

My father appeared in front of me. Somehow, I was happy to see him.

"You want to go up here and meet Steve McQueen?" he said. He looked star-struck.

"Yes, sure. Who wouldn't?"

"Okay. Come with me." He moved fast. We waded through the dense crowd, and I barely managed to keep up with him.

My memory flashed to Encino in 1966. I was taught to swim in the Ambassador apartment's pool at night. I tried to grab onto my dad's back. I had almost drowned after I fell into the deep end of the pool, out of an inflatable PT boat, and he had dived in and saved my life in front of many onlookers. His back was slippery like a whale as he lunged around. I was pried off every time, my fingernails raked down his back and across his moles. "Ouch, you scratched my back," he said each time. I became a fair swimmer, enough to save myself in rough water.

We ascended wooden steps. The condo was brightly lit. Steve McQueen was slouched at the dining room table, recognizable by the famous blue eyes and cheekbones, and the hair that I had seen when he was on the motorcycle. Everyone else stood in the adjoining kitchen. To McQueen's right, below the table, were about twenty empty, crushed Budweiser beer cans, in a pyramid pile, and a stack of pop tops on the table directly above that. He drank in slow, massive gulps. The sight of the famous cheekbones and steely blue eyes filled me with a calm respect.

My father, his girlfriend, and Ali MacGraw were in the kitchen, and leaned on the counters. My father shifted his weight uneasily and talked about the party down below and other small things. I inched toward a couple of guys who had just entered and talked with Steve McQueen. Then they joined the others in the kitchen.

I wasn't such a big fan of his. One of my brother's favorite movies was *Le Mans*, in which McQueen wore a little "Gulf" patch on his shirt as he drove around a racetrack. I was told that he could fill up all his cars for free at any Gulf station for the rest of his life. My father told us he saw him on Malibu Canyon Road and he passed around him like he was parked.

Mr. McQueen finished his beer and picked up another from a paper case to his right on the table. He cracked the beer can and dropped the top.

"Do you know if we're going there tomorrow? Should I make reservations?" he called out.

"I don't know. If you want to do it, that's fine. I'll go," Ms. MacGraw answered.

"What are you going to do?" asked my father's girlfriend. Mr. McQueen slowly stood up, a bit overweight.

"We're flyin' back east to watch the fireworks shoot off in the harbor. We'd have to get out of here tonight, though. We have to find out about security."

"We can call in advance and work it out," said Ali MacGraw. Mr. McQueen shifted his weight and thought about it.

"Maybe I'll just shoot across the length of the harbor on roller skates!" Everyone laughed. Mr. McQueen stood away from his chair, crouched, and put his right arm out.

"With Ali tucked under my arm like a surfboard!" He acted

it out. My father laughed the loudest and couldn't stop; his face was red. Mr. McQueen sat back down and opened another can of beer. The room had wall to wall windows as big as doorways on all three sides. Each window was black in the night.

I stood in a shadow to the side of the room. Mr. McQueen glanced at me and then away and looked at me again. I cautiously looked back at him. He did that three more times and I figured he must be deep in thought. I moved across the room and I noticed those eyes darted over at me still. Mr. McQueen looked me in the eye and spoke.

"You keep up that acting. Don't ever let it go. Just keep up that acting. You hear?"

Steve McQueen had a voice that penetrated, and everyone in the kitchen heard him. I saw Ali MacGraw look at me. My father stared at the floor with folded arms and a concerned face.

I looked at Mr. McQueen and answered quietly, "Okay, yes, thank you." I smiled weakly.

"I mean it. Keep up the acting," he said. I nodded.

His eyes were clear, his voice and balance steady. Maybe someone had helped him drink all those beers. I didn't know. What a beautiful sense of style he had.

He raised his elbows, stretched and yawned as he stood up. He wore a short-sleeved, faded, Hawaiian shirt and faded Levi trunks.

"Ready to go, Al?" he asked over the kitchen babble. He moved toward the door and I happened to be in his path.

"Are you really going to fly to New York tomorrow?" I asked.

"Huh?"

"That's what you said."

"Yeah. We're gonna have to call and find out," he said.

"That's a long flight," I said, as I reached for conversation.

"It ought to be a hell of a show. *Al, you coming?*"

BICENTENNIAL

"Coming," said Ali MacGraw in her great movie voice. She smiled and strutted across the carpet. They went out the door together and I stood in the doorframe and watched them glide briskly down the narrow, wooden steps. They huddled close with their heads down and arms around each other as they attempted to be invisible.

(Journal entry)

'IN CONGRESS'   July 4, 1976
           BICENTENNIAL EDITION
For countless years now I've hated the present and have only loved the past. I thought all the important dates were over and done. I predict that when future nostalgia kicks get started, this day, July 4, 1976 will be THE day to look back on as the day our America... Land we love under God turned, for the first time, TWO HUNDRED years old. This is not "a" day to remember. This is THE DAY!!!

>>><<<

"McQueen is one of the big, big, stars, you know."

"He sure is. I wonder why he said that to me last night." My father shrugged and looked away.

"I wouldn't be too encouraged by that if I were you. I think he had a few too many."

I never knew whether my father was going out for the night or staying in. It would be last minute. Frank slept over and my father cooked us grilled cheese sandwiches that were thick with cheese and fried dark with extra butter. He handed each of us a plate. They were burned and shiny. Frank didn't want his. My dad stared him down from the head of the table.

"I am going to make you eat it. What do you think about that? You have to eat every bit of it." He finished his and got up and stepped to the other end of the table and stood over Frank's shoulder letting out a one syllable laugh through a septic smile. I had finished mine. We listened to the crunch of Frank's teeth.

He took snapping bites and chewed slowly. He never did eat all of it. Later that night in my room, we sat on the floor in our boxer shorts and t-shirts with blankets around our shoulders.

"Sorry, Frank. My dad is a son of a bitch."

"I'm glad he didn't make me anything else to eat. I can imagine how it gets for you." I rested my neck against the edge of my bed and changed the subject.

"My mind is my only surfboard, and crazy is my waves," I said. Frank's left eyebrow shot up.

Frank's dad was a director of commercials and owned Water Barrel Productions in Hollywood. We followed behind him into a building, past large plants and a life-sized black and white poster of Burt Reynolds nude on his side. Mr. Kratovil's suite was up a flight of stairs, down the hall, and on the left.

"Jeff, why don't you try something in front of the camera? I will give you fifteen minutes to work something out. Then I'll come back, and we'll film you," said Mr. Kratochvil. I turned to Frank.

"Let's act together!"

"This is just you. I am only funny off stage."

A chalkboard and plastic chair were my props. I went to the bathroom mirror to practice Marlon Brando in *The Godfather*. I stuffed my mouth with toilet paper and stuck out my chin to the left. I drew on a Charlie Chaplin mustache with a felt pen that stank.

Bicentennial

"Okay Jeff, it's time to shoot it," said Mr. Kratochvil from the hallway.

Chaplin, Godfather, and Laurel and Hardy, were schoolteachers brought on one at a time to teach a history class. Charlie Chaplin taught his class in silence until he uttered a single syllable, slammed his hand over his mouth, and ran out. They all began by saying, "The first world war..." and never got much beyond that.

All the characters tripped over the chair, but none of them had sense to move it. I had seen my father do this. Mr. Kratochvil laughed every three seconds from behind a large video camera.

He played it back on a TV screen. My timing was good. Mr. Kratochvil laughed about it all the way home.

(Journal entry)

July, 11, 1976

8 months ago (about), I first saw Lynn. The second I saw her I couldn't believe what a goddess I saw. From then on, my mood depended on her. For 8 straight months in a row she was my guiding light. Everything I loved was in her hands. She had power over me. I gave her a note some weeks ago asking her if she liked me. She never answered me back. I figured the reason was she was shy. I started calling her frequently and things went fine. Last night, Joel and I went to her house to spy. She caught us at it and for some unknown reason, as usual, got furious and changed her opinion of me 100%. Joel was by my side as I called her up. When she got on the phone I said, "Hello, Lynn?"

Then she said, "Just a minute," and came back after a while. She then said, "Who is this?" (as if she didn't know.) "This is Jeff," I replied. Then she hung up on me. In shock, I waited a while. And then called her back. This time I was given the air worse than ever. She told me she wouldn't go to the movie with me, that she never really liked me anyway, and that she has found someone new! I've been a wreck ever since the phone call. I suppose I'll continue to be for a long time. But in Ron's words: It's her loss!

⸻

I slept over at Frank's place on the living room floor side by side as usual.

"Do you take your responsibility as my agent and manager seriously?" I asked.

"Yes. I am more of a manager, though."

"Okay, good. Just don't try to shoot my eye out with a BB rifle ever again."

"Okay," he said.

Me, with my insomnia. I unzipped his sleeping bag and hugged him lightly. I glanced up in the scant light through two dark windows. It was quiet and serene. Then I could finally sleep. In the morning he refilled Life cereal into my bowl.

"Life cereal is the best thing I ever tasted," I said.

"I know you want four more bowls, but we have to go shopping. My dad wants to set up another video shoot with you."

"How many more are we going to do?"

"I don't know, but that's what he wants. He thinks you are good."

"Well, hot damn."

BICENTENNIAL

(Journal entry)

July 31, 1976

I was horribly blue with the loss of Lynn to me. I've decided to set girls aside for a while and concentrate on my main goal I was on last year at this time – and that is to catch up to and conquer Tatum O'neal! Frank's dad has a girlfriend that writes movie scripts. She's THINKING of giving me a small part that doesn't require any talent, which kind of hurts I guess but at least it's better than where I am now. She told Frank that she doesn't feel very comfortable around me and I don't like that.

※※※

"Now my Dad said he wants to take acting headshots of you," said Frank. "Saturday at three o'clock; he wants you to meet him here."

"On Saturday? I'll be here. Shit, I hope this goes okay."

On Saturday my father and I argued. "I gave you a camera for your birthday. Why don't you use that instead to have acting pictures taken?" He seldom made gestures with his hands when he talked. His clenched hands looked like they were always ready to kill.

"Thank you for the Vivitar camera, but it's not the same thing. Frank's dad is a professional, and he asked me to be there today."

"Well, unfortunately, I want you to clean your room first."

"I don't know how to clean my room!"

"Don't give me that! I don't care what you are doing today, or the next day, or the day after! Clean it up! And while you're at it, I want you to call up your mother and tell her you're on your way!"

I ran away from him out the door. When the R.T.D. got to

Sycamore Park, I was late.

My orange plaid shirt that I didn't like was wrinkled. Mr. Kratochvil complained about the flat collar, and I offered to come back another day.

"No. We'll go ahead with it. Stand underneath the sycamore tree," he said. I felt awkward but tried hard to look okay. The sun set directly in my eyes and I covered it with branches. The pictures were swathed in shadows.

I got the contact sheet.

"My dad didn't think much of the pictures," said Frank.

"I don't think much of them either. Thank God I didn't get my dad's ugly nose. I kind of like my nose. You have a good nose, Frank."

"I have a *perfect* nose," he said.

There were times when my brother and I were alone in the house, and he was always stoned.

"You are the only un-stoned person I can communicate with when I am shit-faced. That's a compliment," he said.

"I don't like drugs very much," I said.

"I always think you are stoned anyway, natural."

"You're probably right. All my worries are in coming down."

Steve and his Santa Monica friends tied on their headbands for a summer's end party. I was lonely and asked if I could go. We drove to an abandoned parking lot adjacent to the Los Angeles airport at sunset to examine the invention of flight.

A pipe was passed around. I kept quiet and held my breath. I gave in because I discovered that the generation I loved in the 1920s smoked lots of "Muggles," Bix too. I took a long hit and coughed. It went around again, and I took another hit. *It would be great if I could just stand here and look cool and not get a buzz*, I thought. We piled back into the car. I was in the left back seat.

A photo from a headshot session Frank Kratochvil's Dad took of Jeff outside their Sycamore Park condominium. 1976. Photo by Frank Kratochvil Sr.

We went around some corner, and I was hit by five avalanches in a shock wave that was like a bullet through my head. I couldn't move.

When we parked, I was pale as death and panicked by every ingredient in the Universe.

"*All right!*" they whooped and climbed out of the car. I was plastered to my foundation. The sound of my blood blotted out all else. For minutes on end I couldn't talk yet tried to with all my life. I was cold.

"*I can't move,*" came the essence of panic.

"You can't? Well here, man. We will help you!" One guy leaned in, put his arms around me, and pulled me out. I tried to assess the horror and I got on my rubbery legs. To stand there was only just bearable. When I could move forward, they turned into mad monkeys bounding along the sidewalk. They danced in circles around me and took turns making spastic ape sounds two inches from my face.

The party went on like an eternity. I would not come down. Most of the time, I held onto a tall wooden fence in the back yard of the house. Everyone knocked into each other and transformed into a kaleidoscope of confused images. I shut my eyes and it got worse as my mind chased its own tail. I was exhausted and had spastic twitches when I did come down at sunrise.

(Journal entries)

Aug. 10, 1976

Tatum O'Neal has placed herself in my life again. Just like last summer. Oh well! At least it gets my mind off Lynn. Her new film, The Bad News Bears was just released about a month ago. She's now doing a film called

"Nickelodeon." I still think I'm better than her in more ways than 1 and I intend to prove it (as soon as possible)! I will do all I can and face up to anything almost in being her toughest competitor.

They're taking fabulous pictures of Mars these days. I included 1 that I particularly like.

Aug. 19, 1976
It looks like another love has crept into my life again. Her name is Laura Holloers and as usual is only 12. She is friends with the Nicoletti's (namely Angela) and went with them to Del Mar. It just so happened that Mom and Jack also were flying out to Del Mar. I went to them and from them, at a hotel close by, went to her. When I first saw her, my reaction was as quote, "She can ride with me in about 10 years." But after a few hours I couldn't help but to fall for her. Even though I was with her just a day I'm trying to get Bea to tell me I can stay there for a while before summer ends.

August 23, 1976
Exactly 50 years has passed since Mr. Rudolf Valentino died. There was a big gathering today in the Hollywood cemetery. Many who remembered him and even some who knew him was at attendance.

The Winds of Malibu

He began his career in the early 1920s. Before long people could recognize his face anywhere. He was the household word. Young ladies around the globe fell madly in love with him and the gentlemen did what they could to copy his style and elegance. Then came the ultimate explosion when his most celebrated movie was released, "The Sheik of Araby." With that movie a new word was added to our dictionary. The word "Sheik" was heard everywhere and Valentino? He was now the ultimate image of America. But perhaps The Sheik of Araby was too great a hit because just about every movie he did after that was almost identical to it. Only the names were changed.

In the mid-20s, he married a woman who was to wipe him out financially and then divorce him.

His career was slipping slowly and surely and his wife talked him into buying a huge estate which he could not afford and his illness began to show. He developed ulcers and appendix problems. Both of which grew so bad that on August 23, 1926, he barely made it to his car and died on the way to the hospital. He was ½ a million dollars in debt and America gave him 2 of the biggest funerals known to modern man. There has never been another "Sheik" since.

※※※

Against the beige wall at Zuma beach, near Tower 11, I turned up the Bix Beiderbecke on my tape recorder over the breaking waves. I had a notebook and pencil. The pale skin on my body shiny with Coppertone fairly sizzled. I began my autobiography, subtitled *The Story of Jeff Lucas and How He Made It*. Part of it came out in third person. I erased "he" and put "I" instead. The main title was *My Struggle*. Then I remembered that is what Adolf Hitler titled his book in 1924, translated into German, but my struggle was different and one hell of a lot nicer. I wrote the words *Mein Kampf by Jeff Lucas* on the cover anyhow. I couldn't think of another title.

I got through four pages and my head hurt, even though the process was like the slow removal of a spear lodged in me. It was more than I could take to spill it out. The task would have to be left until I was more able.

Steve's friend, Greg Wilson, came by.

"I heard the music before I even saw you and followed it, knowing it could only be coming from one source," said Greg. My lips parted into a proud smile. He sat and listened with me.

"How is your brother? I haven't seen him in a while."

"I haven't been seeing much of him either. He's hanging out with the Santa Monica crew these days. I'll tell him you said hi." Greg sat with me through three recordings of Bix Beiderbecke with the Wolverines; a scratchy retake came to an end and the next scratchy retake began.

"Big difference," he said.

I counted the half hours the day before school started. My father drifted out of his room in his cashmere sweater, hands in his pockets to the knuckles. He moved with the dust in the living room toward where I sat on the couch with his disintegrating face looking down and a Beethoven frown.

"There is never any change. One generation just passes its poisons on to the next. It just keeps going," he said somberly.

"Isn't there any way to turn it around somehow?" He shut his eyes.

"No. We are helpless to it. One generation bleeds right into the next, ruining our children's lives forever. It is a no-win situation." He turned and settled back into his room.

I had no center piece to fit in the hole of the 45 rpm record "Tell Laura I Love Her" by Ray Peterson, so I tried to balance and center the record with my fingers as it spun. It was one of those dramatic songs. My dad stared at me in my doorway as the record lost control and sounded warped. He laughed at me. He laughed louder than the record. I wanted my moment and tried again to play it and he laughed harder. It went on and on. I shut the record player off and, on my back on the floor, closed my eyes, and only played the song over in my mind.

(Journal entries)

Sept. 14, 1976

Last night was the 14th anniversary of American Graffiti. Tonight marks the end of an era. That era is the summer of 1976, the era of pure nostalgia. As for me this summer was a kickback time. I was bored a lot, the 4th of July wasn't as good as I wanted it to be and it went too fast. The best time I had was at Del Mar in Aug. I sent off a letter to Laura today. I think it was a little too korny. This 9th grade year will be very hectic for me. I know it will.

BICENTENNIAL

Sept. 15, 1976
Lately I've been getting very nervous stomachs every night. I don't know what my problem is! I've a feeling 9th grade won't be as tough as it seems. My schedule is pretty easy. BOY, is my stomach NERVOUS! I passed Lynn 1 time today and all I heard was "Oh my God!" in disgust. But what the hell.

※

I was forty minutes late to school on most mornings. My schedule put Theater Arts first period. Mr. Thacker scolded me.

"Marilyn Monroe also was always late, even though she was the best actress at the studio. People would not forgive her. They eventually got rid of her. So it's very important to be on time."

Emilio was not there at the outset of ninth grade. Nobody knew anything, and I hoped that he hadn't moved away. Maybe his dad had finished that movie in the Philippines and he was now on another movie set with him. What did I know about Hollywood?

A few weeks into the semester there he was at the edge of the parking lot. He looked at me and shook his head slowly but didn't say anything. I put my hand on his shoulder.

"You made it," I said, and we walked to our PE class together in silence.

Coach Bennett had the class going over wrestling techniques. He gave the whistle a short blast when wrestling commenced and two short blasts when a headlock was achieved. Halfway into class, I saw him smirk and find me.

"*Lucas!*" He would always draw out the "s" when he said my name.

"You fight Flaherty. Let's go!"

Big Flaherty had been my main bully in seventh grade, and he was still a lot bigger than anybody else. He was the same quick-tempered guy with the look of someone who had been held back a few grades. Flaherty and I got along okay these days because I made him laugh a few times, but that wasn't much of a reason to show any mercy.

Flaherty's feet dug into the blue mat. We circled four times. He was hairy, and his teeth were yellow. I eluded him, and he tripped over himself. I jumped over him. The class laughed as I ran around him fast in circles like Groucho Marx.

Flaherty faced me and spun around and got dizzy. He finally sat down and put his chin in his hand. The coach blew furiously on his whistle, but the class laughed and applauded too hard to notice. Coach Bennett turned crimson and waved his arms. He looked like he wanted to kill. I stood in one place so the class would calm down. The coach shook with rage and glared at me.

"This isn't a stage, Lucas! Turn in your suit and go sit in the dean's office!" The class unanimously booed. I walked out of there and changed but stood at the top of the main steps until the third period bell rang.

Emilio laughed and shook his head.

"I can't believe you did that. That was great! The expression on Bennett's face was priceless!" For days afterward, he laughed about it to me. It seemed Coach Bennett went easier on us wimps after that.

Emilio was relieved to be back. It reminded me of my own return to Malibu. He looked like he had gone through experiences none of the rest of us ever had. He held his head more still on his shoulders at all times, and he had kind of a deep look to his eyes now. Everything about him appeared like he had grown up. I didn't pry, and Emilio didn't go into details about his summer vacation.

"Is your dad still working on that same movie?" I asked him quietly.

"Yeah! It's turning into kind of a mess." He sighed and rolled his eyes. I looked at him and he rolled his eyes again. There was silence. He rolled his eyes a third time and slightly shook his head, as if to say; no one would believe me if I told them about the summer I have just had.

(Journal entry)

Sept. 23, 1976
This is the first night of the debate between Jimmy (all Smiles) Carter and Jerry Ford. They were really at each other's throats throughout the whole thing.
I keep telling dad that there is something really wrong with me but he keeps telling me it's nothing.
        Dear LORD
      Please keep me going
      Until I'm old and gray.

     Don't let this corrupted
     childhood finish me off.
        Jeff Lucas

>>><<<

My friend Kevin Wilson was the best part of band class for all of us. He was the son of comedian Flip Wilson and one of the few black people in our school. He got on a roll as the professional class clown, and we couldn't laugh hard enough to get it out of us. The teachers all loved him, and he was the only student who was allowed to disrupt class any time he wanted. He was *that* funny, and his timing was that good! Kevin played tuba at the back of the band, and he disappeared in the middle of class once. We looked for him for half an hour and gave up.

"I want to show you the instrument that I can play," said Mrs. Honey, the substitute teacher. She walked over and opened one of the big green cupboard doors and there was Kevin Wilson in a pantomime jam on the stand-up bass, with his eyes closed and his head in rhythm like he was into some jazz!

Emilio leaned over to me in Thacker's class.

"Have you seen the movie *The Comic* with Dick Van Dyke yet?"

"No, I have not. Is it good?"

"Yeah, it was! I think you should see it."

"I will, then, I will," I spun my wrist in circles as I balanced on the back legs of my chair.

Over the next week, he asked me, "So, did you see the Dick Van Dyke movie yet?"

"Not yet."

"Dad, I was wondering if we could go see a movie at the Malibu Cinema."

"When? Tonight?"

"Whenever you like, as long as it's still playing there."

"All right. What did you want to see?"

"It's called *The Comic*, with Dick Van Dyke."

"Okay. Let's go." He put his newspaper down and picked up his keys. He seemed almost cheerful.

"My friend Emilio from school suggested I go see it. You know, Martin Sheen's son." He clenched his jaw and got ready more slowly and glared at me. I didn't know what was up, and that was the way he wanted it.

"Are you glaring at me?"

"Maybe I am."

"Well, knock it off."

"No, I won't"

The Comic was about a 1920s comedian who becomes an alcoholic. The most memorable scene is when the comic drives his car into his own mansion and up a flight of stairs. Dick Van Dyke does a Dr. Jekyll and Mr. Hyde act, and I wondered if mine was better. It was hard to tell, because his act was so short in the movie. I could really draw that skit out. There was so much you could do during the transformation from one to the other,

The movie ended, and my father and I went in the men's room together and stood at two urinals side by side. He glanced over at me.

"Don't do that."

"Do what?"

"Lay it down on the porcelain like that when you pee."

"I'm not. It's in my hand!"

Someone in a closed stall beside us farted loudly. It echoed across the men's room. My dad stared ahead and farted louder. The guy in the stall floated another one. My father blasted another. We laughed quietly. It went on and on. The farts were loud, the laugh was quiet. They took turns, the two of them. They were not high-pitched ones, either; these were low growlers in short blasts. My father laughed hard and all the gas came out of him and the guy in the stall let it all out at the same time and both of their farts built to a crescendo.

"Thanks for the concert," I managed to say.

On Sunday, I listened to every Bix record that I owned in chronological order. My father put up with it right up until Bix's most famous solo in "Singin' the Blues."

"Jeff, I don't know whether this is some marathon of yours that you think you have to listen to, or what!"

"Your mouth sounds worse than your ass." I muttered so he didn't hear me.

"I want it off!"

"Just let Bix Beiderbecke finish this solo."

"Shut it off! And I don't even want you listening to that garbage when I'm not around! Don't let me hear it when I am coming up the driveway! Now turn it off!" I shut it off. It would be easy for him to destroy my records, just break them into pieces. I could so easily picture him doing that.

A new student named Nanette Sachar proved that she could act as soon as she got on stage. Mr. Thacker found a one-act play for us to do. Nanette portrayed a little girl who made up imaginary friends because her family gave her no attention. I was the imaginary friend, known as "Clown." The play ends at a family dining room table. The imaginary friend says goodbye to the girl because he decides that he will no longer be needed in her life. The Clown bows out and the girl is ready to move on and grow up. Rehearsals took up most of the class period for a week, and our classmates were given small assignments to keep them busy. Or else they could, in Mr. Thacker's words, "watch and learn."

"Hey Dad, Martin Sheen is making a new movie that should be really interesting. It's called 'Pa-crop-of-tits,' or something like that."

"Huh, interesting," he said.

"Who is your favorite actor?" Emilio asked.

"Rudolph Valentino."

He smiled. There was a pause. "I could ask anybody I know, and no one would give me that answer. Why?"

"I live in the 1920s, in my mind. I can't help it, and Valentino's face embodied the era. If Bix was an actor, I would say Bix. Who is your favorite actor?"

"Marlon Brando." I nodded as if to say "Good choice." "I thought maybe you were going to say your dad."

"Him too, of course."

"Is your dad still working on that same movie?"

"Yes. It is a *huge* production."

"I know you have told me the name of that movie seven times, but I keep forgetting the title. Write it down for me." I gave him my notebook and pencil.

"Okay I'll spell it. It's called, A-p-o-c-a-l-y-p-s-e…and then the word, 'Now' after that."

"A-pock-al-lipsy."

"*Apocalypse Now*," said Emilio crisply.

"*Apocalypse Now*."

Martin Sheen went on an evening run at the junior high track. I saw him nod his head and say "Hi" to strangers before they could say "Hi" to him. He said "Hi" to me and I said "Hi" and stopped and watched him run past me. He was friendly, even though I knew it was a difficult time.

"Do you think maybe *Apocalypse Now* will never be finished and be discarded like his Bix movie was?"

"No, they are *going* to finish it. They *have to*," said a serious Emilio.

(Journal entries)

Oct. 2, 1976
Yesterday was Lynn's birthday and talk about coincidence, my No. 1 movie was on TV. "Paper Moon" with THE Tatum O'Neal (I always saw a resemblance between

the two). Lynn was eating at her usual spot in the cafeteria with her fat friend, Monica. I passed her with my arms full of lunch and stopped short at the end of the table. I turned slowly to face her, my D.A. shining in the light, I bent slightly over the table, smiled a little and said, "Lynn" (pause), she looked up surprised, "Happy birthday." And with that I nodded. She nodded the same way I did. But so much for that. In a little while, I'll be going to the doctor for these terrible stomach problems I've had lately. I'm a little nervous about going because it seems like there are so many things wrong with me!

Oct. 1976
For stupid reasons upheld by my dad, I didn't go to the doc. So I have to wait again. I wrote my mother today. I think I will go back to Alabama when I enter high school in '77. There's a new girl in Drama who's finally proved herself competition against me. Her name is Nanette. I'm doing a big production with her now about a clown (me) and a little girl (her). I think we will really go places together. My first 9th grade dance is Friday, I might ask Lynn to dance.

※※※

No Lynn at the school dance. Even Frank hadn't shown up. I walked back outside to get away from the Led Zeppelin song, "Stairway to Heaven," and saw a white car pull up in front of the school. Emilio got out of the back with a girl I recognized: Marsy Nichols. I was about fifty feet away, but he looked like he'd had a few drinks. He was well dressed in long pants and a nice white shirt. He looked upset, and I thought maybe I shouldn't approach him. She walked through the gates ahead of him.

Marsy walked directly up to me.

"Hi, Marsy."

"Hi Jeff. Are you alone? You shouldn't be." She didn't look bad at all, and I wondered if she had mistaken me for someone else. She took my arm, and we strolled toward the direction of my home.

"What are you thinking about?" she asked.

"Thinking about you, really."

"*Jeff!*" yelled Emilio twenty feet behind us. He walked up and separated us with his hands. He was wild-eyed, and his hair and clothes were mussed.

"Marsy, go stand over there. I've got to talk to Jeff alone. Just go! I need to talk to Jeff!" She stood quietly fifteen feet from us by the lunch tables. Emilio walked me in the opposite direction.

"Look, she is trouble. Trust me as a friend. She poisons everything she touches. I'm tellin' ya because I love ya, that's why!" He hugged me tightly, then walked away. "I mean it," he said over his shoulder.

"Yeah, but Emilio, I just wanted to get...."

"Stay away! Take it from me!" he hollered, and then he was out of earshot.

"...laid," I said low. I glanced at Marsy and then back to where Emilio had gone. I shrugged my shoulders and walked away from Marsy and left her there. I headed toward home. I glanced back at her. She wore an old-fashioned long light-blue dress with a cloth flower on the lower back, her blonde hair was braided up, and her hands were folded in front of her.

Nanette and I could hear Emilio's uncanny laugh out there as we performed our play. I entered from stage right unhindered by gravity. I floated along, masculine like a father figure. At the dinner table where the girl was ignored, I sat invisible and delivered lines that helped the girl's self-esteem. I felt a good sense of timing from both of us at the end where I left her and tiptoed out backwards, and bowed out silently off stage right.

They applauded, and I walked down from the stage. Emilio rushed up to me at the bottom step. He had tears in his eyes and stared at me and spoke slowly, almost whispering.

"That was the best thing you ever did… I mean it… the best thing ever… it was unreal." He shook my hand and held on to it.

"Thank you, Emilio. Coming from you, that is the best compliment I could get." For the rest of the day, when I looked at him, he shook his head and smiled.

"You wanna do a scene together?" he beamed.

"Yes indeed! How about a skit about flying an airplane? How would that be?" We pulled up two chairs.

"I play a senile World War One German fighter ace that flies recklessly because he wished that he had been killed in the war and you are my copilot and student." We got our classmate, Lisa Teel, to play the stewardess who interrupts us and ends the play.

"Mr. Thacker told me we didn't give enough notice, so we aren't going to have a big audience."

"Why?"

"He said that takes a long time to prepare, and he doesn't think we are going to be able to find a time slot."

"I hate him; he's an asshole."

"He's all right." I smiled.

"Yeah, he is."

We performed the airplane skit in the auditorium in front of a seventh-grade class of about fifty students, and they loved it.

Mr. Thacker laughed the loudest. Two chairs faced the audience, and we rigged a curtain behind us. I took the plane up and down and Emilio acted woozy. I spoke in a German accent, and Emilio used his own voice.

The audience was at a fever pitch when Lisa made her entrance through the curtain early and cut us off when we were going great. Emilio and I winced and slowly looked at each other at the same time with one eye shut as our audience laughed their heads off.

Mr. Thacker enjoyed it so much that he had a hard time forgiving Lisa.

"Jeff, why don't you have a little talk with Lisa and teach her *how to act*," he said angrily. Lisa and I took a stroll outside the back of the auditorium together.

"So, how do you act?"

"Well, you see, it's like this: You have to have this kind of awareness of your own presence on stage and then you feed off the other characters, sort of. Project it to even the farthest one out there in the audience."

"What do you mean, 'feed'?"

"I mean, like chewing… I don't know what the hell!" I spun back toward the auditorium. "It's always been natural to me. I don't get it when it doesn't go good for everybody else."

Twelve

WANT

(Journal entry)

Oct. 20, 1976
Steve, Ron, the master supplier Dave Meador and maybe Andrea's brother, Chris Allgreen are getting ready for a typical teenage turnout. And what a crazy one. Steve has staged a marathon type endurance test by running from Trancas to Santa Monica (23 miles!) They plan on leaving here at about 1:00 or 2:00 and make it to school at 9:30 am. This is the worst part - They actually think they will make it.

⇶⇶⇶⋘

WANT

My three favorite Bix recordings were "Sweet Sue" by Paul Whiteman and his Orchestra and "Jazz Me Blues" and "Royal Garden Blues" by BIX BEIDRRBECKE and his GANG. I tried to get Steve into the music of Bix Beiderbecke and Paul Whiteman. He bent an ear with his bandana in place. He pretended he got it, but he didn't get it. My father would never get it at all. When we were in the driveway in the car together, I found some jazz on the car radio.

"Now, just tap your foot to the rhythm and fall in love with the *syncopation!* That is the way to begin to like jazz, dad. Tap your foot to it." I watched him tap his big, ugly foot on the floorboard of his car and he could not keep the beat and his face looked like the music wasn't playing.

Adam Shapiro was not as sensitive as his father Steve Shapiro, who was Newsweek magazine's cover photographer. I did appreciate his eccentric style though. He idolized Harry Houdini in a way that even surpassed my love of Bix Beiderbecke. He looked a lot like Houdini, with intense eyes. And he was, for his age, a brilliant magician.

(Journal entry)

Dec. 12, 1976

I've been getting some bad vibes about writing in this book up till now. I can't understand why either. I guess it's because almost everything is going so good. A 13 year old magician, who never has appeared in this book before has drastically changed my life - all for the better of course. His name is Adam Shapiro (Amazo). He is the best magician I have ever seen and that's not all. He also has 1 hell of a lot of connections into show biz. He knows Tatum O'Neal quite personally along with

tons of other stars. We are putting together an act with the slogan - 'Entertainment at its best !' The Magic Castle is soon to come.
Jeff Lucas

⸺※⸺

I thought about the relationship between Emilio and his dad as I walked home from school for Christmas vacation with my report card. Thacker had made sure to give me as much of an A as a student could possibly achieve, and the rest was as low as a student could get except music was a C. My hand trembled with another D notice. This time it was from the attractive blonde, Mrs. Honey. I tried like hell to talk her out of it. No soap.

There was an invisible barrier around the house. A spell of hatred.

I couldn't do it anymore, not once more. I sobbed, yet straightened and braced myself. Couldn't I just forge this? I wavered on dirt clods at the edge of the driveway. He was due home.

I clawed the air with my hands and gritted my teeth.

"I can't do this. No! I can't. No!" I whimpered. If only I knew a form of self-defense, I would knock him on his ass. His wheezing motor made the climb again. I ducked out of sight with my back against the garage wall. I listened to him get out and stomp into the house. I went in to face him.

"Dad?"

"Hello."

"Hi. Could I have a few karate classes?"

"No."

"Please?"

"No."

As he was going through the mail, l I handed him my D notice.

"So, again you have the nerve to give this to me. You have the nerve to hand me this gosh-damn crap?" His head looked like a boiled potato, and he took up the whole floor of the house with his legs.

It was almost comical that he could get so worked up for such long stretches. It was easy for him. He was merely working out. It was a faucet that he turned on, and if he didn't turn it on, it turned itself on. I took it all. If I stayed on the couch, he wouldn't hit me. It was if I tried to get away from him that he slammed me back down on the couch, hard. He stood over me a foot and a half from my face for hours and let it go.

He screamed louder, because he could tell I wasn't quite there.

Slumped, I crawled back inside my brain as deeply as I could. His spit became snowflakes. I looked to my left and clearly saw Bix Beiderbecke there in his tuxedo as snow fell gently around him. There was a brook beside him to his left. I watched him blink his eyes. He was calm and nice. I took a step toward him.

"Where is your cornet?" I asked. Bix raised his right hand and waved gently at me with a little German smile.

"Damn you! Let Puke take care of you!" I was dizzy. He waited for me to come to my senses before he lunged over me and started in again.

"I am not signing it this time! You will get expelled from school, and I hope you do so that we can do MORE of this together!"

As night fell, he went outside, came back in and did his yoga exercises in the living room. First, he stood on his head. Then he got on his knees and stretched back on his hands.

"Dad, are you going to throw me through the sliding glass door?" I asked in all honesty.

"No, not quite that bad."

I got up from the couch and got his father Eugene's bathrobe out of his closet and put it on over my clothes. I knew it never helped when I wore that robe, but I felt perversely crazy and it was a 1930s antique with art deco designs. He signed the D notice on the table, put it in the envelope, then stood over me and whipped it into my face. I removed my hand from my right cheekbone, a dot of blood. It rested by my leg. I sat still as he paced from room to room.

"Do I remind you of Mom sometimes?" I asked calmly.

"Yeah…yeah, maybe you do."

My mom had flown in for New Year's Eve.

"This is great! I can't believe you are in town!"

"I'm here, honey. I have decided I am leaving Jack. John and I are going to live here in California from now on. I am going to have to start all over again, but I want you with me."

"But how are we going to survive? What about money?"

"You don't worry about that. We'll be just fine. All I know is I want you with me, honey."

"I am sure she will be selling her box to get by!" yelled my father from the kitchen.

She picked me up in a rented car and we drove to my uncle Paul Nicoletti's mansion in Northridge. I brought my diary along and spent the day with my cousin, Angela, and Laura Holloers, who looked like a brunette Tatum O'Neal. In the evening, the adults drank, laughed, and danced in the kitchen to "Sh-Boom" by The Chords and then they played a 1950s red jazz record by Earl Bostic. They all piled into a few cars and drove away somewhere.

The entire mansion became quiet. The lights were still on. I had the place to myself. I noticed a dozen bottles of alcohol left out on the kitchen counter. I chose Bacardi Gold with the bat on it. I swallowed gulps of brown rum straight out of the bottle.

I got my sacred diary out of my back pack in the living room, savored the weight of it in my hand.

"A boy's best friend should be his diary. God bless Terri," I said to the empty dining room. I took another swig and clutched my gut. I went to the refrigerator and poured milk into my mouth from the carton. I drank milk between swallows of rum.

I went into the TV room with the bottle. I felt light, like my feet weren't quite on the floor. I noticed a bronze wall plaque. My speech was slurred when I read it aloud.

"To all my critics. When I'm in a sober mood I worry, work, and think. When I'm in a drunken mood, I gamble, play, and drink. And when my moods are over, and my time has come to pass, I hope they bury me upside down so the world can kiss my ass." I copied it down in my diary and drew a curvy frame around it.

I opened the front, double doors of the pillared Nicoletti home and pretended that it was my house and that I was a famous Hollywood actor. I leaned in the doorway and opened my diary to the last page under December 31 and scribbled away in a messy scrawl.

(Journal entry)

December 31 1976 12:09

Happy New Year I'm drunk as hell The bicentennial is out the door and it can kiss my ass. Laura Holloers was jolted when I put my arm around her. I first put my hand on her hair and she got up and told my cousin Ang. what happened and Angela told her to sit by me and without any hesitation, she did and I put my arm around her but she didn't move a peg. Then she got up cause she had to leave. I'm Jeff and going to marry Laura Holloers.

The Winds of Malibu

>»«<

Then I blacked out. The sun was up, and I was on the couch in their living room, my stark naked body covered with a blanket that I didn't recognize. My clothes were bunched in the middle of the floor, ten feet away, with my socks inside out on top of the pile. I could hear the adults in the kitchen talk about the horse races at Santa Anita racetrack. I vaguely remembered masturbating. I sat up and put my feet on the floor.

(Journal entry)

January 1, 1977, at the Nicoletti's.
I've been having the strangest of moods lately. From depressed to moody to sort of happy. Right now I feel terrible. I think I forgot to mention I'm at the Nicoletti's if you hadn't already guessed. I got here Wed. at 8:15 pm. Things went as follows. I had to tell Margaret and Stacy Kim from band class about it and they were overly encouraging and told me to be "warm, gentle & aggressive. Things just didn't go as planned or maybe they did. I don't know? All I know is that I spent all 3 days and nights with Laura on my mind. The one big night was Thursday. Even with me being shy, her silent hinting (or at least that is what I took it for at first) persuaded me to make my move on her. Angela was on one couch watching TV with Laura, me and Bridget on the other.

>»«<

When I got back to Malibu my father stood in the center of the living room.

"Our neighbor, Frank Allgreen, is supposed to be stopping by to wish me a happy new year. He's had cancer, you know."

I was wearing a $4.95 T-shirt that I asked my mother to buy for me. It was a deep red and just said HOLLYWOOD on it, with klieg lights on the top, and framed with little black stars. My father kept staring at it silently and his scowl grew worse. I went to my room, took it off and stashed it in my dresser drawer and slipped on a long sleeved striped shirt instead. I sat on the couch.

There was a light knock on the kitchen door.

"That must be him."

"Hi. Would you like to come in?"

"Hi, Paul. No, thanks; I just stopped by. I just had a couple of big ones."

"Yeah, gee. Cancer, was it?"

"Yep. They think they got it all."

"How are you feeling?"

"I'm getting stronger. How are you doing? How is Jeff?"

"Steve is doing fine and Jeff… is *okay*. He is trying to pursue acting, no matter how much I try to discourage him." He half laughed.

"Some of them make it! There are a lot of big names who live in Malibu! He should run with it if he is interested. My daughter, Andrea, says Jeff is really good!"

"Yeah, well, I am sure he is, but even with his aspirations, the odds are terribly against him, I'm afraid. I pretty well know how this stuff goes because I grew up in it, unfortunately. So, how is Helen?"

"Oh, fine, fine. Well, I just wanted to wish you a happy new year, Paul. I'd better continue on my walk."

"Well, thank you very much for stopping by, Frank."

"Bye, Paul."

My dad snapped up five Kleenex tissues with one hand, leaned back into his big brown recliner, and sneezed loudly.

"Kazuntite."

"Thank you." He swiveled and looked at me.

"So, Jeff… how is your acting going? Have you met any more acting friends?" I cleared my throat.

"There is Emilio Estevez, Martin Sheen's son. He is still the main one, and there is a new girl named Nanette, and a magician named Adam Shapiro. He is good at what he does. I'll have to see who else comes along."

He blew his nose on my last word, spun around, and tossed his snot rag into the waste basket.

"Okay, let's vote as a class, to see who will emcee this year's Talent Show!" Mr. Thacker announced. "All in favor of Emilio, raise your hands." I was the first to raise my hand. Emilio got eighteen hands out of twenty-four. Every female voted for him. Mr. Thacker counted them quickly and mouthed the numbers. "Eighteen hands, okay. Now all those in favor of Jeff, raise your hands up." Every hand went up, mine too, and Emilio's. "Okay, twenty-four," he said, not surprised. "Jeff, it's yours."

Mr. Thacker called me over to him.

"You are going to create the theme and do the coordinating for the entire show. You also have the privilege to do one of your solo numbers and write yourself into any of the selected acts. You have carte blanche."

"Wow… thank you," I beamed. Mr. Thacker kept a low key look on his face and shuffled papers.

I caressed my first love letter and smiled to myself. She signed her name "Jade" and wrote down her phone number. She was

WANT

a seventh-grader with red hair and looked enough like Tatum O'Neal, with a round face and a lot more freckles.

(Journal entries)

Jan. 13, 1977

The 1977 Talent Show is due soon. I will M. C. and do a Bix Beiderbecke number. I've noticed that I'm getting kind of sick and tired of Shapiro. He reminds me of a genius mad scientist who's willing to step on anybody to get discovered. A girl named Jade is head over heels about me. This is the first love note I've ever received but hopefully not the last. Recently I've been feeling quite nice about life which is certainly a change!!!

Jan. 21, 1977, Friday

This 1977 may be my most exciting year so far! Things are going just fine and getting better as time goes on. Though I'm still kind of a disturbed kid. TONIGHT another landmark! I went on my first date!!!! And frenched for the first time — it was DELIGHTFUL! She was Jade Kulka. I went to the Malibu Cinema and saw Marathon Man. I was scared at first to do anything but then I said to myself — "I could just sit here and do a lot of "wheat" or I could get off my ass & do SOMETHING!" I'm awfully glad I did and so was she. I hope to God that things continue to look up!!

I was halfway through a pepperoni pizza square from the cafeteria. Kathy Kendal approached me with her big-lens camera on a strap around her neck. She was one of Emilio's admirers. I didn't know what she could possibly want with me. I waited for her to talk.

"Jeff, I want to do a story on you, okay? Everyone in my journalism class wants me to do it. So, I am going to need your approval."

Touching my pointed tongue to the tips of my fingers, I said, "Thank you, Kathy! You got it."

I had never considered taking journalism. Kathy and I leaned on a metal rail as others went past into the blue-walled kitchen line. It always smelled like cheap pizza and burnt tamales in there. She asked me a couple of questions and I was so flattered that, out of politeness, I asked about her recent trip to Bethlehem, and there went the rest of the lunch period.

The next day, when Kathy met me and asked more questions, I answered them and kept on the subject.

"How do you feel when you walk on stage?"

"Quite excited."

"Are you scared?"

"At first, yeah, I am. But then there is a bolt of electricity surging that happens. It's like it whooshes out of the clouds. A sense of timing rolls in, I'd say, and then I feel the moment."

"You feel the moment," she wrote down, cracking a smile.

(Journal entry)

Jan 25, 1977, Tuesday
Jade called me up Sunday and asked me if I would go to her house in Paradise Cove with the same couple

we went to the movies with. I did. I've noticed that a woman matures a guy. Jade is what I need right now. She gives me the love I need. It almost seems like there is a battery inside me that needs refueling every few days to stop me from getting depressed and heart-broken. Her way of refueling is petting around. It's my favorite thing to do but every time I do it I want more the next time. The M.P.J.H.S. newspaper with "MY STORY" should be coming out Friday.

Super Star Lucas. Great M.P. Actor
By Kate Kendall

Nostalgic is the word for ninth grader Jeff Lucas. It would have to be for everyone who fantasizes about living in the late 1920s and early thirties, prefers jazz to rock, idolizes Rudolf Valentino and Clark Gable and is famous for Charlie Chaplin spoofs. Don't be fooled, behind this wiry, crackly voiced exterior is a shy, good natured, but firm personality whose ambition in life at this age is to become a serious actor as well as a comic. He considers himself a cross between Stan Laurel and Jerry Lewis and suffers from perpetual stage fright. Anyone who has ever seen him perform knows he's an undeniable presence. Like many performers he doesn't understand the reason behind his success. When asked, "In your own opinion how good are you?" he simply blushed and replied modestly, "Well I get a few laughs now and then—but I have a long way to go!" That's the mark of a star!

AGE TWO   THE SURFRIDER, JAN. 28, 1977

History Of A Unicorn
By Teri Swearingen

The dictionary defines the unicorn as—a fabulous animal with one horn, cloven hoofs, and the tail of a lion.

During the Middle Ages he was a symbol of purity. He was a big beast but because of his purity he could be tamed by the touch of a virgin. Also because of his purity the horn (and rhino horn) was used for medicines, and as a protection against poisons. However, a rhino horn cup was experimented with and the result put an end to the superstition. Even so, in France in '89, instruments made of unicorn's horn were used for testing the royal food for poison.

The unicorn hasn't existed since Noah loaded his ark and the unicorn, who was playing, was left behind. Was he really?

Messages To Sweetheart . .

Do you have a problem telling your "beau" how you feel? Well some people do. Here are some of their letters. Ready carefully because one of them may be directed to you!

Dear Sweetheart!
You're the cutest basketball player at school. I like you.
Signed,
Your biggest fan

Dear Sweetheart:
My love she abounds me, my heart she does fill. I couldn't live without her, but she's moving to Abbeville. So please tell her that I love her and put in some x's and o's She's the one that wears a collar and has slime around her toes.
Thank you,
Forlorn

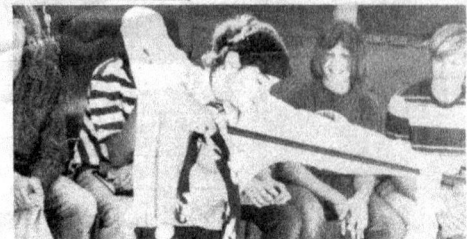

JEFF LUCAS DANCES gracefully before an audience of interested students in the Greek theater.

A Century From Now— Will Earth Be Here?
By Dan Koontz

One hundred years from now, what will it bring? By the time we celebrate our tricentennial, where will we be? Looking back at our country's heritage we see great courage in our leaders and people, recognition of lessons learned the hard way, but we feel pride in what our country has developed into. If we want to continue to move ahead, we must look and plan for the future.

In less than a century we have come from the Wright Brothers to Apollo. Don't be afraid to use your imagination a bit. We will need to look ahead into:

ENERGY—☐ The world's supply of liquid petroleum will be exhausted, and we will be totally dependent on synthetic materials and liquid hydrogen for air and ground transport.

SPACE—
☐ The space shuttle, said by some to be ahead of its time, will be the "Model-T" of our space transportation system.
☐ A scientific base will have been established on the moon and all of the planets of the solar system will have been explored by automated spacecraft. Probes will be on their way to Alpha Centauri.
☐ Military weapon systems will have become so sophisticated, so expensive, and so overwhelming in destructiveness, that they will be finally rejected by world society—or maybe we won't even reach 2076.

Students Resolve . .
By Kathy Burright

Did you make any New Year's resolutions this year? I've been asking people what their's was. To my surprise I've discovered a lot of "perfect" people who don't need to make resolutions. Then again I've heard a few real strange ones like—resolving to slay a few dragons and promising to be perfect. I've also heard some very original ones, such as—disproving Einstein's theory and inhabiting a deserted island.

Remember, it's still not too late to make your resolutions.

Superstar Lucas Great M.P. Actor
By Kate Kendall

Nostalgic is the word for ninth grader Jeff Lucas. It would have to be for everyone who fantasizes about living in the late 1920's and early thirties, prefers jazz to rock, idolizes Rudolf Valentino and Clark Gable and is famous for Charlie Chaplin spoofs.

Don't be fooled, behind this wiry, crackly voiced exterior is a shy, good natured, but firm personality whose ambition in life at this age is to become a serious actor as well as a comic. He considers himself a cross between Stan Laurel and Jerry Lewis and suffers from perpetual stage fright. Anyone who has ever seen him perform knows he's an undeniable presence. Like many performers he doesn't understand the reason behind his success. When asked, "In your own opinion how good are you?" he simply blushed and replied modestly, "Well I get a few laughs now and then – but I have a long way to go!" That's the mark of a star!

Whole World In His Hands

Do you know the story of Atlas? He was one of the Titans in Greek mythology. When the Titans were overthrown, Atlas was forcefully elected to hold the heavens on his shoulders.

Myths have it that he is still down there supporting the earth. I'm sure you've heard about the big earthquake that everybody is predicting, that is because Atlas has his pinky finger under California and he always gets cramps there. He says he is sorry for shaking us up all the time. After all he has been through the Ice Ages and two world wars. We only invented Arthritis Pain Formula and Geritol a few years ago.

The SURFRIDER is published by the journalism class, Malibu Park Junior High School, 30215 Morning View Drive, Malibu, California 90265.

EDITORIAL STAFF
Editor-in-Chief .... Avril Cline
News Editor .... Diana Short
Editorial Editor .... Robin Brees
Feature Editor .... Gillian Karp
Sports Editor .... Teri Swearingen
Photographers .... Drew Digby,
                          Kate Kendall
Reporters: Kathy Burright, Emilio Esteves, Kari Hendler, Daniel Koontz, Lisa Olson, Scott Sparks, Lisa Teel
Adviser .... Mrs. Davida Fonner

You Have Got To Be Crazy!

By Lisa Teel and Teri Swearingen

What would you say if someone came up to you and said "Zeforbs?" He went around the school saying this word to people to get their reactions. A word like this does take some people by surprise. One answered, "Is there a hidden camera somewhere?" and another replied offensively, "I didn't do it!"

Some people say "zeforbs" are food. For example, someone asked, "Does it come with cream cheese?" "Soggy croutons?" "Chocolate covered fingers?" "Black marshmellows?" "Cow clods?" and one grossed out gourmet druled, "Pig snouts!"

Do you like "Zeforbs?" A few people are fond of them. There's one person who answered, "If 'zeforbs' are half as good as I think they are, the whole world should be filled with 'zeforbs'."

What exactly are "zeforbs?" Well they are, "a new kind of whale," "a Cat in the Hat," "A new kind of breath mint," "pitchforks," "doorknobs," "fire hydrants," "lizard teeth," "alligators biting their tails," and "dragons."

They are other animals too. They are zebras, a little mongoose, and gorillas, according to the students at Malibu Park.

Some thought we were pretty strange. Some people asked us, "Are you trying to prove something?" or told us, "You're wacko!" and "You're slightly wierd."

Whatever zeforbs are, they're popular. As one zeforb lover said, "I want one." But the most common answer to this word was "Huh?" So don't be surprised if sometime, someone comes up to you and says, "Zeforbs!"

An article about Jeff in the school newspaper. Public domain.

WANT

(Journal entry)

Jan. Fri. 28, 1977

I was in a pretty bad mood today until I saw the write-up Kathy Kendal did on me. The headline read "Superstar Lucas - Great M. P. Actor." On top of that - I had my picture taken on that Halloween day I dressed up like Clark Gable.

TRAGEDY An overnight star is on his deathbed after shooting himself in the head because of a marriage problem. He's best known from Chico and the Man which was an immediate success. He had many fans and friends and will probably become a legend. This tragic man is Freddy Prinze.

※※※

"Now, move forward, Tommy!" Today was another lesson. I taught Tommy Pringle how to ride a bicycle at no charge. We had been at it for hours on my father's driveway. He rode slowly, and the front wheel jerked around, but he stayed upright.

"I am damn proud of you, Tommy! Now it's time to do stunts!" I took the handle bars and smoothly rode down a narrow slope along the driveway. "Now you try!"

"Oh, gee, I don't know."

"Come on now, Tommy! *You only live twice!*"

"Sean Connery!" grinned Tommy enthusiastically.

"That's right, Tommy, Sean Connery!"

I positioned the bicycle and Tommy sat up there. Finally, he leaned forward and went for it. The spokes turned a little.

"Balls to the walls, everybody! Here comes Pringle! You

can do it, *my Creation!*" I leaped around the driveway with Frankenstein exuberance as I twiddled my fingers together and shook with maniacal glee. My eyes looked crazy. With much concentration, he gripped the handlebars, his eyes wide behind those taped glasses. He made it; he even remembered my instructions to swerve to the left at the end when he got to the ice plant beside the driveway.

We turned our heads and froze at the sound of a familiar engine that tore up the driveway. My father got out of his car and eyed us both with a sober glare. He glanced at Pringle, and his face momentarily had the look of someone at a hideous freak show. Then he looked back at me and his face returned to a mean scowl.

"Come inside, Jeff. I want to talk to you." I followed him inside, and Tommy walked his new bicycle home.

"I found you a shrink… a psychologist. He is somebody I know, and he gave me a good price," he said in a low monotone.

"Oh, that. Maybe I don't need one now."

"Oh, I think you do. I am *sure* you do, in fact. Something is *very* wrong with your mind, quite frankly, so I would appreciate it if you would go."

"Look, Dad, I made our school newspaper with my acting ability!"

He took the school newspaper and read every word. There was also a picture of me "dancing gracefully" above the write-up. He handed it back.

"That's very good. You got any homework?"

"I've got… some." I went to my room. He opened the door as I sat on my bed.

"I'll be coming with you on your first visit. After that, you'll be taking the bus to see him once a week."

"Where is it?"

"Santa Monica."

"Let's celebrate my acting interview! How about cooking those artichokes you got?"

He went in and put water in the pressure cooker and dropped the artichokes in. We listened to the steam escape from the pot until they were ready. He melted the butter and poured too much salt in with it. We ate them one apiece. They were good. I watched him concentrate as he bit into each leaf, down to the heart. He had a gap in his front teeth so there was a line in all the leaves that were piled on a separate plate. I ate my leaves upside down.

After dinner, we were both still hungry. He had cereal and I had a toasted bagel. He noticed among the dirty dishes the remnants of the artichoke butter; a bed of green salt.

"Hey, why don't you use this for your butter?"

"There's too much salt."

"Bullshit! Here!" He spooned all of it onto my bagel. The green salt clumped crystalized half an inch thick.

"Dad, could you eat that? How can you expect me to?"

He tensed up frenetically. "You're gonna eat it, and you're gonna like it! Don't make me angry! Now eat every bit of it, or you're going to be in serious trouble!"

"All right," I said. I always spoke quieter in hopes it might calm him down. It never worked. He pointed his thick finger.

"If I come out here and I find out that you didn't eat all of it, I'll be furious!" He disappeared in his room. I ran outside to the edge of the mountain, stomped one foot down into the valley and threw the two halves of the bagel as far as I could.

I never knew how to throw a ball, but I did throw that bagel all the way to the other side of the canyon.

My psychologist looked like Napoleon Bonaparte. He even brushed his hair forward. He stood about five foot five. My father and I sat on two different couches. I drew breath to speak. My dad talked instead.

"I have very guilty feelings towards my mother," he said.

"Oh?"

"Yes, she asked me when I was a little boy if I would be upset if she divorced my father and I said, 'Oh, I would be so ashamed. I wouldn't be able to face either of you ever again.' So she stuck with him, even though she shouldn't have. He was such an old, bitter man, much older than she was. I forced her to stay with him, which was terrible of me."

My father had slunk down on the couch as the psychologist yawned. They never got around to me at all during that first visit.

He did the same slow yawn no matter what I told him. I was his last client of the day. As I talked on about my painful thoughts, he was bored out of his mind. I never liked to bore my audience, so I started telling him about Bix Beiderbecke. That perked him up a little.

"Our session is up," he interrupted just before his mouth stretched into a long, hard yawn that continued until I walked out the door.

On the bus ride home as we went down the Santa Monica Incline, I sunk entirely into the realm of Bix Beiderbecke like a Disneyland ride that takes you into a new room full of surprises. The rest of my environment got dimmer, lesser, and was a distraction. I decided not to fight it. My kinship with the deceased jazz player, almost fifty years dead, seemed like the only human being I could relate to. Steve had given me a large, red jacket that was too ugly for him to wear. I took a thick, black pen and wrote BIX BEIDERBECKE on the back of the jacket. Beneath that, I wrote THE KING and underlined it with a curl.

It was three sizes too large. I wore the jacket a lot.

"Why are you wearing that? It's ugly. C'mon! Take it off!" growled my father, seizing the zipper.

"NO! The jacket stays!" I tore it out of his hand. He backed off and thoughtfully held his chin sizing me up.

On the way to my shrink, I gravitated into a Santa Monica bookstore, even though I was late.

"Do you have anything on Bix Beiderbecke?"

"Who?" asked the five store clerks. One of them stepped around and lifted up a newly arrived, thick, yellow book, a paperback titled *Bix – Man and Legend*. I didn't have the $5.95.

"Please hold that book for me! I will be right back!" I ran to my shrink and asked him for the money. He unbuttoned his coat and reached into his shirt pocket and pulled out a five and handed it to me.

"I've got to go. I won't tell my old man I left early, if you don't."

"Okay," he said sleepily.

"He looks like Napoleon." I smiled at the receptionist.

"I know he does." She smiled back. I danced to the bookshop. It felt like there was an electric current between that book and myself.

I imagined what Bix would do with various melodies, even David Bowie or Led Zeppelin songs. Wherever I happened to be, I played the improvised solos in my mind. I got scared, because I couldn't stop the music. It was real.

I wrote an essay about Bix's life and read it to all of Mr. Loyd's music classes and all of Mr. Leonard Vincent's Social Studies classes and all of Mr. Thacker's classes with a slide show, and two of Bix's songs: "Big Boy," and "I'll Be a Friend With Pleasure."

"He looks like a vampire!" said a girl as she looked at the blown-up slide of him in the dark.

And to think, Bix's life story was almost made into a movie

with Emilio's dad as Bix! If he had done the Bix movie, maybe he wouldn't be involved in this *Apocalypse Now* movie. I considered possible titles. My favorite title was *In a Mist*. Bix's music had a unique eerie quality. I found out that Bix had devoted fans worldwide, but it was tough to find anyone near fifteen years old to share it with.

I didn't notice Emilio ahead of me. We would have collided if he hadn't sidestepped.

"What is that, your Bible?" he said. We stopped. I glanced down at the yellow book, looked up at him, and we both smiled and continued on our own way.

We were in the school library together, and he sat beside me as I read my Bix book. I read three sentences and sat back to let it sink in quietly.

Greg Sully was in our grade. He was as good at physical comedy as I was and he could do a few things I couldn't. He refused performance of any kind though except for class clown. Emilio and I sat and watched him do his usual routine of standing at a bookshelf and swallowing air and swallowing air and swallowing air and then he opened his huge mouth and out cascaded the loudest, longest, wall-shaking burp ever. When Emilio and I had finished laughing we caught our breath and resumed our conversation.

"I know about a musician who died who I think is great," said Emilio. I looked around for a bookmark as I didn't want to damage my precious property by turning over a leaf. Below my chair was a small red strip of construction paper, bullet-shaped. I picked it up, blew on it, and marked my place.

"Who is that?"

"Jimi Hendrix. The best guitar player who ever lived."

"He was? And how old was he when he died? Bix was only twenty-eight."

"He was twenty-seven," said Emilio.

"Are you sure?"

WANT

"Yes. He wasn't twenty-eight, he was twenty-seven."

"Twenty-*seven*? That's hard to believe. How could anyone make a big mark like that and die so young? You have to think about it because what if we croaked early, you and me, Emilio? What if we died like Bix or your Jimi Hendrix? What kind of mark would we leave? I think about that."

He mulled that over.

(Journal entry)

Feb Thu. 17, 1977

Career wise, my life is shooting skyward. Some days ago I was asked to gather some talent show fruits together for a show in front of boy scouts and the parents. I had a lot of response at first but when the night of the show came, there were 4 performers, all of which will make the big time soon enough. Amazo was one of us — then Greg Allen played a bumble boogie on the ivories. Then John Ufland and I did The Dentist's Office and I finished the show with the "Sugar Blues" and "That's My Weakness Now." In the middle of my dance number I spotted the great Mr. Emr in the audience, laughing his heart out. After the show, he came up to me, looked me in the eye and said, "I've got a dance solo for you in my next movie.

I REALLY think I'm going to make it.

⇶⇷

I danced the mile home in the cold night. All the winds of the earth blew in my favor. I glanced behind me at vast misty clouds above the ocean.

The curtains in my room were colorful illustrations of the fanciest 1920s cars in profile and from the front. The most beautiful cars in history waved in the Malibu breeze. I dreamed I owned each automobile. I raced each automobile through different cities of the world.

(Journal entry)

Sunday Feb. 20, 1977
I'm lying here on my bed in the middle of the day thinking about my career in front of me. I've always thought that the most important thing to me is to be vividly remembered, but I'm not only going to be remembered for my work but for my reputation as well. All my life I've lived in the past and particularly recently I've been in a roaring 20's craze. As I was looking at the cover from my record The Great Gatsby, and as soon as my acting money comes in, that is how I'm going to live. I will be a Sheik and my wife a Sheba.

⟫⟪

Staring at a Bix record spinning, I fantasized Bix Beiderbecke as the most famous star in the world. These were newly discovered recordings of Bix on cornet that sounded worn out, like they were coming over a radio station in 1931. It was an album on a label called Nonesuch.

I envisioned, as the album played, that it was Bix's last concert. It had been advertised for months and the world was listening through advanced radio technology. The tone of his cornet was tired, but it was Bix, and nothing was better than Bix. My eyes were wide.

WANT

I envisioned the next decade in my life to be another 1920s utopia, where the greatest artists in all the fields would blend together perfectly in a Hollywood environment where true genius could reign once again.

I would be in my twenties then, and I would join that echelon somehow as a performer of some kind. I envisioned young, brilliant performers like a band of 1920s musicians. It would be youth and exuberance.

I clenched my fists in a prayer for this to happen.

The last song Bix performs is "Deep Down South, take two." Bix collapses soon after the red curtain falls, and dies three hours later, at age twenty-eight.

My wrap-around bowtie was almost worn out. Still, the only place that sold wrap- around bowties was costume shops, never a tuxedo shop anywhere. I had to make this one last. The fastening hook slipped out, and the bowtie went crooked. I got ready for the talent show. The morning had been a forgetful mess.

I held on to a new Styrofoam straw hat down the muddy path. I forgot my cue cards I had worked on last night and turned around and hiked the mile. Got to the house and couldn't find them. I ran back to school.

Doom was in the air. I could see various classes line up in the halls, and I sprinted to beat them to the auditorium. I bumped into acquaintances, and they were all so nice.

I saw nervous anger in Thacker's face. He had never been mad at me, and I felt bad as he frowned into my eyes. I rolled into whatever would make it the best show.

"I don't have my cue cards."

"I will write the acts down for you, and it's up to you to write your dialogue!"

He had wanted a dress rehearsal that morning, but I was featured in seventy percent of the talent show, so the workshop had to wait for me. He gritted his teeth. I saw his mouth form the word *"Motherfucker!"* five times as I scribbled three half sentences on the back of his list. I heard the audience file in. I did my usual peek through the curtain. Thacker leaned closely in my ear and yelled harshly, *"They're all yours!"* I jumped in the air, and my thumb poked my eye. It was just a little pimple of tension between a teacher and a teacher's pet.

Every student, the faculty, and some parents, were out there. Curtain time, and I walked out. The timing was on a deformed path and I tried to recover it. After I had announced the 1920's, the audience rose to the usual Jeff Lucas pitch.

"That's My Weakness Now" was more varied a dance number than "The Sugar Blues." I could mouth along to some great syncopated vocals done by the Rhythm Boys as I strutted and jumped over my cane forward and backward. I didn't have dance skills like Fred Astaire and Gene Kelly, but I held a trance over the audience. They applauded through the roof in the middle of the song. The Paul Whiteman Orchestra boomed as brilliantly as Led Zeppelin's "Trampled Under Foot" had at the last school dance. I licked my lips.

"Here we are in the 1970s and relationships just don't work out, so….How many of your parents are divorced? Mine sure are. Here is a skit with Lisa Teel and myself to tell ya where it is." The audience talked amongst itself and by the end of the skit when we stare each other down behind a worn-out couch, we lost them.

Shelby Basso was Lynn Craig's best friend's mom. She looked like a cozy mom. Shelby had become my confidante and kind of a mother figure, and she knew I loved Lynn and she helped me with that. She told me how my emcee job had looked.

"It wasn't that bad. You just looked like you were on drugs."

"I printed something for you. This reminds me of you and your dad," said Frank in my bedroom. He handed me a sheet of paper. For a long minute there was silence between us.

It was a cartoon of a hawk with talons out and beak wide open as it swoops down on a scrawny mouse in a bare field. The mouse stands calmly on its hind legs and flips off the hawk with a swollen middle finger. At the bottom of the page reads the caption, "The Last Act of Defiance."

"Thanks. We have just got to keep going." Frank nodded solemnly. I taped it up beside my bedroom door. Malibu was getting worse and worse. Frank would not be able to save me.

My father appeared in the bathroom doorway as I slicked down my hair 1920s style. Best of the Talent Show was due to start in three hours.

"I decided I don't *want* you doing so many shows. You are doing too much acting, so until I can see some improvement from you in your other studies I *want* you to stop all this. You are just getting carried away with all this nonsense."

"I'll graduate and make it to Santa Monica high school just fine," I informed him.

"I'm not talking about graduating! I'm saying I don't want you to continue this! I guess you didn't hear me!" He leaned in the doorway, eyes ablaze. I put the hairbrush down.

"Dad, I've got quite a few people depending on me tonight to be there for this show. It's been planned. Let me just do this." He clenched his fists and slowly moved down the hall. He slammed the breezeway door and left for the night.

I straightened my bow tie and Steve came out of his room.

"You need help getting ready?" The sound of our dad's car grew distant. We went into my room and he straightened my left pant leg over my sock and smoothed out my shirtsleeves.

"Thanks for helping. You don't have to do this."

"That's cool. I'll probably be doing it for a living one day anyway."

He stepped back and looked me over.

"You're a real party animal, Little Luke."

The performance made me feel good—another standing ovation. Afterwards, I went into the audience and an old, thin woman held my hand. I was enchanted watching her old lips.

"My name is Peg Doos*e*. I have been wondering who to give my father's record collection to, and now I know. I will give you my telephone number and address."

I phoned her the next day.

"Come over and I will give you the records, all of them."

"Come by right now? All right." She lived in Paradise Cove, in the same trailer park that Sam Peckinpah had lived in.

Then I remembered the news event of the week; all RTD bus drivers were on strike. There wasn't a bus to take anywhere in Malibu or Los Angeles. I slowed my pace as I tread over dirt clods. "What the hell," was what Bix used to say and I agreed with Bix. I would just walk the whole way there and back. I went into the even, swift, famous Malibu pace with the level head in quick steps. Move with purpose, like Lawrence through Arabia, with lots of thoughts, fun thoughts,. It occurred to me that I could never get depressed so long as I had a show to work on.

Upwards on the Point Dume incline, I slowed my pace. Paradise Cove is still a trek after you pass Point Dume. I arrived and the mobile homes still all looked alike. A crowd of men in their eighties crossed in front of me. The oldest one asked me, "Hey, hey. Do you know where the main drag is?"

"There's a larger street down that-a-way," I said with 1920s youth and vigor. They liked that.

The mailbox said Mrs. Peg Doose. She answered the aluminum door quickly and showed me the records. She sampled one

WANT

on her turn table titled "The Copper and the Gunman".

"I even have one Enrico Caruso. It goes way back the farthest." They were mostly in good condition and from the mid-'20s, or before with two from the '30s. There were nineteen records in all.

"Oh yes. You can have them. I already know you can appreciate them."

"Absolutely…thank you. I am very grateful." The records weighed easily thirty pounds collectively, and I knew about 78 RPM records. If you dropped them two feet off the ground, they broke. I took my time. I was afraid the records might get warped, so I attempted to shield them from the sun as I carefully walked hunched over. When I got home, I placed them on my bed and just hugged them.

(Journal entries)

Tue. Feb. 29, 1977

It looks like Amazo's career is well on the way. He was asked to do 3 TV specials saluting Groucho Marx. Naturally he accepted and he said that he has been trying to get me on the show. He says this weekend we will go to Marx's house (I guess) and give them an idea of my talent and they're supposed to dream up something that revolves around Groucho for me to do. It all sounds crazy to me but exciting all the same. I'm not getting my hopes up too high. I'll do the Sugar Blues and Dr. Jekyll and Mr. Hyde.

Tue. Feb. 29, 1977

Well, the talent show came and went. I think that the '75 was better. I was M.C. for the show and did a dance number called That's My Weakness Now. I talked to Mrs. Emr the other day and she said that I positively will be in their low budget film called Buckaroo. It's rated G and I will be doing a dance solo with a little boy who sits there and doesn't open his mouth. They'll begin filming in about a month or 2. I think that will be real neat and it might launch my career off too. I got nineteen 78 RPM records from Mrs. Doose Sunday.

Jeff entering his room after a school performance.
Photo by Steve Lucas.

WANT

My 78 RPM record collection: "Carolina Moon" by Emil Velazco, vocal by Scrappy Lambert, ukulele and organ accompaniment. "Home in Pasadena" by Al Jolson, with "Mr. Radio Man" on the flip side. "Painting the Clouds with Sunshine" by the Benjamin Franklin Hotel Dance Orchestra. "I Can't Get the One I Want" by Ben Bernie and Orchestra. All recorded in the 1920s. They were all so good. Their sound was visual. They were not just a disc of wax in my hands from that time. The labels in the middle of the records spoke beautiful volumes. I got lost in and was stunned by their glory. When I put the record player needle on the fast disc, I breathed in the syncopation, a solid trance of love. An absolute connection.

I checked out Beethoven's Ninth Symphony from the Malibu Library and rested on the couch as it played. My father entered the living room and added his two cents with his index finger up as the second movement rollicked.

"The second movement of the Ninth has been described as sounding like a giant skipping through a forest. I think that is the best description I have ever heard," he said.

"Yes, I can visualize that." For the rest of my life, I could never listen to the second movement of Beethoven's Ninth Symphony without the vision of my father skipping like an idiot through a forest.

Then I listened to George Gershwin's symphonic works brought home from the Malibu library when my father came out of his room again. His hands were stuffed halfway into his jeans pockets.

"You are still listening to that goody?"

"Yes, it's almost as good as Bix Beiderbecke."

"It was considered a tragedy when Gershwin died. I remember when Gershwin died… but it didn't compare with music's greatest loss, which was when Mozart died."

"I see."

It didn't happen too often, but I managed to calm him down when we listened to classical music in the car on errands, and it was a pretty good moment together. He popped my leg with his open palm as a sign of a good mood.

"Ow!" I laughed, when he did that.

He listened to his Brahms and Mozart in the living room. I sometimes sat with him.

"To think of the treasure trove of classical music that you will be hearing for the first time in the decades of your life to come, I envy you. I really do," he said in a dignified manner after a crackly record ended.

WANT

On various nights when the weather was calm, I hooked up a fifty-foot extension cord and listened to my record player and rested on the chaise lounge chair under the Malibu moon as it glistened across the sea. I played an album of light classics titled *25 Most Beloved Melodies*. The music settled clearly across the canyon. The gentle ocean breeze made me envision 1920s high romance. My father came outside and briefly stood there beside me.

"You've got it all set up out here."

"Yes," I said. He listened for a minute. Then he slowly went back inside the house. That was as close as we ever got.

Thirteen

Mr. Thacker's first period class settled in and I got there before Emilio, which was new. The door flew open and Emilio entered with heavy steps, terribly upset and dazed. He looked like he had slept in his clothes. He hyperventilated, fell into his desk chair and leaned back. He was reclined in his desk chair, with his head back, his eyes at the ceiling. It was so unlike Emilio that no one had the courage to speak. His eyes were wide, he was pale, and I was the only one who stared at him ready to help. He was right next to me on my left. The whole class had stopped.

He breathed a little slower and then yelled out to the ceiling, "My dad had a heart attack on the set!" He looked as though his entire life was about to cave in. Mr. Thacker was the first.

"Is he going to be all right?"

Emilio raised his head. "They don't know!" Mr. Thacker looked away to the left and shuffled some papers.

D

"When was it?" I managed to ask.

"*Yesterday,*" he said. He did not look at me; he looked at the ceiling and continued to half-lie there. He was too distressed to say one more word for the rest of the class period. Mr. Thacker told us all to read a book quietly. Emilio leapt out of his desk and ran out of the room when the bell rang.

"Jeff, come here, please." Mr. Thacker motioned me over. "Do you know what's wrong with Emilio?"

"His dad is Martin Sheen, you know."

"I know that." He nodded.

"His dad has been filming the same movie since… I don't know how long. It just goes on and on and on. Something is up with that movie. It is not…the average movie. That is all I know. I think it is unlike any film that he has ever been in."

Mr. Thacker nodded. "I will keep an eye on Emilio and see that he is all right."

"Yes, do that," he told me.

Emilio was shocked and silent the rest of the day. The next day, he was quiet and depressed. He sat still and stared straight ahead into space during lunch and didn't eat. He did not smile once. For the first time, he was inactive in PE. He sat out against the gym wall on the ground, still in his street clothes, with his head down and his arms crossed. Coach Bennett went over and said something to him that I couldn't hear, and Emilio glanced up at him with a closed mouth. Coach Bennett walked away from him. We all left him alone.

A few days later, he slowly walked up to me and nodded his head. I nodded gently back.

"They *think* he is going to be okay. His heart attack happened in the Philippines, and it wasn't as bad as they had thought, at first."

"Whew…I don't know what to say. If that had happened to *my* dad, I probably wouldn't have felt as bad…as all that."

It was then that I realized that the bond between Martin Sheen and Emilio Estevez was far stronger than any father-son bond that I had ever seen. They truly cared about each other's feelings.

We all read the *Surfrider* school newspaper, and if I saw Emilio mentioned or written about in there, I clipped it out and saved it. I didn't have a scrapbook. I saved mementos in a paper grocery bag just like the one I put my cornet in. Emilio could make me laugh. He was easier and more comfortable to be around than any friend I have ever had. When he sneezed in school, he yelled "HorseSHIT!" If anyone irritated him, he did this great pantomime where he loaded bullets in the cartridge of a handgun, put it to his head, and pulled the trigger, the gun flew out of his hand. I started doing it too.

He had a quiet intensity. The classroom was never as quiet as when Emilio performed a monologue. He had this low, mystical energy that pervaded the classroom. We all felt a sense of calm that stayed with us for the rest of the day.

We both did the same monologue from *Requiem for a Heavyweight*. I did mine first. I tried to puff out my arms and chest. My acting was exaggerated, and I got a lukewarm response. Then Emilio walked in front of the class, sat down, and performed the role much better. I comically sank in my seat and gave a red-faced, sheepish grin to the class.

"Look at Jeff's face!" laughed Eric Lovaas, next to me. Mr. Thacker laughed, too.

(Journal entries)

Tue. March 15, 1977
I think my life has turned over a new leaf – this time for sure. It sure was unexpected. I was working on

D

a play in my drama class about a week ago with Lisa Teel. And we got to talking about each of our lives and I told her all about my hard life at home and that I was painting the clouds with sunshine all the time. She told me that her story made her feel sad and the next day she wrote a poem about it. It was really quite good. Today she really straightened me out and knocked some sense into me. First, she suggested some hobbies to occupy my time while I'm alone and for every suggestion that she said, like becoming interested in a sport or something, I said, "Nah, that's not for me." Then she suggested joining the Marines!! And to that I said a loud no and said that if they ever tried to draft me, I would move to Canada! She said that was the most cowardly thing she ever heard of and that my problem was that I was too lazy. I stewed over that one for a while and then sadly agreed with her. She told me something that I will never forget. She said,

Lisa's law

If you don't feel any pain from working, then your efforts are being wasted.

PAGE TWO   THE SURFRIDER, APRIL 1, 1977

Emilio Estevez Has Ooomph!

By Kate Kendall

According to those who know, Emilio Estevez, our blond and deeply tanned ninth grade boys' vice president, is a lover. Watch Emilio's face light up when he talks to a girl and you can see what they mean. Emilio is a very sexy person. He is also a gentleman.

Besides his reputation as a ladies man, Emilio is just as well known as an actor, and that we can judge for ourselves. As an actor, Emilio is outstanding. He is so talented that it is difficult to understand how he can be so good so soon.

Emilio gives much of the credit to his father, Martin Sheen, one of the screen's finest actors, for coaching him. Emilio says that his father, whom he regards as his best friend, has given him the opportunity to gain first hand experiences on movie locations around the world. This association has permitted him to observe some of the most gifted performers and directors in the business.

EMILIO ESTEVEZ, aspiring actor, poses Burt Reynolds style for fans.

Jeff snipped this out of the school newspaper and kept it. Public domain.

D

March 1977

Today was Bing Crosby's 50th anniversary in show business. I like to think of him as working with Bix Beiderbecke as he did when he first started his career as a singer for Paul Whiteman in 1927.

March 25, 1977

The girl that was the most common thing in my life is starting to make a comeback. Who else but LYNN CRAIG. Shelby Basso, a lady who has become a good friend of mine and is Monica (fat friend's) mother volunteered to help me with Lynn. So it looks as if it's starting all over again. This time, with hope, it will be successful. Wouldn't you know it, there's a dance tonight at the school and Monica's mother said that I should ask her to dance—both fast and slow! That is going to take about 1000 more nerves than I have. She also agreed to take me home next to Lynn. This will either be a breakthrough or a downfall.
 EVERYTHING FELL WITH A HORRIBLE CRASH.

※》》》《《《※

Emilio and I talked about our future at Santa Monica High School.

"They've got bigger facilities for us. I've heard that," he said.

"Maybe they've got decent acting teachers too. We've both got to keep an open mind. Who knows? Maybe someday we'll be Academy Award winners like Art Carney!" I smiled, and he laughed.

The Bix look. Photo by Steve Lucas.

"My dad couldn't believe he won for *Harry and Tonto*."

"I know. You told me," we laughed.

I told Emilio how far I had hiked to get those 1920s records.

"Sometimes, I'm close to your house when I'm up there… spying on a certain girl. I walk by and count all the Citroens in your driveway."

"Yeah, my dad collects 'em." He smiled.

"I love Citroën cars. That's what Richard Dreyfus drove in *American Graffiti*. Have you ever met Richard Dreyfus?"

"No. Why don't you stop by?"

"It's okay if I do?"

"Yeah, you can drop by the house any time!"

A few days later, I did. I knocked quietly. A man who looked like Martin Sheen, but not quite, answered the door, and he didn't quite sound like him either. I figured the heart attack might have physically altered Mr. Sheen.

"Hi, is Emilio home?"

"No, he isn't right now. May I leave a message for him?"

"Yes, would you please tell him that Jeff stopped by?"

"I sure will. Thank you, Jeff. Bye-bye."

"I stopped by your house and your dad said you weren't home right then. How is he feeling?"

Emilio laughed. "That was my dad's brother you met at the door. He's staying at the house while my dad recuperates. I was over at John's house when you came by."

"Oh."

My father hadn't signed another D notice. He set a higher level of antagonism.

"I am not giving you any more haircuts until your grades improve, since you like them so much."

I went to the window and adjusted the curtain so that light fell on the wall in one precise beam like a cross with no arms, that moved and shifted when the trees moved, something like a shaman's dance. I felt an impassive silence between us which was, in its way, more frightening than when he blew his stack.

"Want to join me for a walk?"

"Not really."

"Come on! Let's walk!"

We headed down the driveway together, him slightly ahead. Malibu looked sad. The way the wind blew hard across the grass and trees toward the top of the mountain and mingled with the sound of the mighty, soft crunch of the ocean.

"How is your job going?"

"Oh, I think I can do quite well with it. It's somewhat difficult right now, but I think once I get used to it, it should work out quite nicely. Thank you for asking."

I pushed the stupid excess hair out of my eyes and looked at him. "Listen, I was thinking maybe we could try something more constructive in dealing with this D notice."

"I've already thought it all carefully through. I am not allowing you to walk on any stage or to act in anything, not any production, nothing, until I see straight A's out of you. I know I have threatened that before, but now I am going to vigorously enforce it. I won't be satisfied with what you're doing, Jeff."

"Do you really mean that?"

"Absolutely I mean it, and you bet I will enforce it! I don't want you appearing in anything until I see a vast improvement from you. I have put up with this laziness of yours long enough."

"I am acting with Martin Sheen's son, and we are making progress together, we are both working on being Hollywood actors together someday!"

I stopped, and he continued his big steps ahead of me and didn't look back. We were on the dirt trail that led off of Philips Avenue. I watched him stride into a charcoal sunset. When he was 50 feet away, I wrung my hands.

"Why do you always take away everything I love?" All I could see was the back of his head.

"Because you are not doing well in school!"

My mind was numb. I was pale and nauseous. Emilio looked enthused. He had brought two scripts of a play from home and handed me one.

"This Pinter play, *The Dumb Waiter*, is a two-hander."

"A who?"

"A small production. It would be just us. No one else on stage."

"Okay, let's do it."

I read it over. It was a heavy, brainy play for two adult characters, Ben and Gus, who were in a basement. There were no time lapses, just one continuous stream of consciousness. I would be Ben, the older experienced hit man, and Emilio was Gus, the younger protégé. We told Mr. Thacker about it together.

"Okay. I will find you an audience," he told us cheerfully. Emilio knew that I did better with comic roles.

Mr. Thacker kept an eye on us, interested in the chemistry. I felt lazy in rehearsals, and my mind wandered. We read from the script and we got distracted and looked up and saw the Carradine girl walk past us with a nice wiggle in furry boots that went up to her knees and short shorts.

"And here comes Puss-in-Boots," I said to Emilio. He got a good laugh over that.

My copy of *The Dumb Waiter* had penciled in script ideas that might have belonged to Martin Sheen and for a bookmarker there was a card from Donald Pleasance to Emilio's mom. I rehearsed lines by myself outside of the house. I paced around and went over it, read three sentences, put the book down, and spoke the three sentences out at the ocean. In rehearsal, I forgot my cues. We went over it all the way through once or twice with our noses in the script when we got together.

I got home from school and put my books down and accidentally placed *The Dumb Waiter* on the dining room table by the phone and left it there.

"*Jeff!* What is this? You remember what I told you—no more acting."

"Do you want to know who that booklet there belongs to? Martin Sheen, that's who. Do you know who Martin Sheen is? *The real* Martin Sheen!"

"Don't talk to me like that, Jeff. I know who Martin Sheen is, and you know it."

"His son asked me to do this play with him, and it is a difficult play to act in, and I believe Martin Sheen would like to see if Emilio and I can do this play together in front of an audience at school. Will you help me with it a little bit?"

He stood back and placed his hands on his hips, sighed, and focused on a list of business phone numbers in his personal phone book. "Martin Sheen, huh?" he said under his breath as he dug some food out of his back tooth with his tongue.

"This is a difficult play, Dad. Will you help me with my cues, please?"

"And what makes you think I'd want to do that?" He put thick-sliced jack cheese between two buttered slices of Orowheat bread.

"Because Emilio and I will be performing this play whether you help me or not, and Martin Sheen is going to hear about how it goes."

"Well, let me think about it then." He flipped his grilled cheese sandwich over in the pan.

I waited until he finished. I watched him lean over his food at the head of the table. As he was about to move toward his room, I said, "Just a few lines with me, Dad, please?"

He did an about-face and we both pulled up a chair at the dining room table. He sat to my right. I handed him the Pinter script opened to the highlighted page.

"Where? Here?"

"Yes, right there, two sentences back." He looked the page over first. He read me Emilio's lines.

I do believe my father was the worst actor I have ever seen in my life, even just to read a sentence out loud. He sat still and spoke in a whiny monotone that I had never heard from him. It was as if he was trying to be lousy, but he wasn't. He gave me a few cues and I wracked my head and got some of the lines out.

"Thanks, Dad; this is helping a little."

I lay in my bed that night, puzzled. Did Emilio know that people like my father even existed? How could I act so well when I came from this man? How could that happen with genes and chromosomes? And to think, he gave Tom Pringle a hard time for speaking like a retarded moron.

Before I left for school the next morning, he stopped me.

"But I *want* this play of yours to be the last one until your grades improve." I walked out the door like I didn't hear that.

The Dumb Waiter was booked for a Friday night performance. My father didn't know I was there. I told him that I slept over at Robert Mirabilio's house. I knew I would be a lot less nervous if I danced to "The Sugar Blues" instead of this. Our characters were twenty years older than we were, so we tried to dress up and move like grown-ups. Adults moved slower than kids, I noticed, and I told Emilio we should slow down all of our movements.

My palms were sweaty. We didn't talk about stage fright. We took our places on stage, looked at each other and nodded

The Winds of Malibu

our heads. The curtain pulled back, and my first thought was of Frank Kratochvil. I had to get him out of my mind, or I would laugh hysterically. This play was not a laugher, which made me want to laugh.

It started out good, and then drifted far sideways. I tried to bluff that I remembered my lines, but really I couldn't remember them. I think what was in our favor is that it is an off-the-wall play, and that is what we gave them that night, a lot of it. What I liked about only two actors on a stage that big was a lot of room to use, so many choices. We had rehearsed some loose blocking, but we didn't force ourselves to stick with it and as our lines got away from us we threw the blocking out the window, even though we were supposed to be in a basement and there was no window.

I spoke a line from further into the play. Emilio folded his arms and looked off toward stage right with his back to me as he leaned on one foot and appeared deep in thought. I stayed mostly stage center left and faced the fourth wall. It would be nice if some Bix Beiderbecke music would kick in from the speakers, I thought.

We knew we had to find a conclusion, and how it ended would be a surprise to both of us. There was silence as if no one was in the building, except for sporadic coughs. I looked at him, and Emilio spun around and looked at me. I nodded. He nodded. That was supposed to be the end, but the curtain puller stood there with his hands in his pockets. I could see him!

I stared at the curtain puller and gave him a face that said… Come on, what are you waiting for, the twenty-first century? He finally saw me and pulled the curtain slowly closed. Emilio and I stood where we were, ten feet apart and stared each other in the face. The curtain puller finished his job and Emilio went down the right side of the stage steps and I went down the left side and we went into the audience. As soon as we saw each other Monday morning, we laughed.

Emilio found me.

"I've been looking for you. My dad wanted me to give this to you." It was Martin Sheen's Bix Beiderbecke double album that was as rare as it was beautiful. The liner notes were in French.

"My dad used it to prepare himself for the movie. He wanted me to give it to you."

"Thank you! This is *so* beautiful."

The next day, he gave me the screenplay for the Bix Beiderbecke movie!

"This was my dad's screenplay for the part. He wanted you to have it." We were standing in the hall near the library entrance.

"This means everything to me. This means absolutely everything. Thank you."

"Thank my dad." He walked away.

I poured over the text slowly. The elation I felt as I turned each page was like what the local surfers felt on the best waves. The screenplay was done in flashback form, which wasn't as good as chronology form. In one scene, Bix plays Dixieland jazz on a riverboat going down the Mississippi River. A rainstorm comes in, and Bix and his gang of musicians calm the crowd. The people dance and laugh. A big tree rams up through the middle of the dance floor and the riverboat sinks amid screams. The musicians swim to shore, but they can't find Bix. They look back as people straggle ashore. Bix is submerged but holds his cornet out of the water and he glides smoothly out of the river and onto the shore with the others.

I slept with the Bix screenplay next to me. My father came into my room and switched on the light. He stood and looked at me.

"If you are finished reading Martin Sheen's book for the

night, why don't you take it off of your bed?"

I closed the screenplay on my forefinger. "It's not a book. It's a screenplay about Bix Beiderbecke. It helps my anxiety to keep it when I sleep."

"As long as it means that much to you," he said. He switched off the light and backed out of my room.

(Journal entries)

EXTRA EXTRA EXTRA

April 13, 1977

In the summer of 1975 my loving sister Terri watched me write a letter to Tatum O'Neal that took me all day. She told me privately that I might meet Tatum but not probably and she didn't want it to hurt my feelings if I never got to. Over a year later. I got on the RTD to go into town. It started out the usual boring ride and I was going to sleep when the bus stopped at Big Rock to let a girl on the bus. It was a little red headed girl and she sat right by me. At first I saw her through the corner of my eye and she didn't look like much. She glanced over at me and then looked away, I did the same. She then crossed her legs the way a man would, 1 second later I did the same. (I guess I was trying to mock this girl a little) The next time I looked over, her legs were crossed more feminine like. I looked over at her again and caught her looking at a 45 degree angle. My legs uncrossed, my breath grew short, my eyes widened and I broke out in a cold sweat. I was looking my future competition and childhood idol right in the eyes. This little brownish red headed girl was none other than Tatum O'Neal (pride of Hollywood) A sense of panic quickly came over me. What should I do? What should I say? How should I act? I knew that I had to do something for this was my pot of gold! She looked out towards the highway and put her leg up on the seat. She sat up and waved to someone as the bus came to a halt. That someone got on the bus.

-Tatum and her friend got off the bus at the same stop that I did in Santa Monica. I followed them. Tatum looked back at me and laughed. I smiled at them. Every time that they slowed to let me nearer, I slowed down too, keeping about twenty yards away. Tatum stopped and looked at me. I stopped too. It was just a fun game. I certainly wanted Tatum to feel safe. "The famous must feel terrified sometimes," I thought to myself. I smiled kindly at them and decided not to follow any farther. I comically dove into some bushes and saw them laugh. I walked away and did what I was going to do anyway and went looking for buildings that had 1920's architecture. I found a good one and leaned against the bricks and smiled and thought of Tatum.

Monday April 25, 1977
Something is really troubling my mind. I've got a horrible premonition that something drastic is happening to Lynn Craig. It's like something drilling in my mind, telling me to go there and see what's happening to her. I feel very tempted to and if this feeling continues I just might.

The Winds of Malibu

Extra extra

Tatum Tatum   May 4, 1977

Exactly 3 weeks ago I was completely dazzled out of my mind over seeing Tatum on the RTD but everyone whom I told the story to was disappointed because I didn't talk to her but at that I said something like that just couldn't have been accidental and that someday she would be mine for a time. Today at Sunset Mesa she got on the RTD again and again she sat close by. I started to freeze up again but I knew I had to say something. This is how it went. She had a few more pimples on her face than the last time but she was still the same Tatum O'Neal that I know of except she was a little less talkative.

    Jeff- Where are you going?

    Tatum- Home.

    Jeff (after a long pause)- Do you know when Six Weeks is coming out? Tatum was obviously pleased by this. A slow smile came over her face and she shook her head no. We then passed that big house (Sea Manor)

    Jeff- I used to think that you lived in that house. She looked back and said "no." Jeff- I remember about a year ago I used to go and sit there on the beach. I'd wait for you to come out but you never did. We stopped talking and I just glanced at her once in a while. She missed her stop and got up.

    Tatum- Sir, could you stop please.

D

Driver— Where?

Tatum— Anywhere. He quickly pulled over and she got off the bus. That was positive proof to me that my sister Terri is watching over me. Amen!

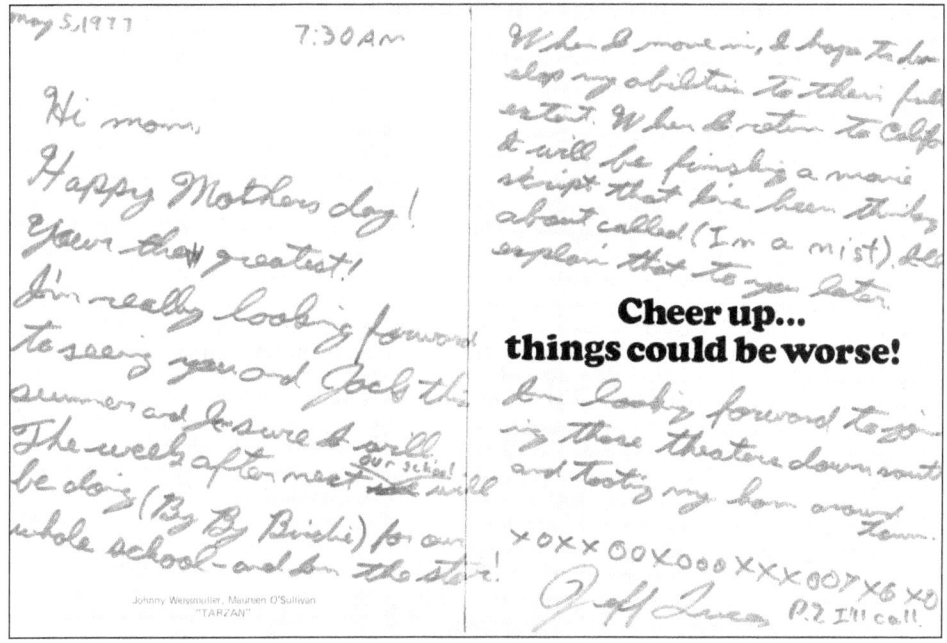

Mother's Day card, Jeff Lucas Souvinirs.

>>><<<

Shane Smith invited me up to his house. My old partner in crime walked slower than he used to, and we hung out in the garage in the evening. The first thing he did was pick up a propane tank and walk around with it.

"Have you ever inhaled propane?"

"No."

"Do you want to try it?"

"I have never heard of such a thing."

He sat against the back wall of the garage and turned up the valve and inhaled propane through a tube. Then he shut it off. He got his lopsided grin on. He laughed a lazy laugh, and I took it from him as I stood, turned up the valve, put it to my mouth, and inhaled away. It had a cold, gassy taste and I could feel and hear my brain cells pop like popcorn. I wondered how I would ever memorize lines after this. When the dizziness subsided, I dragged the tank back over to Shane.

"It tastes like a cold fart," I said. He had another big hit and passed out. His lips turned blue. A puddle spread from under him. Then he came to and saw that he had just pissed his pants.

"Whoa!" he said, and he passed out again and sat there in his puddle of urine.

If I were like Shane, I could understand why my father would force me to live two thousand miles away from Malibu.

"Goodbye, Shane, and don't come back. Don't come back, Shane." Shane waved clumsily. I walked out and went down the mountain and passed six caged, leaping, ferocious dogs along the way.

For our ninth grade play, Mr. Thacker combined dialogue and plot from the musicals *Bye Bye Birdie* and *The Music Man*, and we had no music, not even an overture. He wanted to see me play Harold Hill in *The Music Man*, he told me. Emilio played a drunken scene that was added just for him. I suggested to Emilio that he cut his hair, which was long enough that it sometimes obscured his face on stage when he held his head down to deliver a line. He refused.

"How about just a little bit, maybe around the edges?"

"No, I want to keep it."

"Do you think you will ever cut your hair?"

"No."

I watched him go through his part. He was always fun for

us to watch. Mr. Thacker yelled out from the back of the auditorium, "Let's see your face, Emilio! We can't see your face!" He could still piss off Emilio once in a while. I had brought my Vivitar camera. I took two pictures of Emilio, one with his hair down in his face as he delivered a line, and in the other picture, I just called his name and he looked over at me and smiled in character.

Rehearsal ended, and I went across the parking lot toward home.

"*Jeff!* Wait. I'll walk with you. Which way do you walk home?"

"This way. Up the hill pretty far." Emilio turned toward the running track, and I followed him.

"Going for a run? Maybe I can time you."

"Nah." He dropped down on the grass and I sat beside him.

It was a normal, hazy Malibu day. The ocean was just out of sight. He looked out towards the Pacific. There was silence for a minute between us.

"This past year has been so bad for me, with my dad being sick and all. It's been one thing after another, I swear," he said.

"Yes, if something ever happened to him…my God… God forbid."

"Yeah." Another pause.

"Do you ever think of suicide?" he asked.

"Yes, but I think… it's the combinations. Whatever happens in life, everything combines and interacts and creates what happens. Combinations can create a mountain or a molehill. That's my belief."

He was pensive. "Sometimes, I'll be with a girl, and everybody's got to know about it the next day. It's all over school. Makes me feel like a jerk."

"That's not being a jerk! Most people are superficial. Just look around the field here. Look around the school. Superficial

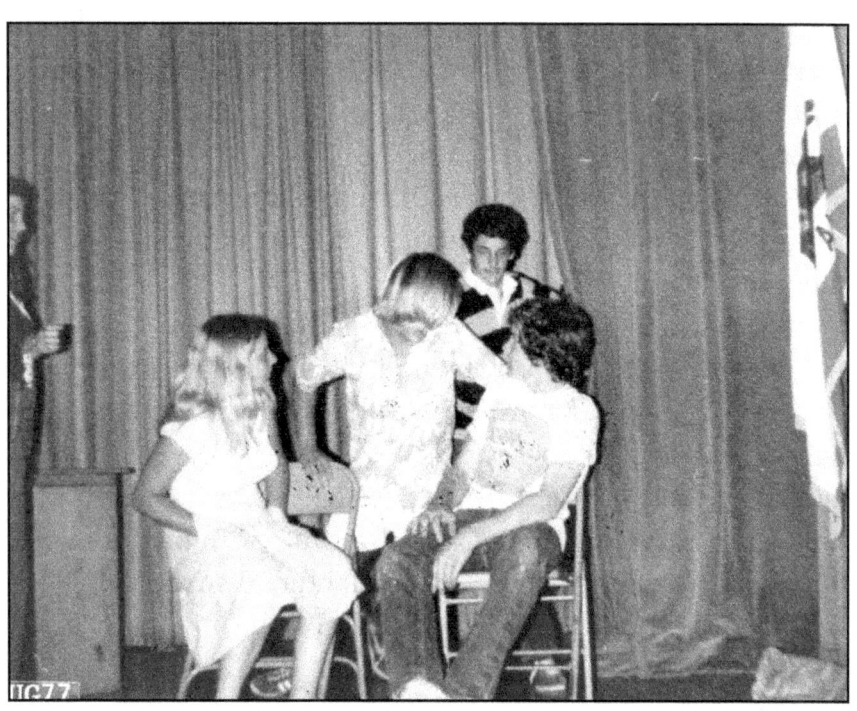

Emilio in the center, with, L. to R. Jenifer Heiser, John Ufland, and Robert Loving. Emilio's hair sometimes got in the way, when he was delivering a line while acting on stage. Mr. Thacker commented and yelled to the stage, from in back of the auditorium, that he couldn't see Emilio's face. I can still see him cupping his hands to his mouth.

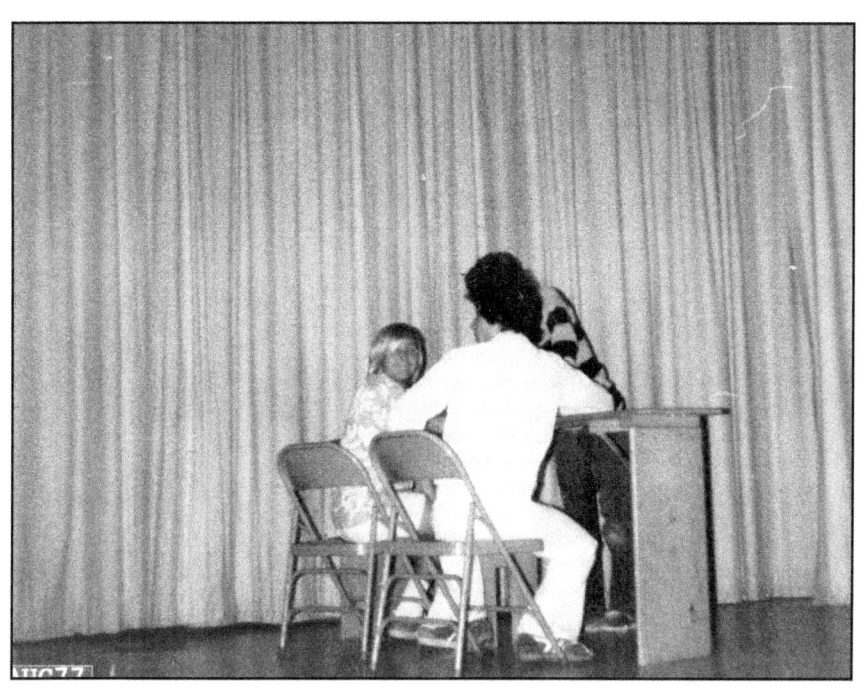

"Hey Emilio, LOOK!" Emilio with Chris Pac and John Ufland. (1977) Photo by Jeff Lucas.

is the main ingredient! I think I'm the biggest jerk."

"What?" He grinned.

"You know what I did? I walked into a nightclub three days ago and it was dark inside and I had sunglasses on. I couldn't even see my drink. I set it down and I missed the table. It fell right on the floor…and broke."

"Did everyone just go, hahaha?"

"Yeah, I can't even get a screw. I can't find a girl anywhere. I'm just the Sugar Blues Kid to these people!"

"I don't know what to do with all the time on my hands. Where do I go? What do I do? It seems like everything is hopeless." He stared into the grass.

"Are you bored a lot?"

"Yeah."

"Well, I'll tell you, there is acting. I mean, maybe we'll be something someday." That perked him up.

"My dad says if you can act Shakespeare, you can act anything," he said.

"I will remember that. I don't think I've ever been bored. Never really. I get too nervous to be bored."

Emilio looked at me, intrigued. "My dad said he always knew he'd be famous. Even when he was young, he knew that."

"What was it, like a feeling?"

"He just knew. He always knew."

"There *is* acting. I will act with you every chance I get."

"God, my life is so fucked up right now. *Whew*," he said.

"It will improve. That's what I think. We'll get it. We'll make it." I smiled. Emilio smiled the same way.

"Let's go." He nodded in the direction we were headed, toward the sea.

"It's the combinations that make everything like that."

"Yeah."

D

"So, ya think *Bye Bye Birdie* is gonna be a smash hit?" I said. Emilio laughed.

"Well there, Meelies, I go home this way." I pointed in the opposite direction.

"Okay. Take care, Jeff. I'll see you tomorrow."

(Journal entry)

May 25, 1977

2 days ago while I was in our music class, Michael Wipranik in the clarinet section and I got into a discussion. I told him that I like the 20s. He said, "Well everyone knows that. You like the 20s as much as Chris Idee likes her horse." I liked that remark. Bix Beiderbecke is my full time idol and I'm convinced I was him. My dad thinks that this is just one of my passing fads but mark my words, I will carry Bix's name to my grave.

⟫⟪

I saw the small pretty girl, Chris Idee, who was never without her horse, on my walks home from school on most days. I had my thick yellow Bix bible and she had her horse. It's good to be obsessed with something.

I found Eric Lovaas, a popular surfer with a large cranium, and cornered him.

"Eric, I heard there is going to be a typical party on Point Dume for the locals Friday night. Do you know the address?"

"Yes, it's on Dume Road."

"I'm waiting." I copied the address into my history book.

"Thanks. It is the real thing, though? Is it going to be a *typical teenage turnout*?"

"Yes, Jeff," he rolled his eyes and exhaled.

"Okeh." I straightened my bowtie. "That was a 1920s record label. Okeh," I told him. I walked away while I was ahead.

I wore my weed-picking clothes. No bow tie, no Vaseline in my hair, no vest or dress shoes. I set out at six p.m. and watched the sun set as I walked the three miles. I went up the porch of a small, one-story house. It was smaller than my house. The front door was wide open and would stay that way all night. There was a sign on the door that read, "Leave The Lights Off!" The only light came from the moon and from when teenagers lit up their pipes and joints.

I moved slowly down a hallway and didn't touch the walls, the furniture or the people. I could only distinguish between males and females by their breasts. Everyone seemed bored. I wandered through crowded rooms. This was the Malibu elite.

"Aqualung" by Jethro Tull boomed across the house from the record player. I wished Frank was with me. Frank and I had more original fun together in any ten minutes than these poor guys had all night long. Wait until I told Frank about this party.

I saw Sean Penn as he leaned against a wall, cool and just naturally in charge. I went up to him and hesitated before I spoke.

"Hi, Sean."

"Hi."

"Are all Malibu parties like this?"

"Yeah… some are slower, actually," he said calmly. I smiled.

I got myself a can of Budweiser from a tub with water in it on the kitchen floor. I pulled off the top and wore it on my index finger like a ring. Not many in the house drank, but there was plenty of pot, and I saw people swallow Quaaludes with water from the kitchen faucet. They bent down into the spigot to get water.

At 1:00 a.m., everyone still leaned on walls and furniture

without much movement. I stayed for most of the party and expected an orgy or a fight, but neither happened. People went home. I asked around for a ride home.

"No, dude, sorry," was all I got. I went down the porch steps and moved toward Malibu Park. I was not the only partygoer on foot, but most lived on Point Dume.

When I got to the dark Pacific Coast Highway, I turned around and saw two barely recognizable figures behind me. One was tall and buff, and the other guy was a little shorter than me. Both had hair past their shoulders. I stopped to let them catch up. It was Steve McQueen's son, Chad, and his big, lethal, dark-haired bodyguard friend. They were inseparable.

"Hi, Chad! It's me, Jeff Lucas from Malibu Park! You don't mind a short-haired guy walking with you, do you?"

"Yeah, why not," said Chad.

"We don't mind," said his friend politely. I gave them a closed-lipped Bix grin.

"I was wondering, how is the acting department at SamoHi?"

"It's good," said Chad.

"We really wouldn't know," said the bodyguard.

"Are you going there next year?" asked Chad.

"Yeah, I'll be a freshman there."

"Well, we will see you there then," said Chad. When we came to Morning View Avenue, I turned right.

"Well, bye, Chad. Take care, you guys."

"Goodbye, Ned," said Chad.

"Bye, Jeff," said the bodyguard.

I turned on the television set in my father's room after school and caught the last two-thirds of a black-and-white movie about a giant passenger liner that stupidly ran into an iceberg. A long *Zachary All* commercial came on, but it didn't sink my spirits. As was my custom, I studied the movie credits with pencil and paper in hand, and learned that the movie was based on a book, also titled *A Night to Remember*."

When I had the house to myself, I made a ship out of aluminum foil and filled up the bathtub with cold water. My aluminum foil boat was two-and-a-half feet long and floated well enough. I took a pin and jabbed a few holes along the front side and timed it to see how long it took to sink. I twiddled my fingers in excitement as the bow went down first. When the aluminum foil *Titanic* hit the bottom, it shivered across the length. I crunched up the boat into a wet ball and threw it away. I did this twice a week. The water level was rising fast in our septic tank.

"Where is all the aluminum foil, Jeff?! There never seems to be enough! I just bought this roll!" I gave him a bland and innocent face.

"How should *I* know? Why don't you ask Steve?"

"I think you'd better call up your mother and tell her you're on your way."

I didn't. I decided I would stay in Malibu just to piss him off. He had a new girlfriend over, and the two had spent the day in his room with the door shut. I had met her that day and we politely said hello in the kitchen. She had a continual grin on her face. All my friends were busy. I made myself scarce in my bedroom.

It was unusually quiet. No rattling windows and the crash of waves from the surf were small. I shut my door and studied my Bix script and listened to a library record of the radio broadcast of the *Hindenburg* disaster.

At sunset, I heard them walk out on the patio. I joined them there. We made awkward conversation. A long garden snake slithered by our feet. The snake saved the conversation. My father bullied it with his feet. I joined him and lightly derailed it as his woman laughed obnoxiously in the north east corner of

D

the patio. He laughed and ran to the garage and came back with the hoe. I stepped back as he smacked the snake around roughly while his girlfriend wiggled and giggled and goaded him on.

"Oh, Paul, I can't believe all this!"

"Come on, Dad. Let it go!"

I got between him and the snake.

"Let the snake go, you *shit-ass!*" I snarled into his face.

She gasped with an open mouth. He scowled and smacked me across the right side of my face. I held my face and ran into my room. The house was quiet for an hour as he talked to his girlfriend, quietly. He came in somber.

"Sorry I slapped you, but that was one word your mother used to call me, so don't ever do it again."

"Okay, I apologize, Dad. I won't."

"See that you don't."

She stayed the night and the next day. I watched her watch me as he ordered me around. I moved plants and pulled weeds at his beck and call. In the evening he made us stroganoff for dinner. The Malibu night sounds were getting to me; the coyotes yipped up in big packs.

"We are going to a movie at the Malibu Cinema."

"Can I go with you?"

"You're welcome to."

We watched the movie *Slapshot* with Paul Newman, about hockey games. We noticed the comedian Flip Wilson several rows ahead of us to the right. He wore a flashy suit that would look great if he was on stage, but he didn't even have a date with him. He sat quietly alone in the dark, and I don't think he spoke to anyone. He had sparkling rings on his fingers, maybe even his thumb, that shot off rays. His suit was white with a mass of sequins. It was hard to pay attention to the movie, because the dim light of the film reflected off his outfit. The rays distracted everyone. I got fidgety. I looked at my father. His eyes alternated between the movie and Flip Wilson every ten seconds.

I stood up quietly and went into the lobby and a girl I knew from school was there, Debbie McCollum. She seemed to be a deep thinker. I could never tell what she loved or what she thought, and she was beautiful, with dark wavy hair. She seemed happy to see me.

"Is that movie boring you?" she laughed.

"Yes. All they do is beat each other up in an ice rink."

"Do you want to sit together?"

"Yes."

We sat away from my father and his date all the way in the back row of the theater. I started to feel cool. I moved in my seat like I was the Lord of Flatbush, and Debbie was relaxed and just naturally cool.

Suddenly my father loomed over us. He had found me easily, that face of his took the place of the characters on the screen. *Slapshot* had become a horror movie!

"Come back and sit with us now! You came with us and you will stay with us until the last second! I don't ever *want* you getting up like that and walking away ever again!"

"What is it, Dad? I'm sitting with this lovely girl." Debbie smiled.

"You sit with us this very second, or you are walking home… and don't expect there to be much left of you when I am finished with you!" He whispered loudly, and throaty shouts poked through. He bounded away down toward his seat. Debbie's eyes were wide, and she looked scared.

"What the hell was *that?*" she asked slowly.

"That's what I go through all the time these days. I better go." We waved goodbye.

I got up and moved down the grade of the theater and sat

D

next to my father, silent, and pretended there was an indestructible wall that separated us.

On the way home from the movie with his date in the front seat, my father talked on.

"You know, you *always* see that large list of unknown actors at the end of *every* movie! The list is full of actors that *never* made it in Hollywood and won't ever make it in that business!"

"You are so right, Paul," said his girlfriend as I crouched in the back seat by the right rear window and stared up at the dark mountain.

Emilio and I leaned on a rail quietly together, meditative outside the cafeteria as students bustled around us.

"Marlon Brando had dinner over at our house last night," he said. He looked off into space for a minute and quietly said, "Wow." John Ufland waved me over to him.

"Wow is right." I walked over to John.

"Hey Jeff, buddy, I got a tip for you. There is an acting class my dad told me about. I think you ought to check it out."

"Well, hey hey, big bad John—lay it on me." John laid it on me and gave me a half sheet of paper with a phone number on it. I made sure the paper didn't blow out of my fingers on the walk home.

"Hello. I heard about your acting class from Harry Ufland. Harry Ufland, the talent scout, and I was wondering if I could maybe join up with your acting class."

"How old are you?" the man's voice said.

"Fifteen, but I look a little older!"

"Sorry. You've got to be at least eighteen to join!" he said coldly.

"But… uh… do you know Harry Ufland, the talent scout?"

"I'm sure… but thanks for calling." (click)

"Yeah… thank you." (click).

I held the phone number of an elderly violinist named Kurt Deiterle (pronounced Dee-ter-lee) who played alongside Bix Beiderbecke in Paul Whiteman's band in the 1920s.

I phoned Kurt Dieterle.

"Hi. I am studying cornet with Herb Sutro, and he gave me your phone number."

"Oh, yes—he told me! How's things with you?"

"Okay," I said in a shaky voice. "I was going to ask you about Bix."

"Oh, yes. You can come to my apartment if you want and discuss it."

"That would be great! I read the book that you are in--*Bix, Man and Legend*."

"Oh, the Bill Evans book!"

"Yes! Did you know Bix very well?"

"Yes, I knew him well enough. He was in the orchestra I played in. Everybody liked him."

I was nervous and star struck. "Well, gee, thanks, Mr. Dieterle. I would love to see you at your place. I'll call you back!"

"Alright. I'll be here, unless I am playing golf." He paused. "I am seventy-eight years old."

"Okay. I truly look forward to meeting you, Mr. Dieterle!"

"Thank you. I look forward to meeting you, too. I will see you."

"Okay then, bye." We hung up. I closed my eyes. He had that 1920s serene air about him. I looked down at my arms. I had big goosebumps.

D

(Journal entry)

June 12, 1977

Because of suffering conditions it looks like I'll be going back to Alabama. This time for a much longer period. I'll leave some time this summer as soon as my part in 'Buckaroo' is completed. I'm leading a pretty shakey life right now and my future is so blind I can't see to the end of my nose.

    When I leave, I will be entering a completely new phase of my life. I shall never return to the old phase. In the past years in Malibu, school has been the only real thing that has kept me going. I'm only now beginning to realize that with M.P.J.H.S. gone, what am I going to do?

Fourteen

"WHAT THE HELL," SAID BIX.

Bye Bye Birdie promised to be a crappy play. We sloshed through it. As the lead I hit my marks and got through my lines. I spoke them quickly. It was hard enough for the students to vocally project when the audience was interested. With over seven hundred students more than ready for summer vacation, I was the only actor that everyone could understand in the back row. Emilio's spontaneous performance as a drunk who walks up to people at a table and says *"Hi,"* as they lean away from his breath, brought the audience's interest back into the show.

Bye Bye Birdie ended to a muted round of applause. I had a feeling that my hero, Martin Sheen, had been in the audience. When Emilio confirmed this, I clasped my hand over my face and put my head back.

"How come he is only here for our worst shows?"

"Don't worry about it. It's okay," he said calmly.

"WHAT THE HELL," SAID BIX.

The phone rang.

"Analog Devices." My father put the phone back down. "Hmm. They hung up."

"Maybe they just weren't in the mood."

"That's what she said."

We sat at opposite ends of the dining room table. We had a good view of each other. When he had to conduct business, he couldn't get angry, so he might get used to me in his line of vision and be calm at the same time.

He slouched but still looked at me as he did a little piano exercise with his right hand on the table.

"Dad." A negative omen was simmering around that name for me. "I got you a present for your forty-ninth birthday."

"You did, huh? Thank you." I handed it across the table wrapped in newspaper. It was a grey statue six inches tall of a naked bald man who weighs himself on a scale but his gut is so big he can't see the scale and frowns. He put it aside and looked at me.

"Don't you think it's funny?"

"You've got a real sense of humor there."

"I didn't mean your present looks like you. You're not fat, not that fat. How old were you when you went bald?"

"At your age, I had more hair than you have."

"Then there is your nose. That is *some* shnoz. I'll never have that. That's good."

"Your nose looks like it was cracked in half and glued back together in two parts," he said. He let out a false laugh. I reached up and felt my nose. He was talking about the small cleft at the bottom of my nose.

"It makes me feel like a cat. I like it." He rolled his eyes. "I did get your musical ear, though. I will always be grateful for that."

"See? I did something nice for you." He stood up and turned toward his room.

"Aren't you going to take your gift? It cost me five dollars." His eyes ready to turn to anger, he left it there and went in his room.

I found in the Los Angeles times that Gershwin's operetta, *Porgy and Bess,* was coming to the Pantages Theatre in Hollywood.

"Dad, look!"

"*Stop sneaking up behind me, JEFF!*" he shook, his face a look of anger.

"Okay, I'm sorry…I was just really excited about what I found in the Calendar section! Please take me to see this? It would mean a lot to me!"

"*Porgy and Bess,* George Gershwin's music."

"Come on, Dad. This might be my last show I get to see in California!"

"Well, since you put it that way, okay. You can consider *Porgy and Bess* your going-away present."

I entered the most beautiful building that I had ever seen—the lavish, 1920s Pantages Theater. My 1920s were here! There hadn't been any restoration done, and the lobby was darkened with half a century of cigarette smoke. One of the airplanes was gone that a statue holds in its hand at the base of the grand staircase. Bix Beiderbecke had performed here.

(Journal entry)

June 15, Wed. 1977

Last night, my dad surprised the hell out of me. He took me to the first professional stage show I've ever seen, and I'd much rather have seen this stage show

"What the hell," said Bix.

than any other. It was at the Pantaiges in Hollywood. It was PORGY & BESS - a full-length operetta. I never thought I'd get the chance to see it. I sure enjoyed it.

Today was the awards assembly at M.P.J.H.S. I'll describe it. I was sitting up on stage with the intelligent Bryan Stearns next to me and the group of trophy winners around me. At first I was fumbling around for a chair and finally found one - sitting next to Mr. Poole. Quite a few awards were given before mine, including Bryans for Principal's Award. Then Mr. Thacker walked up to the platform and said, "I've got some certificates to give out. The first one is Best Comedian to go to Jeff Lucas." The applause wailed. I got up from the stage, grabbed it and sat down quickly.

"The second is for Best Actor and I'm proud to present it to Emilio Estevez." The applause wailed as Emilio got up from the audience, got his award, and sat back down. "But the real award of achievement this year goes to a student whom you all know and have seen perform on the stage. He's done a lot of acting as well as comedy at Malibu Park. I'm proud to present this award to Jeff Lucas." Just as he said my name, he pulled off the tape to the name plate and the name plate came with it and stuck to his hand. As I got up and realized what had happened, we both broke down with laughter. He shook my hand with the name plate

Still stuck to his. I grabbed both and sat back down, knowing full well that this was to be my last applause on the MPJHS Stage.

The name plate of the award that came off in drama teacher Bill Thacker's hand as he handed it to Jeff during Malibu Park Junior High's award ceremony. From Jeff Lucas souvenirs.

I found Emilio outside and handed him my trophy.

"Here! What am I doing with this? You deserve it!"
"No, it's yours. Congratulations."
I combed through the campus getting my yearbook signed. At the gymnasium, I found white chalk on the ground. I reached as high as I could, and wrote across the bricks, JEFF LUCAS WAS HERE. One word per brick.
On the tennis court I said hello to everyone's favorite teacher, Mr. Leonard Vincent. He looked a little bit like a very kind walrus.
"Everyone is saying you're going straight to the top," he said, lifting a shaky finger skyward. "And I believe them!"
"That would mean everything to me. I hope I can give it a true shot... I might be moving real far away though, soon."

"What the hell," said Bix.

"One thing is sure. Entertainment will always be there. We don't know what form it's going to take as it changes, but it will always be there." I shook his hand, smiled and waved, and moved toward home.

I passed the wall where I had written my name in chalk. Underneath, someone had added, "AND IS GREAT!" A tall, blond ninth-grader came up to me.

"I put that up there under your name. My friends and I agreed to do that."

"Thank you." I got misty-eyed.

Slowly up the mountain I went. How many more days would I be able to call this my home? I read through my yearbook and didn't watch where I walked. Every page was filled with best wishes on an acting career.

(MPJHS 1977 Yearbook)

> *Jeff, It's difficult to put in one paragraph how much you have become a part of my life this year – to mention that you are special isn't enough. You are "chosen" and the world will be blessed when you share yourself with it. I'll always be a fan! Love, Shelby*

> *Jeffery, Have a great summer. Good luck next year. I know you will miss me but all these tears – haha You are a neat person, (one of a kind) I mean it too! Love you much, Karen Clark*

> *Jeff, This year has been really good and I'm soo glad you won the acting award. You really deserved it. Thanks for helping with the talent show. Love you forever, Cherie*

Graduation day outside the auditorium, with Tim Otterman and Dan Harris. photo by Adam Shapiro

Jeff, Good Luck Mr. Drama. You will make it in the big time for sure. Keep up the Jazz talk. Maybe someday you will play like 'Bix'! Well, have fun, David C.

Lots of luck to Jeff. On the stage he was the rage but in history, maybe it's best that he left. Mr. A. Martinelli (History Teacher)

To an actor of life and a giver of happiness. Be what you are and never change. Friend, Chris Pak

Jeff, don't get too wasted with your brother and frank, Doug Ashford

Jeff, Have a great summer and a great 10th grade. Pat Bader

Hey Jeff, I believe I am signing the yearbook of a star. (what luck) best wishes, Kevin Stratton

Jeff – You're a real nice guy and funny too. Keep up the good work. You'll go far in life. I know everything you want will work out for you. I hope I see you at a party. Love always, Kathy Hoover Have a great summer.

To Jeff, You're the best and I mean the BEST comedian in this school. I wish I had the talent you have but I don't. You better keep up your acting or I will kick your butt. I hope I see you next year. I'm moving so I don't know. Keep up the good work. A friend for life, Michael Bryant.

"What the hell," said Bix.

Hi Jeff, (most nostalgic) Hey, it's been a great year and I don't see why we can't do it again! Ok! I hope to see ya in Samohi. Although it's a great, huge school, I'll try! You've got a heck of a lot going for you, not to mention the "gals." I'll see you for sure. Have a great summer, and teach the girls how to surf, I'm sure they will all be waiting in line! Love always, Laura.

Jeffrey, Thanks for the memories ! It's been great getting to know you. See you in Hollywood, Kevin Wilson

Jeff, You have been so much fun to be around! I will miss you a lot. If I'm not at Samo, Have fun! Daisy.

See you next year! Bryan Stearns (He drew a picture of a cornet)

Jeff, It's been really fun knowing you through these years, especially Mrs. Bolton when you imitated her on the side wall at Cabrillo & Dr. Jeckle & Mr. Hyde. Those were so good. Have a good summer. See you at Samo. Craig Conklin

Dear Mr. Gable, When I get my mats, I'll come over to your house and we will party together. Have a great summer. Later, Bea.

Jeff – have fun at the beach & have a nice time finding your classes at Samohi. Keep up the acting. Scott Stirling.

Jeff, Have a great summer and I'll see you at Samo and keep up the laughs, B. Dugger.

Jeff, Have a super summer, and too bad you have to move. Stephan K. P.S. Keep on acting.

Jeff, I really admire your dancing! You're really gonna make it big! Have a great summer, best comedian!! Love always, Theresa Hunt 6/16/77 457-7851

Jeff, Have a cool time this summer and don't go to the sticks, okie doke? See you this summer and good luck with your movie! Signed with much dignity, Arthur Mortel.

Jeff, good luck in a long lasting acting and comedy career and have fun in Alabama (if it's possible) Frank Kratochvil

Hey Jeff. How's it going? I hear that you's headed out to Alabamy to live with your Mammy (do tell do tell). Now I want you to go out to Alabamy to all those whiskey runnen idiots and to make them say 'Cathro', and to give them a piece of PIE. Dan Harris.

Lucas, I think you have a future in Jazz. Robin.

Jeff, good luck in your entertainment career. You are very funny and a great actor. Have a great year next year, Chris Ostin

"What the hell," said Bix.

Jeff, Have a radical summer toking pot, snorting coke, & shooting up with Pringle and Kratochvil. Jeff Sutter. Jeff Sutter wasn't here.

To Jeff, one of the greatest actors to come out of Thacker's workshop. You earned a well deserved award, congratulations. Thank you for being a friend as well as a fellow actor. Thank you for all the good times and good luck on your obvious road to fame as a great comedian. Take it light & later on. May the wind at your back never be your own. Later, Emilio.

Monsieur Lucas, So I hear your father is a fruit-cake. Well, knowing you I can believe it. It must be very true. Have fun at Samohi. Kip Shreiber.

Have fun in Samo and I'll see ya around. Keep up the acting and good luck in your career. Well, see ya around. Joel Anderson.

Jeff – I want to keep in contact with you. I hope you enjoy whatever you do. My address is 7981 Broview Dr. Malibu CA. 90265. Take it easy. I think you will enjoy yourself in whatever you do pretty much. Robert Younis

Jeff – You're a good actor. I hope you go far. Love always, Karen.

To Jeff – to whom I feel like a brother to. We shared the stage, let-downs, and the wonders of life together.

Until we meet again magically, The Amazing Amazo. Write Adam Shapiro 22548 Pacific Coast Highway, Malibu, Cal. 90265

To Jeff. Everything best, Alan Lloyd. (band teacher)

Jeff – Congratulations for that Drama award. You will become something in the future. I can… anyway… I can feel it in my bones. I can see the headlines now, JEFF LUCAS MASTER PERFORMER! Bye. Love, Margaret Jerebek, Trombone fanatic. I hope I see you next year at Samohi.

Jeff, See ya next year, Chris LaCagnina. Post. Script. Have a nice summer. Post Post Script. It's been nice PPPS. Knowing you. PPPPS. Hope you have a good PPPPPs. Next year & Forever. PPPPPP. Keep in touch.

Lucas – Have a hot summer. You're a Ham. Haha. Later on, Scott.

Jeff – When you tip toe through the tulips of life, stop and smell the flowers. Mrs Babich. (math councelor)

Jeff, This is my favorite teacher, Ol' Uncle Garibaldi, Lemon Mouth Sauce, Old Stew. After looking at this picture I know there is no way you could have a good summer but try. David Boy Bernstein. (beside a photo of Mr. Martinelli, History Teacher)

"WHAT THE HELL," SAID BIX.

Jeff – What a pleasure it has been seeing you bring joy to so many students. Remember yourself though, and give yourself some joy too. You've done great things here and I know you'll continue. God Bless. Mr. Newcomb. (Chorus music teacher)

Jeff, When you're in Alabama, look me up! Ph. (???) 993-9444 Ad. 1412 Huntingford Dr. Marietta, Ga. 30067 Justin Kocher aka Wolfman Jack!

Jeff – LOVE your routine both on and off stage!! Sorry I can't know you longer – Maybe you can stop by and say hi some time – Mrs R. (attendance office)

Dear Jeff, Have a good summer. Keep up your acting career, don't let all that talent go to waste. Keep in touch. See you around (hopefully) Your future Agent, John Ufland 457-7036 7055 Fernhill Dr. Malibu, Calif. 90265

Jeff, really the best of luck in acting! You're a gas and I really like ya! Love, Nanette.

Jeff, You really have a lot of talent in drama and acting. I hope in the future you can share that talent with others. Have a good summer & where ever you go, whatever you do, good luck. Luv, Kathy Kamath.

Jeff, have a hot summer and to the next Karry Grant, Later, Ray Gonzales.

The Winds of Malibu

Jeff, Thanks for a fun year. Get tan during the summer. Luv, Jade.

Dear Jeff, You're such a great actor. You really deserved that award. I know some day you'll be really famous. All you need is a luck break but please when You're rich and famous, remember me. Maybe one day you can invite me to your yacht or your penthouse apartment. Have a nice summer. Love you always, Donna Leslie Candice Sanders.

Jeff, I hope you don't take this wrong but I got to say it. I really like you AS A FRIEND! But I don't want to go out again cause 1. I'm going to be pretty busy this summer with summer school and Track & 2. I only like you as a friend and I don't want you to like me any more than a friend. Bye, Lisa Teel.

Jeff, You deserve that award you got. You are so funny. Have a great summer. See you around, Love, Kelly.

Jeff It's been fun in Drama. You've done a good job. Hope I see you in some upcoming movies. I think you will be a GOOD ACTOR. I bet you'll get an Academy Award someday. Just hope and never stop trying. Congratulations for your award. You deserve it. Love, Cindy.

Jeff, (Gene Kelly) I think that you are so talented. I can just see me 20 years from now going to see you perform. Have a great summer. Love, Michelle.

"What the hell," said Bix.

Dear Jeff – Looks like everything will be "up" for you. My very best always, Mr. Newcomb. (Chorus music teacher)

Have fun picking your nose and feeling your left pocket with your right hand. Chris Thomas.

Jeff, You're a really funky person and I'm glad I met you. Good luck in the future. Love ya, Monica.

Mucas, How's the snot business. I mean Stanley, I mean Jeff. Congrats on your award. Have a great summer, Drew Digby.

Jeff, Congratulations, you really deserved Drama Student of the Year. You're a great actor and a really nice person. Have a great summer. See you next year. Love, Jenny Heiser.

Dear Jeff – I know we've had our differences but lots of love, Tracy.

Jeff, hi! It was SOO fun knowing you! I'm really glad I met you! Have a great summer! Love, Lisa Olson.

Jeff, It's been great knowing you. You have a great future in acting. Wish you luck. Enjoy Samohi and have a great summer, Scott Hunter.

To the greatest actor – comedian I know (not too many) Have a great summer! See you next year! Jim Engel.

The Winds of Malibu

Jeff, Entertainer of the Year 19__/20__ but certainly bound to come true one way or another – always believe in your natural talents – you'll never be sorry (and neither will the audience) My best to you in all things (including memory) Mr. V (Leonard Vincent, History teacher.

Jeff, I clapped when you got that award. Aren't you proud of me? Try to have a good summer without the great Coyote. Shawn Wiley.

Jeff, Have a super summer and good luck at Samohi. Congratulations for getting the drama award! See ya at Samohi next year! Always, Chuck Cruise.

Jeff, I've known you for so long and I'm glad I've known you that long. Does that make sense? Probably not. Well, see you later. Love, Jenny (Powell) alias Dingy, Shortstuff, Smiley, Shortie, Brat, Piyamoas Penen.

ffeJ, sihT si sdrawkcab rof uoy. ylaicepse esuaceb I ma yzarc, Siln Nosrac, alias, Nils Carson.

I placed the tall, golden acting trophy in front of my dad and the certificate for Best Comedian. He remained at the head of the table and talked business loudly. When he hung up, he stared down at the phone. He glanced at his reflection in my trophy.

"The reason my certificate says Best Comedian, is that Martin Sheen's son also got an award for Best Actor. So we kind of split the award. I told you we were best friends."

"What the hell," said Bix.

"Nice…proud of you," he frowned, and leaned over a sheaf of papers from Analog Devices.

I waited until he reclined in his easy chair and I placed my yearbook in his hands with its rich, blue cover.

"Please read this. It's my yearbook, and what my friends and teachers write in there should convince you that maybe you should let me stay on in Malibu."

He clacked his tongue and slowly opened the yearbook from the first page and carefully read each entry and signature. I sat quietly on the couch and listened to the glossy pages turn. I watched him read every word. His index finger dipped into his lower lip in slow motion each time he turned a page.

He read the full page that Emilio wrote to me as well as the praise from prominent teachers. After the last page, he gently shut the book and handed it back to me without looking at me.

"You said in there that you think your father is a fruitcake," he said seriously.

"I was just joking, you know. I don't mean that. I mean, not really." He shot up from his chair and went over to his piano and pounded out "The Entertainer."

My brother's graduation from "Samohi" was one week later. All of his buddies met at the Malibu house and a brilliant array of drugs were held out as they stood in a communal circle. I kept a safe distance. I had one hit of pot and watched them swallow a new pill called "Canebinol."

I got a chance now to check out Samohi. I studied the rusty fences and the drab, hard expanse of it. It had a mean look. Malibu locals and Valley Dudes were made to attend together. Hopefully Emilio and I could try to create some sort of acting, performing nucleus that would have a hard shell on it to the gruff surroundings.

The graduates who walked around me were as stoned as my

brother was, maybe more so. I had to talk to Emilio. School was out. I focused on the nameless faces to find Steve. The sun was down.

"Got to get back to the house, while there's still time."

I walked down to the junior high sometimes. Summer school was in session. When no one was around, I went up to the main stage and with asinine care, hugged the curtain goodbye.

Fred Grossman walked up. "I want to capture 'The Sugar Blues' on Super 8 film! I believe it is one of the most important acts this school has ever seen! But we can only film it in one take!"

He filmed me dancing to "The Sugar Blues" in the middle of the Santa Monica High School campus during lunch hour. I had my record player plugged in with an extension cord out of view of the camera. We did one rehearsal, and it was great. Then he filmed it and three students put their arm around each other's shoulders and stampeded the camera and ruined it.

Mr. Thacker invited me to speak to his TV production class. I stood in front of the class and felt like it was my funeral.

"The advice I have is to stick with acting, just keep acting, follow your talent through and discover where it leads you."

There were six long-haired surfers there, and five of them were stoned. I looked over at Mr. Thacker and he turned away to let me continue. He was always busy.

"When you are on stage or on camera with other actors, you are all partners."

I rummaged through the classroom cabinets, opening anything that could be opened. I found a sleeveless album that had an obscure Bix song. I would never find that recording anywhere else. I tucked the "licorice pizza" under my left arm and walked

"WHAT THE HELL," SAID BIX.

out the door with it.

I paused in the door frame and glanced back at my acting teacher. He gave me a slight wave and a smile of approval. I smiled in the same way back and walked out with it. It was a Jimmy McPartland recording of a band arrangement of Bix Beiderbecke's "In a Mist."

(Journal entry)

July 13th, 1977
Last night marked the end of our three bicentennial years.

⋙⋘

I wandered Malibu aimlessly. I didn't want the sun at the beach and I didn't want to walk up and down those steep hills through the brush and streets with loose dogs either. I ran my thumb and index finger along some Wild Oats Grass and tossed the seeds to my left. Near Trancas, I chased a Roadrunner so I could watch it comically sprint. They were impossible to close in on. I fell on my back in the sand and laughed as it ditched me. A man in a colorful shirt approached me in back of Trancas market with a stack of flyers in his hand.

"Hello there! Would you care to be an extra in a movie?"

"A movie? Sure, where?"

"On Paradise Cove Beach…tomorrow. You've got to get there early though…eight a.m.!" I took a flyer.

"Count me in!"

I showed up on time and was glad I brought a visor to shield my face. When the fifty or so extras assembled, I glanced among them and didn't recognize anybody. The director stood on a chair and spoke to us through a megaphone.

"Now you all fully understand that there will be no pay except for this T-shirt, if you want to think of that as payment!" He held up an ugly yellow shirt that said, SAVE OUR BEACH on the front in black block letters, the three words scrolled down.

"Now, I want you all to find your approximate size and put these on! You ladies can change inside of your cars and the men can change right here! Come on over and get your shirts out of the box!"

We formed a quiet line, everyone slightly humiliated, as we reached and picked our shirts up out of the deep square box. I lifted off my buttoned shirt and stashed it under a rock.

All we did for the next nine hours in the stabbing sun was shout, "Save our beach!" in unison. The director repeated through his megaphone that we weren't loud enough. By the time the sun had set, my voice, and everyone else's, was hoarse from those three words. I picked up my shirt from under the rock and took the bus to Morning View Drive.

When I got in the door, sunburnt, I held out my T-shirt and showed my father.

"I got this shirt for being an extra in a movie near the Sand Castle. It sure made me wish I was a Hollywood movie star."

"Tsk...I am sure it did, Jeff. I'll tell you...those extreme few who do finally make it in that business after *years* of pursuing their dreams, usually say it wasn't worth the strife that they had to go through and all those countless years of struggling endlessly." He jerked his head forward in a nod, his left hand jammed in his front pocket.

I stayed in bed for two days, depressed. I could barely move. My dad brought me a few simple meals. His passive then turned to aggressive.

"I am tired of this, Jeff! Get out of bed! Get out of that bed!" I got dressed and went into the living room.

"What the hell," said Bix.

"Do you still have a girlfriend?" I asked.

"That remains to be seen." I put on a sweater and headed out the door. He blocked the front door.

"Where do you think you're going?" came the crazy low murmur.

"Out!"

"Unfortunately, I want you to stay here tonight."

"I stay home all the damn time," I said in a stifled voice.

"Are you arguing with me, Jeff? Don't try me. That's a warning." His eyes stared evenly through to the back of my skull.

"Okay," I said, so angry I was ready to mutilate myself. I shook all over and backed up. He moved slowly toward his room. I clutched my sweater tightly and went into the living room and sat on the couch with my eyes pointed to the wall.

"*Jeff!*" He stomped in and held up an accusing finger.

"I'd like to know why you have been shaving in my sink, in *my* bathroom!"

"I've got no stubble on my face. I can't shave! And I don't go into your bathroom because it reminds me of you! So you know I wouldn't go in there."

"Bullshit, Jeff! I use an electric razor! There is shaving hair all around my sink and I know you did it! Now come here!"

I followed him into his bathroom, a place I hadn't entered in weeks. I noticed my ugly birthday present to him was in his garbage pail. There in the basin were thick, black stubble hairs, obviously from an adult's face.

I got dizzy.

"That's your hair," I told him.

"Don't argue with me, you goddamned rotten kid!" He grabbed me and threw me hard out of the bathroom. I don't know where I landed. I think I was between the bed and the dresser.

"If I say it's your hair, then I know!" His veins bulged out his neck and head. I steadied myself. "Clean it up! I said clean it up! Never ever never do you ever go inside my bathroom or my room again! I don't want to think of you anymore! Are you going to clean it up…*or do you want me to kill you!*"

I studied his face. He meant that. I made it back into the living room and sat down on the couch.

My hands came to my face as I passed through.

I tore my face with my nails.

"Useless nothing kid! Get out of my life!"

I heard a zing from my inner ear and wavered on the corner of the couch and didn't breathe. I couldn't hear what he said except "clean it up" was in there, and so was "call your mother." I put my arms ever so slowly down and looked out the sliding glass door.

I sank like never before. My mind glided downward and my depression reached a level beyond known realms. I almost blacked out with my eyes open, just a pair of eyes, blank. I was pulled downward like Saran Wrap through water, out of myself, and down through the couch. My eyes settled into the carpet: a lethal dose of bad combinations.

Part of me that should have stayed in my mind ripped out and went away as I drew a sharp gasp. I shot up from the couch and almost fell into my father's room, breathing fiercely.

"Help!" He lowered his eyebrows and looked me over

"You look pale. My God, you look pale. Huh, how about that?" He put his hands to his hips in a curious fashion.

"Help me. I think I'm dying! You'd better get me out of here!" I crawled on his bed and he came around and sat on me. I trembled like an electrocution and would have flipped onto the floor.

He held down my hands and knees, which took strength. He spoke to me calmly. "It's okay, Jeff. You won't be living here that

"What the hell," said Bix.

much longer."

"Why do you take everything away from me?" I managed to say without biting through my tongue.

"Because you live in a dream world, Jeff. I have got to bring you back to reality. You should thank me."

Fifteen

WHAT THE PEEPER SAW

I would not be able to knock my father on his ass. Quite the contrary is what would happen.

At this point, I needed my prized possessions for my sanity, and they were all vulnerable. Mr. Sheen's Bix screenplay, my brittle 1920s record collection, and the diary Terri had given me were vital.

My adult friend, Shelby Basso, told me that long walks were good for nervous stomachs, so I walked for miles. I saw someone else as I went along on the highway and streets. It was the man who resembled the Frankenstein monster and walked backwards up small inclines and hills. His arms were rigid, as was the lopsided shape of his constantly open mouth. Dressed in outdated farmer's clothes, he didn't speak. He looked at people but seemed to not notice them. Everyone in Malibu knew of him. When I saw him plonking ahead of me, I passed him up, so we wouldn't walk side by side. Word had it he was a shell shock victim from World War II.

All he did was walk all day, every day, for years on end, always at the same zombie pace. We both went around Point Dume, down to Zuma Beach, then to Paradise Cove and back. As I passed him, it felt like there wasn't a hell of a lot of difference between us.

My father was not a shell shock victim. I knew that he had been pretty much unscathed by his service in the Korean War. He had spent most of his service with paperwork in an office and he fucked the general's daughter whenever he got the chance. Her name was Rusty, but he told me that he used to keep her oiled.

I walked along and stepped around my new creature friend and along fences with big dogs that barked hysterically and sprang into the air in a whirling frenzy until my anxiety and depression morphed into an intense monotony. The calmness of boredom was a godsend.

I was close to the house of my friend, Joel, when I felt a terrible surge of fear. I grabbed my forehead and then hurriedly took my hand away. Joel and his mother would soon move away he told me. I knocked on the door and Joel answered.

"Joel, can I come in, please! I feel horrible," I quavered. I started to cry but was too scared to. "Something is wrong with me. I might need an ambulance. You better let me in!"

I barged into the house and stood five feet away from Joel's mother. She had a plate of spaghetti in front of her. Joel had told me his mother had social anxiety. She was determined not to recognize my existence. I stared at her and calmed down. I waved my hand. Her expression was blank, her mouth closed, and she looked straight ahead or down into her spaghetti.

"Fascinating," I said aloud as I held their phone receiver in my hand and stared at her, steadying myself with my index finger wrapping around the cord. Joel took the phone from me and hung it up. He pushed me gently outside and shut and locked the door in my face. I sank on their porch and lay on my side, and then crawled off the porch and made myself stand up and walk like a normal person.

I sat on my bed on an afternoon when I heard my father's car pull up. I heard him enter the house through his bedroom door. He laughed playfully, and his girlfriend giggled.

I thought I should probably leave the house for a while. I worried that they would hear me leave. I heard loud kissing and my father hummed a yummy sound that sickened me. It reminded me of opening an old carton of milk to smell if it was sour or not; you didn't want to smell it, but you smelled it anyway.

I decided to escape through my bedroom window when my father made a grunt. It was the sort of grunt that a lumberjack makes when he chops a tree. Each grunt lasted one full second, and there was a one-second pause between each grunt. Then she began.

"Ah, oh… Paul!

I had never heard a sound remotely like this from my father or any of his women. I was frozen.

"Cork me! Oh, just fuck me now!" I imagined it was two loud tarantulas mating. I thought I might puke. She did have sort of a sexy voice, and once he shut up, it sounded a little better.

"Oh, OH! OH! OH! Come on, Paul!"

He stepped it up. His low, harsh voice went on solidly for minutes and gained momentum like a locomotive from the center of hell. I was either going to vomit or masturbate right then, and I've always hated to vomit. I licked numb lips. I clutched my blue blanket, ran across my room, and when I opened the door;

the woman rang louder.

I sank to the floor of the hallway and screwed my blanket into the floor between the two bedrooms. I humped away and I came as soon as I could, threw the blanket on my bed, buckled my pants, and ran out of the house. I fell into the weeds and stayed on the ground with my eyes shut tightly and shivered.

I hid behind plants and bushes for three hours. The menacing sky was a vast orange sunset with strange cornet-shaped clouds lying almost still at the horizon. I held my breath and went back in the house with ornate carefulness. I made a beeline to my room and stayed quietly in bed.

I heard my father leave with his woman in the morning. I rubbed my tired eyes and ears. I never wanted to hear that again. I got up, got dressed, and made a bowl of granola cereal. I ate and sat up.

"He did that on purpose," I told my empty cereal bowl.

He had been gone a half an hour when he gunned up the driveway with his usual vengeance. I ran in to get my jacket, but he was inside before I could leave the house. I stayed in my room until I heard him tinker with his car. I couldn't believe how sick of him I was.

I opened the front door and ran toward the ocean. I was at the edge of the property.

"JEFF!" His voice cracked like a shot from his rifle. I stopped.

"Why don't I just keep running?" I said sadly to the winds.

"COME HERE!"

I slowly made my way to him. I would just face the same thing later when I attempted to sleep. The hood of his car was open, but I knew he was no mechanic. All he knew how to do was check oil. He stood there and gazed into the engine.

"I'm here. What do you want?" He was silent with a grimace. A full ten minutes passed, and he still had not said anything. I started to walk away.

"I didn't say you could leave," said the hideous voice. I returned and stood in the same place just to his left.

Another six minutes went by. I knew what Frank would do if he were standing here next to this brute. And then I did it; I decided to say the wrong thing. It welled out of me and broke the long silence.

"You sure do know how to screw the lights out of a gal, don't you?"

He rolled his eyes and took a step back and nodded his head. "Huh."

"What? What is it?"

He placed his hands on his hips, stood back from his car in a pretentious pose and focused his eyes on the tops of the trees that lined the driveway. "That does it. You're gone. You're out of here. You will never live here again. Over my dead body will you ever live here again," he said, like a death sentence.

"I am leaving. Goodbye," I said and walked away from him. He didn't stop me, and I realized that he probably liked the words I had just spoken.

I slept over at Frank's, just him and me on the floor of the living room. The look he had on that last morning. We knew. I had hardly ever seen Frank cry. I glanced at him sideways. He didn't look at me, his eyes slightly off to the right and down. His mouth was in a shape I had never seen; oval shaped from side to side, his lips disappeared. He breathed unevenly. and he stood still.

"I'll be seeing you."

"Yeah."

"You know that song. Tell your dad I said hi…and bye."

"Yeah."

"…and your mom too."

"...yeah."

"I'll be on my way. Bye."

"Bye."

I turned and quietly walked out. He stood where he was, as I gently closed the door.

I entered an empty house and went in my brother's room and took his marijuana pipe and a half an inch of Thai Stick and lit up outside. I had four hits and took my chances whether it would set off another anxiety attack. It was a good high. I opened my diary.

(Journal entry)

July 13, 1977

I told my mom the other day that I'm having the funnest time of my life now. I don't exactly know how true that is as I sit here on the living room couch. Lonely and worried – waiting for my bro to return home on his bike. Most of the time I think that everything will be ok but sometimes I have very strange and eerie visions. Since school let out I have been bashing it up pretty much like I said I would. I think I get high too much. I'll be going to live with mom in some weeks. Joel is leaving Malibu tomorrow.

⸎

The school was silent except for the faint patter of one person on the track, two hundred yards away. I meditated on a student-made mosaic that hung over the gymnasium steps. The runner went down the slope and in my direction, muscular physique and long, blond hair.

"*Jeff?*" he yelled out.

"*Hi, Emilio.*" He ran toward me. I looked at him like he was the good angel of mercy.

He looked healthy and happy. The summer must have been good to him.

"Jeff, my dad wants you over for dinner!"

"He *does*? When?"

"Whenever you can come."

"Any time you invite me... except, oh yeah, I forgot. I'm moving away. I think I am."

"Where?"

"Alabama."

"*Again?*" he asked with a tilt to his head.

I looked at the ground, shook my head slowly, and gave Emilio a look that said I couldn't believe it either.

"I know. If it was New Orleans, it wouldn't be quite as bad. At least I'd have my music around me. My dad is...staying here, though."

"Do you still have time for dinner over at our house?"

I straightened up. "I will make time for that! Yes."

"Okay, can you come by tomorrow? Just to see when it might be convenient."

"Tomorrow? I guess so. Sure I can."

"Okay, then. In the afternoon sometime."

"Okay. Thank you!"

I put on my cashmere sweater and tried to look informal but not sloppy. I walked to the Sheen residence, entered the curved driveway and passed the Citroën cars, which were lined up.

I gently knocked on the door. Martin Sheen appeared in four seconds.

"Hello."

"Hi. Would Emilio happen to be around?"

"Come on in," said Mr. Sheen. I entered with big eyes. I had never been in here before. It was not a brightly lit house. It felt comfortable. Mr. Sheen went into the kitchen, where he had cut a big watermelon on the counter.

"Sit down," he said and motioned gently with a knife toward a chair.

"Oh…thank you." I walked over and took a seat in a wooden chair.

"Emilio should be back in a little while. He's just down the street with a friend. You want some watermelon?"

"Yes, thank you." Mr. Sheen placed a moderate-sized slice on a plate and set it down in front of me and went back to the kitchen counter. There was a pause.

"Emilio told me you two are interested in acting?"

"Yes. He's wonderful." He put some watermelon in his mouth, but I forgot I had watermelon in front of me. Mr. Sheen leaned on the counter. He looked concerned.

"There are well over a million who want to make it," he spoke clearly. "Out of that, there is one hundred thousand in the Screen Actors Guild alone. Out of that, there are a few hundred who make it." He took a deep breath. "There are thousands who are qualified, and now Emilio wants in. I told him how hard it is." He looked deep in thought.

"Yes." I listened.

"But he keeps talking about how much he wants in. Still, I guess if a person is *that* headstrong, he has a chance. A *chance*… to make it! A *small* chance."

Mr. Sheen shifted his feet and paused and glanced over at me.

"Emilio tells me you want to be an actor too."

"Yes."

"That makes two of you then," he nodded slightly. "It is one tough, *tough game*. It's *unbelievable*." He slowly shook his head as though looking back on what he had seen and been through. I had to ask while there was a pause.

"You were going to do that movie about Bix Beiderbecke?"

"Yes. It fell through."

"I was wondering what they planned on calling that movie?" I was on the edge of my seat.

"*In a Mist*," stated Mr. Sheen.

The fuzz on my neck stood on end.

"That is so beautiful. It is hard to believe," I said slowly. "That is what I knew it *had* to be called." I almost leaped out of my chair. "I mean, on the brown cover, it just says 'Bix.'" Mr. Sheen stopped and watched me. "Thank you for letting me borrow that, by the way. It means everything… and the records too!"

Mr. Sheen smiled at me, and his face softened.

"It fell through. They couldn't get enough backers for it. It was too bad. It would have been good." He folded his arms in a way that I had often seen Emilio do.

Emilio dashed through the front door.

"Hi," he said. His eyes darted at the two of us. He had a look on his face like he had missed something. He disappeared into his bedroom, opened the door, stood in his doorway and gave me a long, straight-faced stare and motioned me over with his eyes, then closed his bedroom door. Mr. Sheen picked up the watermelon on the counter.

"Maybe I should go knock on Emilio's door."

"He should be out in a minute." He turned and looked at the closed door. "Alright, go ahead." I walked to Emilio's room and knocked on the white door. Emilio opened it.

"Get in here!" he whispered. I went in and Emilio shut the door behind me.

"What did you two talk about?" he asked with urgency. I

shrugged my shoulders. "Bix and acting, that's it. He just gave me some watermelon. Where were you?"

"Down the street at John Kelly's house. Did he talk about me?"

"A little, I mean, he talked about *acting*. That you are acting now and that you are interested in it and that makes two of us. I just got here! Are you going to eat dinner soon, do you think? I mean, maybe I should leave, or stay?"

"Yeah, you had better split."

"Now?"

"Yeah, now."

"Oh, okay."

Mr. Sheen was sitting at a table when I walked out of the bedroom door.

"Thank you for the watermelon. I have to get going."

"Okay, thanks for stopping by."

I gently closed the front door behind me and walked out the driveway as if I had someplace to go. I slowed my pace. I only wished that I could be adopted by any one of my friends. Emilio came out of the house and rushed after me.

"*Jeff!*" He was suddenly happy. I rushed back to him.

"My dad said he wants you over for dinner tomorrow night!"

"He does?"

"He just told me! Be here around five o'clock, okay? I'll see you!"

"I will! Thank you! I will see you then!" I smiled. I watched Emilio stride back into the house, giddier than I had ever seen him.

I got Kurt Dieterle on the phone.

"Hello there, Mr. Dieterle, it's Jeff Lucas."

"Oh hi, Jeff!"

"I just called because it looks like I will not be able to make our appointment to meet and talk about your friend Bix."

"Oh, that's too bad."

"I'm moving pretty far away, and I don't think I will be able to come back, not for a while."

"I am sorry to hear that. Where are you moving to?"

"I'm gonna be moving to…New Orleans," I lied.

"Oh? Good food down there."

"I will be more interested in the music, of course."

"*Oh* yes, they've got that too."

"Well, I hope I can still write you. It would mean a lot."

"Oh, sure! You are more than welcome to." Mr. Dieterle gave me his address and I wrote it down. "Give me a call when you get to New Orleans."

"Okay," I said quietly. I reluctantly hung up and walked over to my father's piano. I picked up the key that he locked the lid with and scratched a two-inch downward gash to the right deeply into the wood beside the keyhole. My face looked like I wanted to kill.

The next day, I held the Bix Beiderbecke screenplay and sat next to my father at the table.

"Martin Sheen, and I, and Emilio, have made a pact. I think Mr. Sheen is going to help Emilio and me with our acting careers."

"That is bullshit, Jeff, and you know it."

"No, it's not. I think he wants me to stay in Malibu, Dad."

He glared at me insanely. "Don't try me, Jeff. You are finished in Malibu. I refuse to keep you under my roof ever again."

"This is my most prized possession that I have, but I think I should offer to give it back to Mr. Sheen. What do you think?"

"What is it?"

"A gift from Martin Sheen."

I looked up at the clock. It was 4:30 p.m.

"It's time now, Dad. Drive me over there, please."

"What if I say no?"

I stood up. "Jesus! I'm going!" Five minutes passed. I went into the living room and tried to breathe evenly.

"Okay, I'll take you… I guess." He didn't face me.

"Okay then, it's time to go now! It's three miles, and it is too late for me to walk there and be on time for dinner and you know it!"

"Alright." He sighed heavily as he tossed a kitchen rag across the table that he had flopped through the air and caught for the past half hour. "But I want to leave right now. I don't care whether you're ready or not. Right this very minute, or forget it."

I guided him to the house and he parked across the street.

"You are sure that this is the Sheens' home?" He was star-struck and nervous as he stared wide-eyed at the house and began to believe that this was really the Sheen residence.

"We are here."

"Are you going to need a ride home tonight?" he asked.

"I don't know. We're going to see." I got out and closed the door on his next sentence.

The sun was still bright as I stepped around a Citroën and walked through the driveway. I knocked; Emilio's mom answered the door.

"Hi, is Emilio here?"

"He just stepped out. Are you Jeff?"

I smiled widely. "YES."

"You're staying over for dinner?"

"Yes, if it's okay."

"Sure! Come on in. He should be back in just a sec."

Mrs. Estevez went in to the kitchen. The food smelled good. It was quiet, and no one else seemed to be home. I slowly tip toed around. I peered into a closet and Emilio's younger brother Ramon sat cross-legged and quietly studied his tap shoes. He looked up at me with a blank stare and closed mouth. We looked at each other and didn't say a word.

I backed up and noticed a large bookcase against the wall. I scanned the shelves. On the top shelf was a hardcover book titled *Remembering Bix*. I took it down and opened it and looked at pictures of Bix I had not seen.

I saw Martin Sheen walk in from the back yard. I looked at a picture of Bix and then at Mr. Sheen as he spoke with his wife. Yes, Hollywood had made the right decision to cast him as Bix Beiderbecke, all right.

An energetic Emilio bolted through the front door. "Put it away," he said, and he took and placed the book gently back in its place on the upper shelf. A friend I barely recognized was with him. "Follow me." I followed them outside to the front lawn. The other guy had a baseball. "Throw it!" ordered Emilio.

I rebelled a little and headed for a hammock on the small front lawn. "Would you mind if I lie down on this?"

"Go ahead," said Emilio amiably.

I licked my lips, closed my eyes, and breathed in Malibu's friendly ocean air. I looked up and saw white seagulls glide in slow motion circles. Emilio let me lie there for seven minutes until he thought I might be almost asleep, and he was right. I felt a push and opened my eyes.

"Wanna go for a ride?" Emilio grinned.

"Sure," I said. He gave me a few hard pushes and then his friend joined in.

I did not attempt to jump off. The hammock rose higher until it was sideways. Then I saw it—a dangerous sprinkler was directly underneath and poked a few inches out of the ground.

"That might be too high," said Emilio thoughtfully.

"Yeah, could be," I answered. They continued anyway. The hammock swung up and straight down like a catapult. The ground came at me like a speeding car made out of grass. Still, I managed to keep my eye on the sprinkler. I landed so hard that my body left an imprint. I looked at the sprinkler two inches from my chest.

My head rang, and my lungs were without air for almost a minute. I raised myself up.

"Are you okay?" asked Emilio. I smiled and winked, doubled over. We stood there while my breath wheezed.

"You guys ought to try flat sprinklers if you are going to have them in wrong places."

Emilio was still giddy. I had always known him as fairly subdued. I could see that the Estevezes were strong enough to endure a lot of adversity together.

"Time to eat," Mrs. Estevez told us from the front porch. I followed Emilio in. His other friend stood there like a puppy shut out for the night.

"Okay, Emilio. I'll see you."

"Okay, Marlin."

People walked in through every entrance to the table. Mrs. Estevez gently seated me at one end. Mr. Sheen sat at the center of the table on my left-hand side and was in conversation with the other guest of honor who was at the other end of the table—a robust, bald actor whom I couldn't quite place.

Emilio's brother, Ramon, sat next to Emilio. A sister and a younger brother sat down on either side of Mr. Sheen. The brother that I had not met looked to be about ten. Never in my life had I seen a father and son look so much alike. The boy didn't say anything, and he didn't appear to listen to much either.

I always knew Emilio resembled his dad, but this younger brother was something else. At first glance, the two faces differed only in age. It was hard to believe that in all our deep conversations over the past three years, I never thought to ask Emilio if he had any other siblings.

My eyes swept around the table. It occurred to me that there was a dominant "Sheen gene." Everyone in the family had small mouths and when the chicken, roast potatoes, and peas arrived, they couldn't fit much food into their mouths at one time.

Emilio was animated, and he ate with a sense of style. He listened attentively to his father. He looked around the table, smiled at me and then at his mom.

"This dinner is really very good, Mrs. Estevez," I said.

"Oh, thank you." She smiled.

Mr. Sheen talked about the nightmare movie that he had just finished. His friend nodded his head and filled his plate with seconds. Mrs. Estevez cleared plates from the table. Mr. Sheen stood up and then everyone followed his lead. Emilio and I left the dining room together.

"Do you have to go anywhere tonight, or can you stick around?"

"I don't know what my dad's up to… I am sure I could stay here for three or four more years."

"Have you got to get home, Jeff?" asked Mrs. Estevez. Mr. Sheen looked over.

"Excuse me," he said to his friend. He was too good of a host. "I'll take him home," he announced.

I tried to reverse the situation,

"I can call my dad… I mean I don't…."

Mr. Sheen waved his hand. "I'll take him." He went out the front door and everyone tagged along, me last.

We were all on the front lawn together, and time stood still.

A little after-dinner conversation in the twilight was a good way to say goodbye to Malibu. I stood next to Emilio. We felt such a strong kinship. I gave him a sidelong glance and he smiled at me. Honesty was in our eyes and drove us forward together.

His two brothers ran out and chased each other in erratic circles.

"You didn't tell me you had another brother."

"You mean Charlie? Oh, yeah."

"I didn't know that. Quiet, isn't he?" Emilio folded his arms and half smiled as we studied Charlie.

"Yeah, except when I want him to be."

I laughed.

Mr. Sheen continued the conversation with his friend and went toward his car. The sun cast shadows across the lawn. I wanted to have my first conversation with Charlie because I hadn't even heard him speak, only laugh. I watched him chase Ramon around the side of the house and back again. Mr. Sheen unlocked the car door.

"How did it feel to get that award?" asked Emilio.

"I thought you were going to get it."

"We were so glad you got it. We were just going, 'Yeah, Jeff!'"

"Thanks, Meels." We smiled.

"Okay, ready?" said Mr. Sheen.

We didn't take a Citroën. Emilio and I got into a Mercedes with Mr. Sheen and his friend. I got in on the right side of the back seat. Mr. Sheen turned from the driver's seat and looked me in the eyes.

"Where is it?"

"Above Zuma beach, in back of the junior high school, up the hill." I really felt like I was in a movie right then, because I had seen so much of him on the screen, but I didn't say so.

Mr. Sheen continued to tell his friend about *Apocalypse Now*.

"Unbelievable! I wouldn't be here now! I told him, I said, 'Hey Francis, that picture nearly killed me. You have got to at least give me half back of what I put into it.' Now we are barely speaking… which driveway is it?"

"The second on the left." Mr. Sheen smoothly pulled up the driveway.

"I sure thank you for absolutely everything, Mr. Sheen."

"You are so very welcome, Jeff."

Emilio followed me out and we stood on my father's driveway in front of the car.

"All right, Jeff." We put our hands on each other's shoulders. We had been through a lot together, and I knew that the future looked shaky as hell for me. I think Emilio could tell that this was a cliffhanger goodbye.

"We'll make a movie together," said Emilio.

"One? We'll have a whole series!"

Emilio's eyes lit up. His smile stopped, and his brilliant blue eyes lit up as though he had seen a ghost. I hugged on to him tightly, broke away, and looked into the car at Martin Sheen. He appeared to have some tears in his eyes. The engine ran and the windows were rolled up. He smiled that great smile and looked at me.

"I love ya… I love you," I saw him say.

I waved. "Good night."

The greatest moment of my life, and I had to walk away from it. I didn't look back because I didn't want them to see me cry. I heard the car disappear. My father opened his bedroom door for me and let me in. He stood back as I entered the house.

He grabbed onto his dresser with his left hand and sank low to the floor. He crouched and shook like a frightened, beady-eyed gopher that had been chased into a hole.

"Who brought you back? That wasn't Martin Sheen I just saw

in the driveway?!" he whimpered as he pointed to his driveway.

"Yes, it was Martin Sheen," I told him, and I walked in a stately fashion toward my room. He leaped behind me.

"So tell me what happened."

"I don't feel like talking to you right now…if you really want to know."

I didn't come out of my room that night, and he left me alone. In the afternoon the next day, I got dressed and walked to the bathroom. I pissed, zipped up, leaned on the sink, and glanced in the mirror at my worn-out face. I walked out and went over to him.

"I should stay here, Dad, and I am not the only one who feels that way."

"Unfortunately, that is impossible. Your plane leaves tomorrow night," he said low and quietly.

"You seem to be recovered from seeing Martin Sheen in your driveway last night."

I took off out the door, and he didn't call me back. I breathed gulps of the Santa Ana winds and went down to Trancas. I sat on the bus stop bench and did what I used to do when I was first grabbed by the acting bug four years ago. I looked like an idiot, doing acting exercises. I watched people and exaggerated their features and mannerisms.

I walked over to the entrance of the market as sunset loomed. I vaguely recognized a few faces as their hair blew around in the wind. I saw Sean Penn walk in from the beach toward me, still wet from the ocean. He was a little out of breath. He was covered in his black surf suit. A flimsy leash was attached from his suit to his waxed surfboard under his right arm.

"Here he comes," I said quietly. He unhooked the leash and set his surfboard on the ground beside the wall of the market and entered through the automatic doors. Sean's hair was blond from the summer sun, and he had white sun tan lotion on his nose.

On the walk home, I grabbed the leaves of bushes and tugged them off, dozens of them, on both sides of me. I stayed in my room with green hands. I fell into a noisy sleep, into troubled dreams.

In the morning it was uncomfortably quiet. I didn't hear my father's usual piano; nor did I hear his rifle shot. I felt dizzy but got dressed and went outside. Under the fiberglass roof of the breezeway there was deadly silence.

I descended the front steps. Where was he? I looked around me. I heard his door open behind me. He came over and circled and paced in front of me as if to mentally barbed-wire me in. A tremendous scowl up under his eyebrows.

"Can you speak?" I said.

"I can speak, Jeff!" He crouched in front of me like a Japanese wrestler, his arms extended, and he wrung his wrists back and forth. His face looked like *The Beast from 20,000 Fathoms*.

"But I don't *want* you here!"

That word, *want*, was four seconds long and the way he screamed it was like the cracking timbers of a roof collapsing.

"How about just to the end of summer?"

"What good is that going to do, Jeff?" he whined.

"I need to thank the Sheens for the dinner and talk with them."

"But I don't *want* you here! Also, I have plans to convert your room into my office as soon as you leave!"

A torrent of rage rattled though me. "I can't go back to Alabama. I had to see my stepsister die when I was there," my voice cracked.

"What's that got to do with anything, Jeff? I need you out of here!"

(Journal entry)

1:05am   Monday, July 18, 1977
1:27am
Well, it looks like I'll be going back to Alabama. My plane leaves Tuesday night. After my dad and Jack finally agreed about the payment. I'd been on the verge of having an anxiety attack a couple of days ago with dad. He started in on me again with the usual this morning. After every fight, he says, "Jeff, I think you'd better call up your mother and tell her you're on your way!" and that's what I finally did. I know Alabama didn't work before, but now it's got to! As the late Peter Finch said, "I'm madder than hell and I'm not going to take it anymore!!!"

I made sure the last song I heard in Malibu on my little turntable was "Take Good Care of My Baby" by Bobby Vee.

He stood in my room at sunrise, his head held high on his shoulders. He was tense with focus.

"Okay Jeff, get out of bed! Your plane leaves in two hours... about!"

I cleared my eyes with my arm. "Wait! You said tonight."

"Well, I thought I'd better get you off earlier, so don't dilly-dally, please!"

"Dad, I've got things to do today! I've got to see Emilio. I want to thank them for the dinner."

"Well, you're not going to get to do it! You're only going to do one thing, and that's pack. So start packing, and don't start with me!"

"You try living back there in Montgomery!"

"This isn't about me, Jeff! It's about you! Everything you see around you here belongs to me—this house, and this property, and you are not welcome here while I am alive! I want you gone! I want you wiped off the face of this property! I *do* hope that is clear!"

"*Why?*"

"Because you are standing in the way of my happiness…*IF YOU REALLY WANT TO KNOW!*" came the ugly moan.

I shut up and stared at my father with a peculiar, distant look in my eyes.

I dropped souvenirs and knotted clothes in the suitcase on the bed. I went into the kitchen and stood in front of him.

"What about my role in the Emr's movie they promised me?"

"So, you can come back for it. Who knows… since you believe in destiny so much, maybe you were meant to go back there."

"Maybe it was meant to be?" I said.

"Maybe so. I'd offer you breakfast, but you're probably not hungry, so let's get going."

"No, I don't want to eat a damn thing. I will have to start my life all over again from scratch."

"I'll load up your stuff." He went into my room and loaded up his car with my luggage quickly, back and forth.

"Don't forget my record player!" I yelled. He stormed back into the kitchen.

"Did you get my record player in the car?"

"Yup! Now all of your prized possessions are loaded up. Everything is in the car. Let's go," he said with calm assurance.

"I have to double-check my room." I began toward my room.

He clutched me and shoved me by flexing his elbows, toward the kitchen door. In case I tried to crawl on the counters, he stuck his arms out to the ends and slid his fingers across the counters like one would lightly brush away dust. I could not get past him, and I couldn't breathe well, either. I backed up.

As we moved out the kitchen door and into the breezeway, he looked like he was about to wrangle a pony into a corral. I was the pony. He herded me forward as his car idled. I staggered ahead of him, numb. I got in and he shut the passenger's door. He got in and fastened his seatbelt. I didn't fasten mine. I sank back with the acceleration.

When we got to the airport, he checked in my suitcase and rushed me to the gate and neither of us said goodbye. He tromped off. I held a brown paper grocery bag. My Styrofoam hat and cane stuck out of the top.

On the plane, I thought about my heroes and how most of them had lousy fathers but not this lousy. I didn't talk to anyone. The stewardess brought me Cokes and food. I sat still. It was beautiful not to see my father's face.

Then it hit me.

"THE BIX SCRIPT!" I yelled on the plane. *"I left it on my bed, I think!"*

People turned and looked at me, and I looked back at them, panicked. I clutched the arms of my seat. Unless my old man had put it in my suitcase, then I left it in his hands, the worst hands in the world! I squirmed in my seat as we rocketed toward Montgomery. An hour later I glanced at the quiet passengers, and I sang out a chorus.

♪"He's got the whole world in his hands. He's got the whole damn world, in his hands! He's got the whole screenplay in his hands! He's got the whole world in his hands! He's got you and me brother, in his grip! He's got you and me brother, in his grip!

He's got you and me sister, in his grip. He's got the whole world in his grip! ♪"

I called the Malibu house right after I dumped out my suitcase on my new bed in Montgomery. Steve answered the phone.

"Hey, Jeff… bummer you're back there again."

"Ain't it though? Is dad there? Is my Bix screenplay there? Is Martin Sheen's Bix script there?"

"There is nothing in your room. He cleared out everything and threw away your bed. There's nothing in there. It's empty."

"*Where is he?*"

"He can't come to the phone."

"*Why?*"

"He's outside. I got him high on some pot," he leaned in and whispered.

"You got him to smoke marijuana?"

"Yes. He's checking out the bark on a tree outside right now. Hopefully it'll mellow him out. I'll have him call you when he comes down."

"He is celebrating," I told him.

I called the next morning. "Yellow," he answered with a sense of ecstatic neglect.

"Dad! Thank God you're home! Listen, what happened to that Bix screenplay, that script that belongs to Martin Sheen!"

"I don't know what you're talking about, Jeff ! What play?" he shouted.

"*The Bix script!*"

"Hmm. That doesn't ring a bell!"

"No! Don't you say that!" I yelled back.

"I may have thrown it away, Jeff. I don't know. I cleared all your stuff out of there, unless I put it in that shed on the side of the house. Anything I would find of yours, I would put in there."

"*If it is* in there, *please*… keep it in that shed. I am going to keep calling you to make sure Martin Sheen's screenplay is in that shed! I hung up on him, ran away from the phone, and drifted around in aimless panic.

Two days later my mother got a letter from him and she showed me the last page.

(Letter from Paul Lucas)

> *"Jeffrey is a slow and a definitely semi-retarded child. He cannot do any of the things that normal kids his age can do. Maybe our efforts to abort him somehow affected his brain. He brings me very much grief and that is why I had to send him to you. I just can't imagine how he will ever make it in the world. Please don't show him this letter but I wanted to explain to you why I have made the decision to send him back there.*
> *Regards,*
> *Paul."*

⸻

I looked out into the Alabama moonlight and listened to the bugs in the trees. It was the anniversary of Bix's death. All I could think about was Bix Beiderbecke as the millions of summer bugs, as big as flashlights, hissed and screamed all night long in the summer trees of the Deep South.

My music stand fell over all on its own in the dark at the opposite end of the room. A shiver went up my spine and out through the top of the roof. I leaped out of my room. I jumped back in, grabbed a pencil and my diary, ran back out, switched on the hall light, and scribbled furiously.

The Winds of Malibu

(Journal entry)

Saturday, Aug. 6, 1931 - '77

Exactly 46 years have gone by since my past life died. It was 9:30 pm. He was suffering from pneumonia in a tiny New York hotel room. It got so hot that his disease became badly infected. Finally, his body could stand no more and the great Bix Beiderbecke died. The legend has never stopped growing since. On Aug. 16, 1961, Jeff Lucas was born and thus Bix's soul could live again. Tomorrow I will write an important letter to Kurt Dieterle.

Sixteen

General Robert E. Lee High

(Journal entry)

Extra   AUGUST 16th Tue. 1977
Extra
Elvis Presley died of a heart attack today! The man had built such a legend for himself that I don't believe we'll ever hear the end of him. As I put on the phonograph his first big hit, "Hound Dog," I went into the kitchen. My mom said, "I think we should have a time of silence, he was the king." It's hard to believe he's lying dead now at 42. Today was my birthday. I had a lot of fun. I took a really cute gal out to eat tonight. At last I found a relationship where a girl can like me back. Her name is Keely.

The Winds of Malibu

>»>«««

I sat at my worn-out, carved-up desk at General Robert E. Lee High School on the top third floor in my history class. Our teacher was a young woman full of Southern sass. We both shared an interest in Elvis Presley. Born and raised here, she was very comfortable with her Alabama environment.

"The first date I ever went on was to see the Elvis movie *Blue Hawaii!*" She beamed. I drifted into space, thinking of Lynn Craig, Frank Kratochvil, Emilio Estevez, Martin Sheen, Robert Miribilio, and Jade Kulka. The student body of my Malibu school was now in class in Santa Monica together. Panic gripped me, seated there in the center of the classroom, and this was only second period. I had four more periods to drag my anxiety through the humidity and then back home to Bowling Green Avenue.

I stood up, got away from my desk, and walked out of the classroom door, while this teacher was in mid-sentence with one of her comfortable anecdotes. The direction I headed in the hallway was west toward Malibu.

With every step, I was closer to all of my greatest friends, scattered across the Samohi campus. I continued west until the hall ran out at the blue wall of the dilapidated building. My shoes banged against the wall, and I leaned my forehead and hands against the windowpane, with reinforcement wire woven through.

I stared out, numbed, at the tops of a few defeated Southern trees, the branches of the trees lie still in the windless humidity. My fingertips slid down the glass to the window ledge.

I backed away slowly, turned around to my right, and made the walk back to my history class and the teacher and the forty students with their thick Southern accents. They looked at me as if I had lost my mind. Wide eyes were full worried amazement at something they had never seen a student do, and the teacher darted her eyes at me and shook her head intermittently for the rest of the class period like she couldn't believe what I had just done. I sat there, as disturbed as I was, and didn't say anything.

I saw *Star Wars* in Montgomery. I liked it less than anybody I met. The part I identified with though was when Obi-Wan Kenobi lets himself be sliced in half by Darth Vader. Darth Vader was my father, and I was Obi-Wan Kenobi. That's all.

(Journal entries)

Sunday, Sept. 18, 1977

For the second time, I'm getting involved in Bye Bye Birdie. Only this time, it won't be put on by M.P.J.H.S. but instead The Maxwell Airforce playhouse. I tried out for the part of Hugo and everyone thought that I was perfect for Hugo (it was a pretty juicy part and I felt I could do a lot with it) but then this other guy stepped in by the name of Chip (a good looking guy with a decent singing voice) He looks maybe 10 years older than me. He tried out for Hugo as well but he didn't get half the approval I did and overall he was a very mild actor. That's why I couldn't believe it when he got Hugo and I was stuck with this bit part of Harry Johnson. At first I was saddened but quickly I accepted it. We've been rehearsing since Aug. 30. On the 15 of Sept. Julie Stevens (our director) told me that she had made a terrible mistake in casting Chip as Hugo and that he was thinking of leaving. She told me today that she will "crawl

The Winds of Malibu

up his ass" until he finally leaves so that I can get the Hugo part.

Tue. Oct. 11, 1977

I always wondered how I would be able to take the news when Tatum O'Neal got her first boyfriend. What a shock when I heard out of all the people, she chose one of the Jackson 5!!! That throws me off completely. I don't know whether to laugh or cry.

GENERAL ROBERT E. LEE HIGH

<u>11:00</u>   Dec. 13, 1977 feeling like shit.   <u>11:20</u>
Because of money reasons and because we did not want to leave Jack alone, we've stayed in Montgomery. I don't mind though. I've slowly grown to religion since coming here. Everybody around here is religious. I met a good friend at Lee high school named Billy who talks normal. In past months I've had many dizzy spells and anxiety attacks. I have an appointment to see a shrink on Friday.

Jeff in his bedroom in Montgomery, Alabama, 1978. Photo by John N. Dick.

The Winds of Malibu

Dec. 31, 1977
This is the last 1977 that I'll be writing under. It's been an awkward year. I was much happier at the end of it. Stars dropped dead like flies; Freddie Prinze, Sebastion Cabot, Groucho Marx, Charlie Chaplin on Christmas and Bing Crosby.

March 9, 1978
Tonight marks the end of the Sugar Blues years. Time has proven that those things are getting old. After Robert E. Lee's Gong Show, which was tonight, I stepped on my hat and said, "It's on to bigger and better things." I can sense a big change is coming. We're moving to New Orleans! Aint that something! Can't wait.

April 6, 1978
It looks like something is finally going to be done about that hernia I've been carrying most of my life. I'm not sure but I believe that it will be operated on this summer. I've decided that I really should not take things like that so seriously. Since nobody wants to remember a coward, I will accept it.
A good day's coming
and it's worth the coming home on stones.

GENERAL ROBERT E. LEE HIGH

April 16, 1978

Just returned from New Orleans and all I can say is "What a town!" This was the first time I heard a cornet player named George Finola. Whenever I say that name I get a feeling of mixed emotions. That man literally ruined my future of becoming another Bix Beiderbecke. Now I know what Bix used to sound like in those night clubs. Finola even looks just like him. Well I've heard the best. Now let's go and beat him!

AUGUST, 1978

A silk, black and silver Western shirt, black slacks, and a greasy ducktail with adolescent sideburns down to the bottom of my earlobes was my look. A young Elvis Presley was what I shot for. My father didn't notice. We nodded to each other. I stepped around him with my backpack. He strode on ahead of me through the Los Angeles airport terminal.

"Come on! Don't slowpoke around!" He whipped his hand through the air. I thought about the Martin Sheen Bix script again as we rode the escalator down; then I cast the thought somewhere else. "Do you have any other luggage?"

"No." I watched him jam a stick of Wrigley's Spearmint Gum in his mouth and put the green wrapper in an ashtray. We got in his big, new, dark-blue Ford and drove out of LAX. It was August in Los Angeles, and even through the smog, the air was easier to breathe than in the humid Southern states.

"Elvis Presley is going to be dead one year on my birthday," I told him.

"You don't say." He drove like he always had, impatiently yet carefully as his jaw worked the chewing gum over violently.. I saw part of his shed as he parked. It was a white shed with green trim, made of thin metal with sliding doors in front.

AUGUST, 1978

Steve wasn't home to greet me. My father walked into the back room and made a phone call in what was now his personal office. I stood in the doorway of my now- unrecognizable bedroom and couldn't breathe too well. He had gotten rid of every remnant of me.

He finished his phone call and pounced out of there youthfully and into the kitchen in five steps and proceeded to make us both cheddar cheese omelets with tap water on the side in those same tall green water glasses that we drank out of when he was married to my mother. I followed him slowly. Steve's room was the same as when I had left Malibu. His large bed was still comfortably placed in the center of the room and the dresser where he kept his stash of illegal drugs remained undisturbed.

"You'll be sleeping on the living room couch tonight," said my dad.

Steve entered with a goofy smile for me and, his hair longer than ever. He was high on weed like the last time I had seen him. How many times had he been high in the year that I had been gone? More than 365 times, I guessed.

"How have you been?" he slurred.

"You should come to New Orleans."

"Oh yeah! I bet it's bitchin."

At bedtime on the couch in the dark, I looked through dusty curtains at the Malibu night out there. I sat up and glanced at dark shaped bushes and weeds and trees. Malibu was no longer my friend; that's what the scenery silently told me. Yet it was still in my blood, my secret home as long as I may live. I fell back to the couch and breathed more dust in from those tired curtains that had been there through everything. Then I slept.

My father stepped heavy-footed and paced early in the morning. He tromped over to his upright piano, sat down, and pounded out Brahms loudly. He still couldn't play that piece correctly.

I put my pants on and closed the bathroom door behind me. As my pee fell, I remembered my ex-stepmother, Jenny, used to say the bathroom was your only privacy. I put it away, zipped up, wiped my hands on my pants, and looked at myself in the mirror. My ducktail was undone. It was time to look in the shed.

I put on my shoes with no socks and flashy shirt unbuttoned and made a beeline for the shed. My father stopped playing piano, and his head turned as I went out the kitchen entrance. In twenty steps I was there. The door grated sideways.

There were a few rusted tools—not enough tools to grow a good garden with. A rolled up green water hose that was cracked and stiff like a fossil. I couldn't even lift up and look underneath the sparse, rusty, and mostly useless items for a chance at Mr. Sheen's screenplay. I listened to the stiff ocean breeze against the walls. I felt like I could be any one of these rusted, broken, and still tools. I felt akin to them.

The sky reeled as I backed out of there. The mild breeze could knock me over. My father was out of the house, to my right. He pretended to be interested in a plant as he paced along diagonally, his eye on me.

I got away from the shed. Dirt clods made for an uneven walk even when you weren't having a nervous breakdown. I stepped on a trail of ants and made it across the concrete and to some trees on top of the slope. I fell down on my back. The moment was one I didn't want. The sky looked sadder than I had ever seen it.

Where was Martin Sheen's Bix screenplay anyhow? Where did my father dare to toss it? The world-respected movie actor, Martin Sheen, where was his Bix script now— in which incinerator, in what garbage dump? I was certain Martin Sheen would understand if I told him what happened to his screenplay. He would prefer if I told him, and Emilio also, but that would take

AUGUST, 1978

more than I had the heart for, and really it was I who would never understand this.

I felt half invisible. I peered up next to some tree branches. There was a small cloud up there all alone. My father could not take a cloud away from me. I reached up and shaped my fingers around the outline to feel it. My hand came down to my forehead. I turned my head to the right and saw the driveway through the tree roots, my father's car there.

I got up slowly and felt different.

I moved along, unevenly, instinctively; I trod the half-mile down to Malibu Park Junior High. The houses and trees looked flat on my way there. It had been just one year, yet Malibu looked dated back to the day I was forced to exit. I couldn't believe that I was the only one who saw it this way. I was glad I didn't see Tommy Pringle as I passed by his house. He would look the same, but everybody I knew might as well be grown up and moved away from Malibu and old.

I stepped onto the blacktop through the fence and moved toward the gym. I had to see if it was still there. I studied the red bricks and there it was. JEFF LUCAS WAS HERE, it still said. AND IS GREAT, it still said underneath. It was the only graffiti anywhere on the fifty-foot tall red square building. I reached up and touched the J and leaned my back against the wall and looked at Juan Cabrillo elementary school in front of me and beyond that, the whelming sea with a fat sun streak. Both schools were vacant. The absence of Martin Sheen's Bix screenplay was like a vapor over this environment.

"Malibu is dead to me now," I said into the wind. I breathed in deep the same cool sea air that was no longer mine. You never had to breathe Malibu air much. It went right up your nose from that constant ocean breeze. I wasn't out here for any reason. I didn't want to see anybody I knew. I wouldn't mention Martin

Sheen's Bix script to my father. He was bent the way he was, and that is all there was to him forever.

I awakened on my seventeenth birthday ready to start over someplace else. Just give me New Orleans, that's all I'd ask. New Orleans and I went together well. I was Kid Creole.

He loved to eat out, so he asked me to choose a restaurant for my birthday dinner, and I chose the crappy Trancas diner. I ordered a burger. He reached for his wallet and with two large fingers hammered a fifty-dollar bill onto the table. I didn't pick it up. It stayed there between us for twenty-five minutes.

"If you don't want that, I'll take it back!"

"Okay…" I said and slipped the fifty in my pocket. I still didn't let my eyes look at him. I just saw part of the sleeve and massive elbow. He stood up to leave.

"Incidentally, I hope you are all packed. Your plane leaves early in the morning!"

(Journal entries)

Jan. 27, 1979

I walked down Bourbon St and stood outside George Finola's "Blue Angel Nightclub." I guess he noticed that I was just staring at him and he stared my ass right back. I went in with Mom and Jack and I said something to him. He said that he couldn't hear me. So I wrote him a note on a napkin, "Play something that "Bix" did." He read it and said, "We close in two minutes. He probably did this song." And then he finished the last few bars beautifully and I gave him my autograph book and a pen. He said in his fast, sometimes stuttering voice,

AUGUST, 1978

"Oh, that's okay, I already have one." He pulled back his coat to reveal five pens in his shirt pocket. We laughed. He signed it and stepped down from the stage and we had a quick, nervous conversation. We spoke of Bix mainly. I shook his hand and turned around to talk with the folks and before I could turn around George had gone to his dressing room up a spiral staircase. He came down in his street clothes and we began to talk. I brought up the movie part I might have with Martin Sheen about Bix. His eyes lit up because he was asked to do the soundtrack before it fell through. I asked him which one of his albums did he think was his best out of his three. He said, "Well, if you like Bix, I think it would be that one." He told me that he had gotten to be a Bix fan the same way that I did; through that first record I bought of his, that first solo. He said he'd been collecting his original 78's for 15 years and that he had most every one. He said that if I would like to tape them to give him a call. I bought the record and said, "Put your number on here." He did. We chatted some more and then he said, "I gotta run!" He ran home, and we started walking toward our car parked on Gov. Nichols.

Feb. 21 1979
Well, the Mardi Gras season is heavily upon us New Orleanians but the asshole policemen had to go on

The Winds of Malibu

strike so most of the parades are canceled. On the 1st of Feb. '79, I called up George Finola and talked to his recorded answering service for awhile. After, when he called me back, he drove from the French Quarter and picked me up in front of Georgetown. He had a slight delay because he stopped to help a friend fix his car. He brought me to his very nice home in his Pontiac Firebird - white outside, red inside. We taped Bix all day for me. He's got Bix autographs and all kinds of incredible stuff. On the way home, he said that our relationship was great because he always wanted to meet someone down here who was interested in Bix.

On Feb. 14, I talked my California brother, Steve into living in New Orleans with us and on the 17th, he showed up at Jack's place. He says that he loves it here and wants to stay a long time, and I feel the exact same way. On Feb. 19th, I had a great time watching George Finola play that cornet. Mom, Jack, and Steve were with me. He recognized me right away and he played more beautiful than anybody anywhere as far as I know. He spent most his time with us between sessions and introduced me to the head of the joint, some head Mafia guy by the name of Carlo Montalbano. All I have to do is mention his name and they'll allow me in. I also talked on the phone with him earlier that day.

AUGUST, 1978

George Finola and I were smoking muggles together in his loft.

"Do you think you will ever leave New Orleans, George?"

"No. Everything I want out of life is right here. God, I sure wish I could see that Beiderbecke movie script that you had, just to read through it one time, that's all I want. I can't *believe* you let it get away from you!"

"I can't believe it either. You were going to be Bix's musical voice in that movie! How come the movie people didn't send you the screenplay?"

"Eventually I would have seen it, if the movie had been made! In the eyes of Hollywood, I am just a New Orleans musician. I can't stop thinking about that screenplay, though."

"I can't either."

July, 1979

I never would be without a notebook and pen in my hands or near me for the rest of my life: this was the substitute, the security blanket, for Martin Sheen's *In a Mist* screenplay. I wrote stuff down in my notebook, but mainly it was just to hang on to tightly. I also swatted bugs with it or opened doors or pushed toilet levers.

Without a notebook, I would go crazy. When one notebook was filled with observations, I would have another cheap one lined up to take its place, usually one of the lightweight standard spiral 120-page school notebooks.

I called my father.

"Which month do you want me there this summer?"

"I am not sure I want you here for a whole month, but we'll see."

"And how long do I get to stay this time?"

"Oh, I guess about a month might be okay. We'll see." He had a satisfied sound to him.

My brother drove his wrecked pickup truck from New Orleans to Malibu, and I rode with him. I wore blue jean overalls, and a bandana headband that my hair rested over in tufts. I had round hippie sunglasses with a peace sign painted on one

JULY, 1979

of the lenses. My taste in music had changed to Jimi Hendrix, Janis Joplin, and The Doors. I played every Doors album and told their story to my brother the whole way there, through a thunderstorm.

I went for aimless walks in all directions and made the inevitable trek down to my old school and stood near the track with my new hippie look. I stood in one spot for twenty minutes, fifteen feet away from the parallel bars. Uh oh, there was a dear friend; Sally Emr.

"*Jeff!*" Her eyes lit up and she threw her arms around my shoulders. I gave her the pat on the back, guilt hug.

"Art and I have thought about you a lot! We still want you for his movie he is going to do!"

"Thank you. Is it still *Buckaroo*?"

"Yes! He is going to do it and he wants *you*… we want you to be in it! So how are you?" .

"Not bad, I'm…getting into music…while I'm living in New Orleans. Acting is kind of on the back burner."

"Oh, how cool! Here, can you give me your address?"

"Okay. I have a pen and notebook right here."

"Art is going to be thrilled that I ran into you!"

"I always loved you both."

We hugged again. Sally looked intensely into my eyes; she was shorter than me. "We will see you," she said and walked away; she turned around at ten paces and we waved, and she left down toward the parking lot.

I didn't know how much more of this I could take. I looked up the mountain toward the Lucas house, and around me. I needed some deep meditation here, but I couldn't get it. I needed to sit in the field at Philips Avenue near Deerhead Road and stay there in one spot for three days, but there was no way in high holy hell that was going to happen. I decided there was something silly about this place. Malibu was deeply mystical, but not many realized that.

Four guys jogged up on the track. One of them descended the tar paved ramp. At forty feet away I recognized who it was; holy mother, here he came! It was Emilio Estevez! I'd better hide! In this new garb he might not even recognize me, so unlike Bix or Jerry Lewis, and besides, it had been two full years. I looked away at the ground. Near the end of the ramp, he glanced over and locked into my eyes; his eyes widened.

"*Jeff!*" He bounded toward me. I froze and wanted to either run or sob. I did neither. He threw his arms around me and squeezed me tightly, in the biggest bear-hug I have ever had in my life. I couldn't even respond with my guilty tap on the back or any other way because my arms were pinned at my sides. He let go, stepped back, and had that smile of his that I hadn't seen in two years—such an unusual, authentic smile.

"How have you been?"

"Not bad." I smiled a little.

"Have you been acting?" he asked, his smile beaming.

"I had the lead part in our…in *a*…high school play in New Orleans, *Ten Little Indians* by Agatha Christie. It's a mystery."

I could sense a self-assurance I had never seen from him. His eyes were on fire with optimism. I couldn't make his facial expression if I tried. I started slowly toward my father's house and he was right beside me; every step he made was full of strong enthusiasm. He had found his place and himself. You almost never see that in a seventeen-year-old anywhere at any time, past, present, or future. It was a shock to behold.

"I should have something coming up!" he asserted with wide eyes. I looked him over. He was like a brother to me just from what we had been through those few years.

"Something? You mean like a real movie?"

July, 1979

"*Yeah!* I want to give you my phone number!"

"Thanks…I have a pen and notebook right here."

He opened to a blank page and tore off a tiny slice of paper at the bottom that was the size of a caterpillar and handed back the notebook. He tugged a bit of paper out of his left front trousers pocket, unfolded it, and used his leg as a table. He wrote down the phone number to the caterpillar-sized paper. Remorse nibbled like crawfish in my mind.

Martin Sheen's Bix screenplay loomed in my mind. The sadness grew in my stomach and my eyes misted over.

"Why do you have to study your own phone number like that? You don't have it memorized?"

"We change it every month."

"Every month?" My eyebrows rose.

"Yes."

"Has it always been like that?"

"Yeah," he said, and blinked.

"Your dad got really famous after *Apocalypse Now* came out."

"Yeah. He deserves it, though."

"Well, yes, of course he does!"

"*Call me!*"

"Okay," I said blankly. I took the paper between two fingers and tucked it into my right pocket with my index finger.

He turned to his left and headed toward the ocean, and I turned to my left toward the mountain. I could not bring myself to look back and watch him vanish.

I stood outside my father's kitchen, my arms hanging limply at my sides. There was no safe place to keep Emilio's phone number in that house. There was not a refrigerator magnet. On top of the refrigerator, it would easily blow to the floor. To put it in my father's new office was out of the question. I had brought an overstuffed backpack from New Orleans which was kept beside the living room couch where I was told to sleep. Best keep it in my pocket!

I placed my hand in my pocket and pinched the paper nervously. It was too soon to dial it, I figured. Should I copy the Estevezes' number in big scrawl in my notebook? Yes, I should! But maybe he didn't want me to do that. That was why he gave me the caterpillar-sized paper!

I needed to believe in myself like I did when I lived here—that was what I really knew for sure. I needed to sleep in my old room. That would do the trick! Three hours spent in my room. Then I would call that number tomorrow and follow through!

At 2:00 a.m., I creaked along the hardwood floor. It took me eight minutes just to make it past my father's door. I had to recapture the feeling of my room. I could hear my brother happily snore in his room, but my father had always been a defensive light sleeper and I did notice that he made no sound.

I got into my old bedroom, now carpeted. The only part I recognized was the window Frank and I sneaked out of. There was nowhere to lie down, but I squeezed in on my left side between his oversized desk and the unnecessary glass coffee table, and I was quiet and still.

"If I can just lie here for three hours, then I should be able to get some Malibu courage that I used to have," I barely whispered under my breath.

I let the minutes drift through me and got something back. My Malibu room; how I had loved it! How I had so greatly missed it! My father had a clock on the wall and I looked up in the faint moonlight. Twelve after two, it read.

I lay there in peace for three minutes and ten seconds when I heard a lurch from my father's room, the massiveness of his bulk stirred. His bedroom door pounded open and he stepped into his office and stood there solidly. I saw the kinky tufts of hair on

JULY, 1979

the sides of his big circus clown head.

"What are you doing down there, Jeff?" he asked maniacally.

"If it isn't the owner of my hatred," I told him in well-pronounced words.

"Get up!" I got up, and he stood in my way.

"What do I have to do to get it through that *weird* head of yours that this is not your home? Those days are over with and finished!"

I wanted to kill him with the gold-plated letter opener that I could see on his desk.

"I am going to get you back to the other side of the country sooner than you think, so get on that living room couch!" He still had those massive hands and arms and chest that could crush me if I tried to tackle him.

"If you weren't built like a heavyweight boxer, I would fucking beat you to a pulp and love it. Move the hell out of that doorway if you want me on your living room couch, before I steal something sharp from your office!"

I got around him and jumped ahead so he couldn't pound me blindsided. He stood where he was, and I went back to the couch. Steve didn't snore when I went past his room, but he didn't bother to come out and face us either.

My steps on my long walks got slower. I stood in the midst of various fields of straw for hours and just stared ahead as the wind swept.

I was in the center of my father's house between the dining room and the living room. I reached in my right front pants pocket for Emilio's phone number. My hand went to the bottom of the pocket, and it was empty. I pulled my pockets out onto the table: a thin wallet, keys to my mother's New Orleans apartment, and thirty-five cents. I gave my pockets rabbit-ears as

I panicked.

How could this happen? I checked with wide eyes in my father's office, and his carpet was clean. Emilio's little piece of paper was not on or in my father's couch. If it had fallen out on a long walk while I was spaced out, I could never retrace those aimless steps, and even if I did, the winds of Malibu would have blown that slip of paper from one hill to the next.

Out of terror, I phoned Shelby Basso, whose phone number I still had written at the back of my diary. I knew she didn't have to change her number every month. She invited me over. I put my right elbow on the arm of her couch and my heavy head in my hand.

"Where do I even fit in around here anymore? I swear."

"Oh, you are a legend," she said.

I laughed.

"I just feel like if I go stand in front of Martin Sheen, I am going to cry my eyes out before we even say hi. Do you realize how big of a star he is with *Apocalypse Now* in movie theaters! He is *huge!*"

Shelby shifted in her chair. "Well, there have been times I have been told when people have seen him drunk, just sitting on the curb with a wine bottle, staring into space."

"That makes me idolize him even more. He *is* like Bix. I can't cry in front of him before I can even explain myself. He is intense, and…I don't know what to do."

"Maybe you should just show up at their door," she said.

"I know I should. I just can't seem to bring myself to do it. No matter what happens, I am not ever allowed to live in Malibu again. My father has made that real clear."

Shelby pressed one hand on her forehead, arranging her thoughts. "Tell me more about your father."

"I have never met a monster like him. I don't even have a

JULY, 1979

driver's license, because he refuses to sign his approval to allow me to drive because he thinks I am retarded. Now I am turning eighteen in two weeks, and I won't need his signature. He signed my D notices, but he won't sign for my driver's license."

My father walked in with momentum that night while I was on his couch.

"I talked with your brother and convinced him that you both should leave here tomorrow morning. If he were alone, it would be different, but since you are here with him, I want you both to leave! So, you will be getting back to your mother's in plenty of time for your school semester to begin in Louisiana. That should make you happy."

I sat there. "And what if I don't need that much time for my school semester to begin in Louisiana?"

"You will both be ready to leave by nine sharp in the morning! I don't want you lagging around here."

I got up early while Steve was asleep and joined him, with calm disinterest, for his morning walk. He made conversation.

"So, how is your mother? Does she talk about me?"

"I guess so...once in a while."

"What do you mean, once in a while?"

"A little bit."

"And what does she say about me?" He turned vigorously up a trail. I followed behind him.

"Don't you ever get tired of asking about my mom?"

"Quite frankly, no," he sneered. "What does she say about me?"

"She says she doesn't want me to ever behave like you do."

And what did you tell her about me?"

"Not much. I never bring you up."

Jeff on the front page of the Metro section of the New Orleans Times-Picayune newspaper, while living in New Orleans, Louisiana. 1979. photo courtesy of Times Picayune | The New Orleans Advocate file photo.

February, 1980

Marlon Brando toward the end of *Apocalypse Now* was what I was going for. Most important, I had to look scary. I was in the bathroom of my New Orleans high school at night. I had my brother's acrylic paints. This would not be a cute performance. I used a green base and swept black circles and hooks across my mouth and forehead with a sponge. I put some white across my eyes and painted my ears black. I fastened my rolled-up white kerchief headband over my long hair and brushed some dark paint across it.

Outside in the auditorium, the clean-cut drama teacher, Mr. Gabb, was Master of Ceremonies of our high school talent show.

"Good evening ladies and germs, and welcome…to the Abramson High School annual talent show, featuring the brightest talent that the youth of New Orleans has to offer. Here is a young man who is a contender for this year's Optimist Award, Vernon Ketry, and his band, The Knifers, singing and playing "Crazy Little Thing Called Love".

The band went into it. A tall blond singer belted it out. He was a nice enough guy with a simple look on his face all the time. He sang the song well enough, dressed in a sweatshirt with cut off sleeves. I was a singer now too and found out I was good at it, and tonight, I would sing the angriest song I had ever heard.

I had narrowed it down from a list.

My song was "Masters of War" by Bob Dylan. I knew the simple chords on my family's acoustic guitar, and I hadn't told my mother about this because I had plans for our family guitar tonight. I pampered the guitar in the boys' bathroom because the guitar was about to die.

Across the front I spilled drips of red paint from the little glass jar, below the strings and sound hole.

Mr. Gabb strode into the boys' bathroom and made a beeline to me. He stood there with his short, comical frame. He looked into the mirror with me. I hid my guitar against the wall by the sink.

"Lucas, you've got me worried tonight."

"Why is that, Mr. Gabb?"

"Maybe it's because you've got your war paint on. I don't even know what song you are going to sing. You never told me." Mr. Gabb did a mouth twitch that he did when in thought.

"We are only interested in wholesome, innocent, family entertainment here, Lucas. Upbeat, happy music like from the good old days. I am sure you can appreciate that kind of music, can't you? Can I trust you that you are going to give us that tonight?"

"Sure, why not?" I said.

Mr. Gabb puffed up his cheeks, raised his eyebrows and walked out as "Crazy Little Thing Called Love" concluded. There was cheerful applause. Mr. Gabb applauded also as he stepped into the spotlight.

"Let's hear it for Vernon Ketry and the Knifers…and now, for a student who hails from sunny California, and then from humid Alabama, and now he is in the gator swamps of Louisiana. He is going to paint us all a sunny California picture with a song he is going to sing while he accompanies himself on guitar. Let's give a warm welcome to Jeff Lucas!"

I secured my guitar strap and walked out. The drummer from

FEBRUARY, 1980

the Knifers stayed there seated at his drum set. We grinned at one another in agreement, and I stepped up to the microphone and looked out.

"I'm gonna attempt to freak you out tonight." My friends cheered like hell. I strummed the gloomy minor chord and kept the rhythm.

"This is dedicated to all the people that uh...want to draft eighteen- and nineteen- year-olds." When the mood of the room felt about correct, I sang. I forgot one line and instead sang, "All the kids' blood runs into the mud." I had good pitch and a full voice. I stood basically still and looked out to sections of the audience in their fold-up metal chairs. There were about three hundred, mostly parents.

After the last line of the song, I kept up the strum of the guitar, I looked over my shoulder and cued the drummer and he nodded and began a haphazard drum beat mixed with a drum roll. I unhooked my guitar strap and untied it at the neck.

I moved the microphone stand far over to stage right gently and smashed my acoustic guitar on the stage. A shocked strum is how I can best describe what it sounded like. The low tones overpowered the high tones, from the right to the left. Splinters flew in outrageous directions and I saw four parents in the front row lean cautiously and then evacuate their seats and scamper to the back of the theater.

My guitar continued to ring out in grand style like a subnormal bell. After the sides had been demolished, I changed my stance and swung it over my head and forward and broke the neck with a sweet crack. It swirled like a lasso squid in circles over my head, and the shards cut my right arm. I held up my cut to the audience so that we could both watch blood drip together.

When I was convinced they could see some blood, I dropped the guitar to the floor and stomped on it as the drummer

continued. I cut my right ankle.

I lifted the mangled splinters of wood and steel and made the remnants dance marionette fashion at the tip of the stage. My drummer had slowed down until it was a heartbeat tick-tock, then he stopped at just the right time. I bowed low in the classic 18th-century style to the applause of about three friends on the sidelines. The rest of my friends were just laughing. The audience sat in their seats, tight-lipped, their hands in their laps, their eyes big.

Mr. Gabb picked up the microphone stand and dragged it back to center stage, too embarrassed to look at the audience. He peered off to stage left without a smile.

"Lucas even surprised me with that one. He broke his promise to me…and…he broke his guitar. Moving right along, you

February, 1980

Jeff in New Orleans, Louisiana, in the spring of 1981. Photo by Patricia Decker

will now be entertained by Mike Aboud, who will pull a rabbit out of his hat."

The show concluded, and the house lights came up for the curtain call. All the parents applauded, smiled, and took pictures carefully and quickly with their cameras. I made my way from behind the performers who gladly let me through. I kneeled at the very front of the stage with the remnants of my family's guitar wrapped around my neck and I smiled a Dean Martin smile.

The reaction to my presence was immediate and fascinated me, as every parent ignored me and looked away to their left or their right or at the floor, and all the cameras dropped at once and were put away into cases or out of sight into pockets or purses. The parents exited the building and away from me quickly, without exception.

The talent show performers rushed to the exit so they could join their parents under the neon lights of the parking lot and hug each other. I moved slowly toward a rubber trashcan near an exit and lifted the mangled guitar off of my shoulders. I held the remnants out over the garbage can at arm's length and let it go.

MARCH, 1982

I leaned on the dashboard.
"All I've got to go on is some place on Point Dume where this is going on!" I told her. We drove along the coast casually in her white Capri.

"So in all probability, we are doing this for nothing," she said.

"Yes, except I am on a mad driven hunch."

"So, let me get this straight," she sighed, "the singer of The Doors, Jim Morrison, had a sister?"

"Right. Anne Morrison."

"And a movie might be made about Jim Morrison because your friend from New Orleans called you and said that she heard on the radio that the auditions are on Point Dume?"

"Yes."

"In Malibu."

"Yes."

"How big is Point Dume?"

"It is densely populated and very easy to get lost there."

"Find what you need within one hour, or we are driving back! I don't have all day to get lost on Point Dume, and you are paying for my gas!"

"It's a deal. You are my roommate's girlfriend, and thank you for doing this. It would take me three days to ride my bicycle to Malibu."

"This is Point Dume here. The real estate companies are trying to pronounce it, Point Dumay, but that is wrong. It's pronounced, Point *Doom*. Turn right here at the gas station. Okay, drive slowly now. I have got to put out my sensors." I peered out the windshield. We went up that incline that is so slight you barely notice. "Dume road is the nerve center of Point Dume. Okay, go about an eighth of a mile, half a mile, something like that." Pull over here and park."

To our left was a downward alley that led into several back yards. I got out of the car and walked down. I zeroed in on the third backyard on the right-hand side, which was a tennis court. Two middle-aged men with long hair played tennis. I went over, opened up the gate, and stood on the court, clearly trespassing. I was dressed to look as much like Jim Morrison as I could: a long-sleeved flowing white cotton shirt that had strings to tie at the neck, black jeans, moccasin boots.

They noticed me and walked toward me and smiled as if I were in on their secret. They held their tennis rackets, looked me right in the eye, and kind of laughed.

"How did you know?" said one with a cool English accent.

"You are here for the Morrison project, right?" asked the other one.

"…uh, yes."

"You are?"

"Yes, I am. I am available for the Morrison project for sure. Jim Morrison, right?" He took my notebook and pen out of my hands and wrote down an address.

"Be at this address tomorrow at one p.m."

"Thank you! I sure will be there on time," I said in my best Jim Morrison dialect.

MARCH, 1982

The next day, she drove me.

"Jim Morrison's sister, Anne, is involved in this project somehow. Come on! Christ, we're late! I will break off your dashboard and throw it out the goddamn window if you don't drive faster!"

"You do, and I will stop the car right now! Do you want me to stop the car right now?"

"Okay, I'll calm down. Just let's get me there!"

We got to the address on Dume Road and I leaped out as we rolled. I had a ghetto blaster on a strap to record myself if I got a chance to sing.

I was let in to a quiet, darkened living room with a full band and monitors set up ready to play. Over in a corner, Mickey Parenti, from junior high, still short for his age, was there, hanging out as a Doors fan. He used to know me right off the bat. Now he didn't recognize me as he studied me singing. Just for fun, I decided to keep it that way.

"I'm blazing on acid right now," he announced quietly as he sat against a wall.

"Light my fire, Mickey," I told him.

The gentleman with the English accent walked up to me.

"What Doors song do you want to sing? What is your favorite Doors song?"

"My favorite Doors song is 'Hyacinth House,' but I can sing any one of them from any of the albums. Just name it!"

"All right. Let's hear you sing 'Moonlight Drive.'" I went up to the microphone stand and the band went into it. They were good, and the amps in the living room were even better than the band. There was no keyboard player, but they played so well we didn't miss it.

They vamped "Moonlight Drive," and I let it play out longer than the record, then dove in. The set-up was clean and professional. I added additional lyrics to the song that were rarely heard, from a Doors bootleg I had from the Matrix in 1967.

I filled the house with a great Jim Morrison-style vocal. I could tell I did, because I could hear myself really well over the speakers which were angled just right. I forgot to record myself, damn it. I had made a good impression on everyone in the room, and that included the young man who they had already chosen to portray Jim Morrison. He was the right age, a few years older than me with a fuller face, and he had Jim Morrison's nose and thick neck.

The song ended well.

"Step outside, will you? And we will call you back in," I was told by the man in charge. I stepped outside for five minutes.

"Come back inside. We are going to stick with him as our Jim Morrison. Great job, though! You can come back for the video we are going to shoot and feel free to stay through this evening. Anne is cooking a turkey for us all."

"Thank you."

A woman came out of the kitchen and walked toward me and held out her hand.

"Hi. I'm Anne," she said sweetly. Yes, I could see the resemblance to Jim Morrison in the eyes and mouth of her great face.

"I am *very* pleased to meet you. Hello." It was getting dark in the part of the house that faced the east and she turned on the light in the kitchen. She went over to the oven and opened it.

"That food smells so good," I said to their main Jim Morrison.

"Yeah, it does," he said.

I watched Jim Morrison's sister baste the turkey with care, and held on to my happiness and freedom, which was smart of me, because they were soon to be cut in half.

MARCH, 1982

(Journal entries)

Thurs. May 13, '82
Absurdities, one acts are performed, supposed 1st and last day after (5) weeks in rehearsal. Pinter's Applicant was fantastic. Some theater booker talked to me after the show about MONEY for this kind of shit.

Thu. Aug. 12, 1982
God, I feel like a fucking Kurtz these days. How the hell could I let my environment lead me to this? I have learned to study 6 hours steady at a piano w/ out realizing it and come up with what looks like less of a product than what I started with. In the past month or around Santa Cruz time with the band, I have had too many close brushes with nervous breakdowns. I can't do my life like this. I am eating but psychologically I am a fucking wreck. I can't get there's from here. Got to change. I have to tell this life...My ego has never been so low. Well now I can't say that. But it's never all come back negatively like it has this Summer - tonite I mean. I just can't leave music alone yet my attempts, so many of them, seem so fruitless. I guess I deserve what I...I can't answer that. I've got to really change completely or something because everything's pointing to dead. Maybe I took too much advice. Jeff Lucas's life has got to change now. It won't be fast. I've got to accentuate what I've already had got, will have.

AUGUST, 1983

I entered the liquor store just after 10:00 a.m. to get either Ruffles potato chips or Doritos plain tortilla chips. I would decide when my hand reached for one or the other. I stepped up to the counter. And there was *Rolling Stone* magazine right beside the chip section. "The Next James Dean" was the cover story, and there was a headshot of Sean Penn, with a 1950s haircut, and he had dyed his hair as black as mine. He stared directly out of the cover, with a burnt red dangerous backdrop across the rest of the magazine.

Chips didn't matter anymore. I wasn't going to eat chips today. I was reminded of ancient stories of Lot's wife, and I felt I was being turned into a pillar of salt. My face went blank. I backed up as I stared at the *Rolling Stone* cover. Sean and I looked into each other's eyes, only he couldn't see me. I bumped into the *USA Today* news stand behind me. I looked down at the front page. Actor David Niven had just died, it read.

I fainted. I fell backward and landed on my side. The floor of the liquor store was carpeted, but it was a hard, tight carpet. My head banged it. I didn't pass out completely. I almost passed out, and I crawled as if climbing out of a hole and away from the liquor store.

AUGUST, 1983

After I had almost regained my composure, I wrapped my notebook around the handle bars and made my way unsteadily on my yellow bicycle to the office where the temporary and worst jobs were offered.

"What are you good at?" the woman asked.

"Acting, and sometimes singing."

"We don't have anything available for that."

"Don't I know it. What I've got to do is hard labor. Give me the hardest labor you have."

She pulled up a card. "It's not really worth the pay. It's $34, and it might take you two or three days to finish."

"I'll take it. I'll do it. Give it to me," I said calmly and patiently. She handed me the card.

I was in front of an acre loaded with tall, thorny, healthy weeds right off of the beach in Ventura. I dove in. I couldn't wait to dive in. I tore them out; both hands gripped hard and worked at once. It felt good! I was just a machine. I was a weed killer! Thorns didn't matter. Spiders didn't matter. I had no gloves. Out by the roots they came. My blood dripped. I wore my white long-sleeved Jim Morrison shirt.

Blood ran down my arms, blood on the rustling weeds. My arms bled more than my hands did, round small holes in my arms. It was all just weeds! Weeds made me bleed! Before I knew it, I stood up and looked behind me, and I was finished! Congratulations! Award of awards!

The euphoria of the sucker punch.

I gathered up all the weeds, stooped and collected them in voracious armfuls, and tucked them down tightly into a dumpster.

I went to the wrinkled woman's door and knocked. She opened it and surveyed the yard from her doorway.

"Let me get my envelope," she said. She came back and pinched some bills. "There is $34. There," she barely said. Her hand moved just a few inches out of the door frame. I took the money.

"Any more work to do?"

"No. That's all I had. Goodbye."

(Journal entry)

End of Oct. 83, Malibu.

I feel like I've lived thru, been thru, everything. I then turn around and it looks like I haven't even approached the starting line. I find this to be unbelievable. Dad said he would not help me artistically. He said though, he would for bare necessities. He's offered to help me support an apartment in West L.A. Somewhere. That deal's been open for two full months and I haven't been able to budge an inch with most of my current opportunities. I just can't believe I never saw myself heading full speed toward such a Rude Awakening. I keep seeing Rob Lowe sport about here & there. Fuck this. Where is my POSITIONING!

Jeff briefly stopped by Malibu with his mother and stepfather and two brothers. Just passing through. Autumn, 1983. Photo be John N. Dick

FEBRUARY, 1984

I called her My Ramona, or Little Miss M 80. I was emotionally attached to her. We walked into the party together.

"Hocus Pocus Lucas Focus," she said.

"Okay. I am focused. Did you really sleep with Rob Lowe?"

She smiled sexy. "Yes. My dad suggested that he take acting lessons."

"He doesn't have anything to worry about in that department," I said.

She knocked on the door. A young man my age with a light-brown dry ducktail answered. He looked like he had been lifting weights. His eyes were ready to turn to anger.

"Hi," said My Ramona. He stepped back with a scowl and motioned us in with a scoop of his hand. We turned right and followed him to his living room.

"Let me introduce you two. This is Jeff. He grew up with Sean Penn." Then she gestured to him.

"*His* favorite actor *is* Sean Penn," is how she introduced him.

"What's his name?" I asked.

"You can call me Sean," he said. His face didn't look like Sean's, but he was trying.

"What's your real name?" I asked.

FEBRUARY, 1984

"His name is Doug. Jeff's an actor," said Ramona. She muffled a laugh.

"HE'S NOT BETTER THAN ME!" he spat. He spread his legs apart and stood solid. His lower lip jutted in a scowl as he stared me down.

There were twenty people at the party with the new Yuppie look, wide suspenders, hats with a wide, flat brim, short stiff hair, no beards, the whole bit. I did not try to look like anything anymore. I just dressed NUMB. I had a George Orwell 1984 shirt on of some sort, charcoal tunic with a zipper over my left tit. I felt apart from everybody. Nobody talked to me, and I sat quietly with my mouth closed.

There was his weight-lifting bench in the center of the room. Everyone moved around it. I sat in an isolated comfortable chair and stayed there, ginger ale bottle in hand. In the middle of the party with everybody mingling, he got down on his bench press and began pumping iron. Then he got up, went over to the coffee table and sat down and glared at me like a dog does, with steely eyes.

He nodded a little bit.

"I want to arm wrestle you!" he said to me and pointed. The guests glanced at me and glanced away. They didn't seem surprised.

"Me? Why?" He popped the coffee table with his open palm. I rolled my eyes and slunk over and kneeled on the floor and rested my elbow on his glass coffee table. He put his arm up and slammed my arm down hard in half a second.

"Try it again! Make sure you are ready!" I braced my arm, tried to put muscle into it.

"I have got a delicate arm, as you can see." He slammed my arm down in one full second.

"Okay. I'm done." I stood. He stood.

"You want to fight?"

"No. I am built like an actor, as you see." I went back and sat in the chair and barely moved.

Four hours went by. Everybody had gone. The Prince had stopped. It was quiet. My Ramona had talked to me a little bit, but I barely answered her. Now I didn't see her, and I didn't see him. They were in his room with the door shut. Suddenly, she was talking loudly just about objects in the room, and he was panting.

"Where did you get that lampshade?"

"Oh yeah," he undertoned.

I stood up. "Well, there is a ninety-nine percent chance they are fucking," I said. I don't think they heard me. I had been ready to leave since we got there, but she was my ride. I walked into the front yard and climbed nine feet up a tree and sat on a branch for an hour and ten minutes. She walked out, and I looked at the top of her auburn head. She peered out at the street, concerned.

"George Orwell would laugh his ass off," I said.

She jumped and looked up. "I have been looking for you everywhere!"

"You know to check trees!"

"Get down out of there. Get down from there, or I'm leaving you here!" I swung by my hands and jumped down.

We moved toward her car. I stared dead ahead at the blank universe, and the words jutted out of me.

"How did they get there? Sean, Emilio, Rob, and Charlie? How?" She got in the driver's seat. I fell into the passenger's seat.

"They all have a look like they are in the wrong business. They just do! Let alone at the very top of Hollywood, all of them, Tom Cruise and his wooden face included! I feel like they are bringing the quality of Hollywood stardom down, which by

February, 1984

the way, and in the way, brings America down, and nobody can see it but me…I think."

"You have got focusing issues! They don't!"

We drove out of there in her new black Volkswagen Rabbit.

"…and I happen to love Tom Cruise to death!"

(Journal entry)

May 10th, 1984

Just push the hunch and don't say no.

Believe it.

I've got to be heading for something at the right time because God would not waste me like this.

If you stick to a certain way of developing, then you may keep your hair.

May 12th, 1984

I drove the blue ice truck into what I remembered was Emilio's driveway, a new mini Toyota pick-up with the name of the ice company on the doors: North Hollywood Ice.

I knew it was Emilio's birthday, May 12th. The driveway was vacant, and I drove in like I owned the place, parked abruptly, and stepped out. I had ten big bags of ice under the tarp in the back. My clothes were damp with ice water and dirt smudges. I had gone to work that morning in what I used to wear in junior high school: nice pants, a tuxedo shirt with a black bow tie, and a red sweater vest. I slicked my hair down 1920s style that morning, but it was messy now. I lifted a fifty-pound bag of ice on my shoulder and walked up the porch.

I had never thanked them for that dinner seven years ago. It was quiet in the neighborhood. Just a few birds chirped; the wind was unusually still. I knocked on the door. A woman answered with a polite smile.

"Hello?" she said. We looked at each other in silence. It took me a slow ten seconds to remember her. It was Emilio's mom.

"Hi. Is Emilio here?"

"No, he's not here right now."

"This is his birthday, isn't it? I wanted to surprise him for his birthday." The ice was dripping down my shirt onto their door mat.

"He celebrated his birthday yesterday. He rented out the back of Barney's Beanery."

"Oh." I put the bag of ice down on my wet shoe. "Well… would you tell him Jeff Lucas stopped by?"

"I sure will."

"I just wanted to give him ice for his birthday party."

"I'll tell him you stopped by. I think I remember you," she said. I smiled a little.

"Thank you. I'd better get back to the ice company. They are waiting for me." Mrs. Estevez looked at the truck. Half of the ice was melted and dripped down in a puddle under the truck that spread out in their driveway.

"Thanks for stopping by Jeff."

"Okay. Bye Mrs. Sheen."

"Okay. Bye Jeff."

I hoisted the bag up and tucked it under the tarp, and she closed the door. I got in the truck and started the engine. It was the best truck we had at the ice company; I had made sure of that. I drove gently forward out of the Estevezes' circular driveway, turned right, and headed out of Malibu.

(Journal entries)

May 21st, 1984
Someday, the exuse my father might give is that he hardly spent time with me and cercumstances were kept so strange that he could hardly have been expected to understand my motives.

The Winds of Malibu

January 18th, 86

It now seems quite unforgivable and what can you do with that but walk away from it. Let it be then. & I'm just gonna have ((fun))

EPILOGUE

Stephen Lucas is a fine arts painter living in Hawaii.

Mathew Peckinpah lives in Oregon and works in Communications.

Emilio Estevez became a highly successful Hollywood actor and a director while in his early twenties and is also a professional winemaker.

Sean Penn became the most famous Hollywood actor of his generation while he was in his early twenties, and also a movie director.

Jeff Lucas disappeared from Malibu and was widely believed to have committed suicide in the mid-1980s. In 1995 he attempted to contact Emilio but was unable to answer his telephone, which rang off the hook. He published two short stories in *Rosebud Magazine* in 2004 and 2005. In 2012 Emilio included him in his autobiography, *Along the Way* that he co-wrote with his father, Martin Sheen.

Paul Lucas met a woman in the 1980s who was slowly able to calm him down. They were married for twenty-four years, until his death of heart failure in 2010.

Frank Kratochvil became a decorated lieutenant in the United States Coast Guard. It is highly likely that he heard and believed

Jeff Lucas had committed suicide. He committed suicide with a handgun in his car at age 46 in 2009.

Lynn Craig got married and had children and has a normal life. Her first boyfriend in Malibu was Rob Lowe.

Vance North died in his early thirties. On his tombstone it reads, "See ya - Vance."

Charlie Sheen became one of the most durable celebrities in Hollywood history.

Index

Abbot & Costello, 42
Abramson high school, 345 - 350
Addams, Don, 31
Big Al, The Bus Driver, 163, 167
Allgreen, Andrea, Vl, 8, 12, 13, 14, 54, 123
Allgreen, Chris, 210
Allgreen, Frank, 59, 123, 217
Allgreen, Helen, 61, 62, 122, 123
Ambassador apartment, Encino, 184
American Graffiti, 42, 43, 44, 61, 62, 247, 198
Anderson, Joel, 172, 189, 283, 297, 298, 301
A Night To Remember by Walter Lord, 265, 266
Annie Had a Baby, Hank Ballard and The Midnighters, 54
Apocalypse Now, 171, 205, 228, 240, 241, 311, 339, 342, 345
Aqualung by Jethro Tull, 264
Armstrong, Louis, 90
Around The World In 80 Days, 106, 107, 111
Astaire, Fred, 94, 232

The Bad News Bears, 152, 194
The Ball family, 19
Barbarella, 42
Basso, Shelby 232, 245, 277, 342
Beethoven, Ludwig Van 68, 238
Beiderbecke, Bix 135, 139, 146, 147, 154, 155, 160, 161, 173, 196, 197, 203,

204, 205, 211, 213, 226
-228, 230, 231, 238, 245,
246, 253, 254, 263, 270,
274, 280, 290, 291, 296,
304, 305, 306, 308, 317
- 320, 327, 328, 330, 332
- 336, 339
Bennett, Jeff, 177
Mr. Bennett, Les, 82, 84, 199, 200
Berle, Milton, 36
Billings, Scott, 6
Ms. Bolton, 34, 43, 44, 63, 67
Bonnie & Clyde, 8, 9, 24, 163
Boy, Did I Get A Wrong Number, Bob Hope, 63
Boyle, Peter, 49
Brando, Marlon, 53, 188, 205, 269, 345
Bye Bye Birdie, 258, 263, 272, 323

Carney, Art, 245
The Carpenters, 3
Caruso, Enrico, 234
Chaney, Lon Jr., 38
Chaplin, Charles, 58, 69, 102, 103 – 105, 188
Cinema-On-The-Mall, 42, 99
Clark, Roderick, V
Conklin, Craig, 65, 102, 109, 281

Craig, Lynn, 132, 134, 136, 133, 137, 152, 153, 169 – 172, 181 – 183, 189 – 191, 194, 199, 205, 206, 245, 255, 322, 368
Crazy Little Thing Called Love, The Stray Cats, 345, 346
Conkrite, Walter, 11
Crosby, Bing, 245, 326
Cruise, Chuck, 90
Cruise, Tom, 362, 363

Daniels, Danny, 164, 165
Deep Down South, 231
Mr. Delkner, William, 81, 102, 132, 179
Dick, Kelly Snow, 29, 115, 116
Dick, Lt. Col. John N., 2, 29, 113, 117, 18, 139 – 142, 325, 332, 334
Dick, John Patrick, 114, 115, 141, 359
Dick, Michelle Wilson, 29, 115, 116
Dick, Reba Cain Lucas, 2, 42, 95, 117, 139, 141, 142, 214, 257, 321, 332, 359
Dick, Terri Lynn, 29, 79, 112, 113, 115, 116, 139 – 144, 149, 172, 173, 254, 257
Dieterle, Kurt, 270, 305, 306, 320

Index

Mr. Digarmo, Charles, 125
Domino, Fats, 61
The Doors, 337, 351, 353,
Doose', Peg, 234 – 236
Dorsey, Tommy, 126
Dreyfus, Richard, 247
The Dumb Waiter, Harold Pinter, 249 – 253
Dick Van Dyke in *The Comic*, 202, 203

Mrs. Edgington, Shirley, 81
Emr, Art, 155, 156, 229,
Emr, Sally, 155, 337
Engelhardt, Louise, 13
The Entertainer, Scott Joplin, 102 – 104
Estevez, Emilio, 71 – 74, 77, 92, 97, 98, 109, 124, 130, 133, 135, 146, 147, 162 – 168, 171, 174, 200, 201, 204, 205 – 209, 212, 218, 228, 240 – 242, 245, 247, 249 – 253, 258 – 263, 269, 272, 275, 276, 283, 288 – 290, 302 – 305, 307 – 312, 322, 338, 339, 367
Estevez, Janet, 307, 310, 364, 365
Estevez, Ramon, 162 – 165, 168, 308
Evil Kneivel, 32

The Execution Of Private Slovik, 72
The Excorcist, 29

Finch, Peter, 315
Finola, George, 327, 332 – 335
Fizz, Ted, 124
Foggy Mountain Breakdown, Flatt and Scruggs, 9, 47
Fonda, Jane, 41, 42

Gabb, Peter, 345 – 349
Gershwin, George, 153, 238
Giants of Jazz, Studs Terkel, 139
Gibbons, Euell, 137, 138
Godzilla, 5, 8
Goldenstein, Joey, 47, 48, 52, 53, 76
Goodman, Benny, 93, 126
The Great Gatsby, 152, 230
The Great Race, 31, 73
Grossman, Fred, 107, 174, 290
Gurak, Pam. 161, 162

Hackman, Gene, 7
Harris, Dan, 279, 282
Hendrix, Jimi, 228, 337
Holloers, Laura, 195, 198, 215, 216

Holly, Buddy, 61
Mrs. Honey, Pat, 202, 212
Hudson, Rodney, 127 – 130

I'm Going To Charleston Back My Way To Charleston, by The Revelers, 152
In A Mist, by Bix Beiderbecke, 238, 257, 304

Jazz Me Blues by Bix Beiderbecke and his Gang, 211
Jaws, 112
Jerabek, Margaret, 170, 284
Johnson, Arty, 32
Joplin, Scott, 102, 127
Juan Cabrillo Elementary school, 7, 33, 34, 38 – 40, 43, 44, 62, 64, 65, 331

Kendall, Kate, 220, 221, 223
Kim, Stacy, 216
Katochvil, Frank, 29 – 32, 38 – 40, 44, 45, 48, 54 – 61, 63 – 65, 82, 90. 98, 99, 110, 111, 116, 118, 125 – 130, 132, 133, 145, 160, 161, 172, 187 – 192, 232, 233, 264, 282, 300, 301, 322, 367

Mr. Kratochvil (Frank's dad) 188, 192, 193
Kulka, Jade, 219, 221, 286

LaCagnina, Chris, 180, 284
Lake, Arthur, 15
Lawrence Of Arabia, 8, 74, 234
Laurel & Hardy, 34, 180, 181
Lester, Mark, 8, 10, 13, 28, 89
Lewis, Jerry, 17 – 19, 51, 108, 155, 156
Lowe, Rob, 358, 368
Lucas, Eugene, 35, 36
Lucas, Ilona, 3, 92, 100
Lucas, Paul, lX, 1 – 4, 6, 7, 11, 15, 17, 22, 26 – 28, 34 – 37, 41 – 43, 45, 50 – 52 – 54, 56, 57, 61, 68 – 70, 79. 81, 86 – 88, 92 – 96, 100, 102, 111, 117 – 121, 123, 125, 130, 131, 136, 142, 147 – 149, 153 – 156, 158, 159, 162, 163, 166, 167, 176 – 178, 181, 183 – 188, 197, 198, 201 – 204, 211 – 214, 217, 218, 224 – 227, 232, 233, 238, 239, 247 – 251, 253, 254, 263, 266 – 269, 271, 273 – 275, 288, 289, 292 – 300, 306, 307, 312 – 319, 328 – 332, 336, 340, 341, 343, 367

INDEX

Lucas, Stephen, Vlll, 2 – 5, 22, 27, 28, 32, 33, 43, 44, 59, 61, 72, 87, 115, 119, 121, 144, 147, 166, 167, 183, 184, 192, 194, 197, 210, 211, 233, 289, 301, 329, 334, 336, 340, 341, 343, 359, 367
Loyd, Allen, 102 – 105, 131, 138, 159, 161, 175, 263, 284

MacGraw, Ali, 184 – 187
Malibu Cinema, 51, 118, 202, 203, 219, 267 – 269
Malibu Park Junior High school, 24, 25, 80 – 82, 85, 93, 94 – 97, 105, 124, 125, 132, 145, 146, 160 – 162, 167, 170, 171, 175, 179, 199, 200, 202, 206, 207, 220 – 222, 227, 228, 231, 232, 241, 244, 259 – 261, 269, 272, 275 – 279, 301, 302, 331, 337 – 339
The Manson Family, 59, 62
Marathon Man, 219
Martin, Dean, 17, 52, 349
The Marx Brothers, 104, 235
M.A.S.H, Theme from, 161
Masters Of War by Bob Dylan, 346, 347

McCollum, Debbie, 268
McKeown, Ladd, 7
McQueen, Chad, 184, 265
McQueen, Steve, 183 – 187,
Meador, David, 210
Mr. Merriman, R., 64, 66
Merz, Egon, 22
Miller, Glenn, 82, 127
Mirabilio, Robert, 104, 109, 117, 180, 251
Monroe, Marilyn, 199
Moonlight Drive by The Doors, 353
Morrison, Ann, 351, 353, 354
Morrison, Jim, 351 – 354, 357
Mortell, Arthur, 131, 159
Mozart, Wolfgang Amadeus, 69
The Music Man, 258

Newman, Paul, in *Slapshot*, 267, 268
Nichols, Marcy, 207
Nicoletti, Angela, 215
Nicoletti, Paul, 214
North, Vance, 38 – 41, 368
The Nutty Professor, Jerry Lewis, 28, 30, 51

OLIVER! The Musical, 8, 13, 28

The Omen, 118, 121
O'Neal, Tatum, 99, 109, 116, 131, 132, 157, 191, 194, 205, 219, 254 – 257, 324
Otterman, Tim, 278
Orwell, George, 361, 362

Pac, Chris, 180 – 182
Pantages Theatre in Hollywood, 274, 275
Paper Moon, 99, 205
Peckinpah, Mathew, 44 – 48, 52, 53, 58, 62 – 64, 74 – 79, 89 – 92, 367
Peckinpah, Sam, 45, 47, 48, 52, 53, 74 – 79,
Penn, Arthur, 8, 47
Penn, Sean, 95, 105, 106, 110, 264, 313, 356, 360, 362, 367
Peters, Michelle, 40
Planet Of The Apes, 8
Play That Funky Music by Wild Cherry, 147, 148
Mr. Poole, William, 20, 26, 275
Porgy And Bess, 153, 274, 275
Presley, Elvis, 74, 126, 321, 322, 324, 328
Prince, 362
Pringle, Tommy, 19, 21, 38, 47, 48, 49, 75, 85, 126, 134, 223, 224

Prinze, Freddy, 223

Rasgon, Mickey, 110
Requiem For A Heavyweight, by Rod Serling, 242
Mr. Rickard, Dan, 85
Richtofen, Manfred Von, 8, 10
Royal Garden Blues by BIX BEIDERBECKE & his GANG, 211
Runaway by Del Shannon, 62

Sachar, Nanette, 204, 206, 208, 285
The St. Louis Blues by Bessie Smith, 90
The Sand Castle restaurant, 74, 177
Shake Rattle and Roll, by Big Joe Turner, 74
Shapiro, Adam, 211, 219, 229, 235, 279
Shapiro, Steve, 211
Sheen, Charlie, 309 – 311, 368
Sheen, Martin, 72, 124, 130, 146, 162, 171, 199, 201, 204, 205, 212, 218, 228, 240 – 242, 244, 247, 249, 250, 253, 262, 272, 302 – 313, 318, 322, 330, 332, 333, 336, 339, 342

INDEX

Mr. Shultz, R. 15, 67
Since I Don't Have You by The Skyliners, 171
Sing Sing Prison Blues by Bessie Smith, 90
Smith, Bessie, 90
Smith, Shane, 19 – 26, 257, 258
Stairway To Heaven by Led Zeppelin, 206
Star Wars, 323
Stearns, Bryan, 275, 281
The Sting, 102
String of Pearls by Glenn Miller and his Orchestra, 127
The Sugar Blues by Clyde McCoy, 93 – 99, 152, 229, 326
Sully, Greg, 228
Sweet Sue by Paul Whiteman and his Orchestra, 211

Take Good Care Of My Baby, by Bobby Vee, 315
Teel, Lisa, 66, 208, 209, 243, 286
Tell Laura I Love Her by Ray Peterson, 198
Ten Little Indians by Agatha Christie, 338

Mr. Thacker, Bill, 32, 33, 72 – 74, 93, 94, 98, 107, 111, 133, 145, 146, 150, 152, 173, 174, 180, 182, 183, 199, 204, 208, 209, 218, 231, 232, 240 – 242, 258, 260, 275, 276, 283, 290, 291
That's My Boy, 17
Thomas – Terry, 87
Thor, Cameron, 105
Times Picayune | The New Orleans Advocate photo file, 344
Trancas Market, 20, 21, 25, 291, 313
25 Most Beloved Melodies, 239

UCLA, 10, 11, 87 – 89
Ufland, Harry, 152, 269, 270
Ufland, John, 152, 260, 261, 269, 270, 285

Valentino, Rudolph, 195, 196, 204
Mr. Vincent, Leonard, 108, 227, 276, 277, 288

The Way We Were, by Barbara Streisand, 120
Weatherwax, Frank, 31, 127, 128, 130

Webster Elementary school, 155, 156
What The Peeper Saw, 10, 28, 89, 122
Where Have All The Flowers Gone, by Pete Seeger, 113
Whiteman, Paul, 245
Wilder, Gene, 49, 75
Wilson's House Of Suede And Leather, 53,

Wilson, Flip, 201, 267
Wilson, Kevin, 201, 202
Wilson, Greg, 197

Young Frankenstein, 49, 75, 85
Younis, Paul, 97

Zachary All commercial, 265

www.ingramcontent.com/pod-product-compliance
Lightning Source LLC
Chambersburg PA
CBHW072130220426
43664CB00013B/2202